The Christian Church: the True and the False

Willis J. Hartman Jr.

The Christian Church:
The True and the False

by
Willis J. Hartman Jr.

Library of Congress Control Number: 2007906703
International Standard Book Number: 978-1-60126-073-4

Printed by
Masthof Press
219 Mill Road
Morgantown, PA 19543-9516

To the children and young adults
of the United States of America and around
the World, this book is dedicated.

CONTENTS

Part One

The Sovereign Rule of God

Foreword vii

1. In the Beginning—God Created the Heavens and Earth (Genesis 1:1) 2

2. The Glorious, Ever-loving, All-powerful and Only God................................. 5

3. The Wondrous Person God Called Man..................... 11

4. The Fragility of Man 13

5. The Manifestations of the Sovereign Rule of God....................................... 16

6. God Reveals the Restoration of the Spiritual Kingdom 46

7. The Parables of the Restored Spiritual Kingdom of God.................................. 65

8. God Makes the Glorious Declaration......................... 70

9. God Calls—We Answer 82

10. *Halakhah*—Way of Walking...................................... 96

Part Two

Errors of the Ways of Men

11. Knowing Right From Wrong 122

12. Traveling Companions 140

13. Soul-searching by Pastors 186

14. The Great Soul Robbery 196

15. The Lingering Mystery—
Satan's Own Men on Earth 223

16. Confusion in the Seminaries—
All Cannot Be Right 245

17. Liberation of Pastors, Priests and Rabbis 256

18. Did God Really Want Man to
Create the Church and Christianity? 274

Epilogue 304

Endnotes 314

Addendum 319

Foreword

"Know this first of all, that in the last days mockers will come with their mocking, following after their own lusts, and saying, "Where is the promise of His coming? For ever since the fathers [Jewish Prophets] fell asleep, all continues just as it was from the beginning of creation." For when they maintain this, it escapes their notice that by the Word of God the heavens existed long ago and the earth was formed out of water and by water, through which the world at that time was destroyed, being flooded with water.

But by His Word the present heavens and earth are being reserved for fire, kept for the day of judgment and destruction of ungodly men. But do not let this one fact escape your notice, beloved, that with the Lord one day is like a thousand years, and a thousand years like one day. The Lord is not slow about His promise, as some count slowness, but is patient toward you, not wishing for any to perish but for all to come to repentance.

But the day of the Lord will come like a thief, in which the heavens will pass away with a roar and the elements will be destroyed with intense heat, and the earth and its works will be burned up. Since all these things are to be destroyed in this way, what sort of people ought you to be in holy conduct and godliness, looking for and hastening the coming of the day of God; because of which the heavens will be destroyed by burning, and the elements will melt with fervent heat.

Therefore, beloved, since you look for these things, be diligent to be found by Him in peace, spotless and blameless, and regard the patience of our Lord as salvation; just as also our beloved brother Paul, according to the wisdom given him, wrote to you, as also in all his letters, speaking in them of these things, in which are some things hard to understand, which the untaught and unstable distort, as they do also the rest of the Scriptures, to their own destruction.

You therefore, beloved knowing this beforehand, be on your guard so that you are not carried away by the error of unprincipled men and fall from your own steadfastness, but grow in grace and knowledge of our Lord and Savior Jesus Christ. To Him be the glory, both now and to the day of eternity. Amen."

2 Peter 3:3-18

Emphasis added by the author.

Part One

The Sovereign Rule of God

1

In the Beginning—
God Created the Heavens and Earth
(Genesis 1:1)

Most of the people who inhabit the earth today do not personally believe an all-powerful being created them and all the wonders in the heavens and the earth. Most of those people allow someone else to tell them what they believe, particularly in the area of religious teachings and thought. It has been said that man uses religion to control the thinking of the ruled and to order their way of life. We do not have to look very deeply into many of the governing systems of the nations around the world to verify the validity of that statement. At the same time, where people have freedom of religion, they also have freedom of their way of life. This too is only partly true, because even where people have the freedom of choosing where and how to worship God, that worship for the most part is ordered by the clergy or leaders of the specific belief.

Genesis, chapters 1 and 2, tells us that God worked six days to bring into being the heavens and the earth, and He placed minerals upon the earth, which is a kingdom of itself. God brought vegetation into being on the earth, which is a kingdom of itself. God brought the animal kingdom into being by placing animal life on the earth in the water and on the land, and God saw that all He created was good. Then God said,

"Let us make man in Our image, according to Our likeness; and let them rule over the fish of the sea and over the birds of the sky and over the cattle and over all the earth, and over every creeping thing that creeps on the earth." (Genesis 1:26) God created man in His own image, in the image of God He created him; male and female He created them. (Genesis 1:27)

What does it mean that God created man in His own image? It means that man was without a sin nature. Man did not and could not know about anything evil, and he could not discern what was good for all was good. Man was righteous. He knew his Father was a righteous Father. Man did not and could not discern anything unrighteous about his helpmeet. Nor could the female helpmeet discern anything unrighteous about her male companion. No animal on the land, in the sea, or of the air could harm man, and man could not harm anything of the animal kingdom. Man could not misuse anything of the mineral kingdom nor anything of the vegetable kingdom. All was good for their use and consumption, for man had dominion over all those kingdoms God put man as husbandman over. Man was in complete harmony with God, themselves, and with all that God created on the land, in the sea, and in the air. Mankind lived in the Father/children relationship of the original spiritual kingdom of God. God communicated with mankind in the Spirit. It is believed that man could not see God in the Garden of Eden. They heard Him walking about in the garden in their presence, but He could not be seen.

God gave man one very simple rule. Man did not have to have book after book filled with rules and regulations and laws to live by, all regulated through other men. We all know what the simple rule was that God gave His first inhabitants in the Garden of Eden. Just think of what it would be like if we did not have to have great concrete structures with mechanical machinery and systems for cleaning our water that we drink. Think about what it would be like if there would be no need for removing weeds in our crop-growing fields. Can you imagine what it would be like if poisonous reptiles, vicious man-eating animals, disease-carrying organisms, and death would not be a reality in our life. Our life with God, in complete harmony with God and our surroundings, would have been continuous love and happiness, as we experience for only very brief moments in our lives at the present place and time. We cannot buy peace, love, and happiness for all the gold or oil in the world.

A time is coming when humankind will be living in complete harmony with their maker again. That time had its beginning when God brought His only begotten Son to earth to make mankind's way straight so that all who accept His Son's shed blood for their sins can become part of God's restored spiritual kingdom on earth and in heaven.

2

The Glorious, Ever-loving, All-powerful and Only God

In the episodes of Star Trek, the actors display actions of superhuman beings and beings created just for a certain galaxy. The program very realistically shows spaceships moving about the universe portraying, in the power of man and in fantasy form, that which God performs in real form. Large objects such as the earth, sun, moon, and distant planets in orderly motion 60 minutes each hour, 24 hours each day, 365 days each year for thousands of years are directed by God without error. Only a being of indescribable and infinite power can perform as our only true God performs in the universe, in the world, in the United States, and in each person's life who puts their trust in the Lord Jesus Christ.

In Acts 17:22-31 we are given enlightenment concerning our all-loving and all-powerful heavenly Father:

> So Paul stood in the midst of the Areopagus and said, "Men of Athens, I observe that you are very religious in all respects. "For while I was passing through and examining the objects of your worship, I also found an altar with this inscription, 'TO AN UNKNOWN GOD.' Therefore what you worship in ignorance, this I proclaim to you. "The God who made the world and all things in it, since He is

> Lord of heaven and earth, does not dwell in temples made with hands; neither is He served by human hands, as though He needed anything, since He Himself gives to all people life and breath and all things; and He made from one man every nation of mankind to live on all the face of the earth, having determined their appointed times and the boundaries of their habitation, that they should seek God, if perhaps they might grope for Him and find Him, though He is not far from each one of us; for in Him we live and move and exist, as even some of your own poets have said, 'For we also are His children.' "Being then the offspring of God, we ought not to think that the Divine Nature is like gold or silver or stone, an image formed by the art and thought of man. "Therefore having overlooked the times of ignorance, God is now declaring to men that all people everywhere should repent, because He has fixed a day in which He will judge the world in righteousness through a Man whom He has appointed, having furnished proof to all men by raising Him from the dead."

This, then, is a great portion of the plan of God for all mankind. It was His plan then; it remains His plan now. In His almighty power and out of His love for His created human beings, he has brought into being, through His Son, the restored spiritual kingdom of heaven.

The true and only God possesses omnipotence—being all powerful. Romans 4:17 reads: (as it is written, "A FATHER OF MANY NATIONS HAVE I MADE YOU") [referring to Abraham] in the presence of Him whom he believed, even God, who gives life to the dead and calls into being that which does not exist.

> 1 Corinthians 1:27-31. But God has chosen the foolish things of the world to shame the wise, and God has chosen the weak things of the world to shame the things which are strong, and the base things of the world and the despised God has chosen, the things that are not, that He may nullify the things that are, so that no man may boast before God. But by His doing you are in Christ Jesus, who became to us wisdom from God, and righteousness and sanctification, and redemption, so that, just as it is written, "Let HIM WHO BOASTS, BOAST IN THE LORD."

This Scripture says, always give God recognition for all that you perform or produce or, in time, you will fall. Any nation that fails to remember God will fall. History has proven this time and time again. (See Isaiah 40:14-26.)

The true and only God possesses omnipresence. God is everywhere at the same time. When lightning strikes in Brooklyn, New York, in Seattle, Washington, and in Tokyo, Japan, all at the same moment, God is there. He does not have to jump from one location to another to be present. God could make a phone call to Himself to each and every phone that exists all over the world, and He would be there to pick up the phone to talk to Himself at each and every phone simultaneously. God is present in each and every breath of air we breathe. He is present when each and every person praises Him (in the manner in which He deserves praise) in the innumerable locations around the world. God is present when men curse Him at all the locations at the same time, when men and wherever men curse Him. God is present at all of the above happenings at the same time. In 1 Corinthians 2:4-10 Paul gives us insight into the power of God working in man.

> and my message and my preaching were not in persuasive words of wisdom, but in demonstration of the Spirit and of power, so that your faith would not rest on the wisdom of men, but on the power of God. Yet we do speak wisdom among those who are mature; a wisdom, however, not of this age nor of the rulers of this age, who are passing away; but we speak God's wisdom in a mystery, the hidden wisdom, which God predestined before the ages to our glory; the wisdom which none of the rulers of this age has understood; for if they had understood it they would not have crucified the Lord of glory; but just as it is written, "Things WHICH EYE HAS NOT SEEN AND EAR HAS NOT HEARD, AND *WHICH* HAVE NOT ENTERED THE HEART OF MAN, ALL THAT GOD HAS PREPARED FOR THOSE WHO LOVE HIM." For to us God revealed them through the Spirit; for the Spirit searches all things, even the depths of God.

Working backwards from verse 10 to verse 9, the question is, what is meant by all that God has prepared for those who love Him and what is it that those who love Him have not seen or heard and have not entered the heart of man? Man has not seen nor heard the restoration of the spiritual kingdom of God. And what is it that the Jewish rulers in Jerusalem at the time of the first appearance of their Messiah did not understand, and why did they proceed to push for the death of Jesus? They did not realize that God sent His son to restore the spiritual kingdom of God. The restoration of the spiritual kingdom of God is projected in Scripture as a mystery, the hidden wisdom, which God predestined before the ages to our glory. It was hidden because it was not prophesied by any of the prophets. What can be more glorious to us than to spend eternity with

God in His eternal kingdom? It is the almighty power of God that brings us unto Himself. Nothing on this earth can bring us to God. We are called by God through the working of the Holy Spirit and the word of God telling us that we are lost sinners and that we need to confess our sins, thank God for forgiving us, accept His son's shed blood which covers our sins, past, present, and future and ask Jesus Christ to come into our life and make Him master of our life.

God possesses omniscience. God has infinite knowledge of Himself, the Son, and the Holy Spirit. God knows ahead of time everything that is going to take place. He knows those who will be born fifty years from now. God knew that His created human beings would fall, but He provided and put into motion His plan of redemption and, at the same time, gave mankind opportunities to come to God and live before their maker in complete harmony with Him.

We are told in Titus 1:1-3 the promise of God long ages ago.

> Paul, a bond-servant of God, and an apostle of Jesus Christ, for the faith of those chosen of God and the knowledge of the truth which is according to godliness, in the hope of eternal life, which God, who cannot lie, promised long ages ago, but at the proper time manifested, even His word, in the proclamation with which I was entrusted according to the commandment of God our Savior,

The commandment of God is to go and make disciples of the people in all the nations of the world. Titus 3:4-8 verifies that God has given mankind that which was promised long ages ago.

> But when the kindness of God our Savior and His love for mankind appeared, [Jesus Christ], He saved us, not on the basis of deeds which we have done in righteousness, [good works] but according to His mercy, by the washing of regeneration and renewing by the Holy Spirit, whom He poured out upon us richly through Jesus Christ our Savior, so that being justified by His grace we would be made heirs according to the hope of eternal life. This is a trustworthy statement; and concerning these things I want you to speak confidently, so that those who have believed God will be careful to engage in good deeds. These things are good and profitable for men. [Clarifications added by the author.]

We can only be renewed by the Holy Spirit when we have Christ Jesus as our Savior and allow Him to be Lord and Master of our life. This can only happen by the fact that the Lord Jesus Christ, by His first appearance and through His life, His death, and His resurrection, did give His heavenly Father good cause to return the Holy Spirit to earth.

3

The Wondrous Person God Called Man

God said in Genesis 1:26, Let Us make man in Our image, according to Our likeness; . . . Man has everything that God the Father, God the Son, and God the Holy Spirit wills for man to have. In other words man has God's unlimitedness at his disposal. God gave man a brain, wherein he has the ability to create and bring into being a myriad of things, nearly miraculously. Man's ability to create substantive objects is limited to using the raw materials that God placed on the earth. But God gave man a creative ability. That ability is limited only by man's ability to trust in God. What man cannot create, God can create for man. The man who creates miraculously is creating by the power of God. That is the reason man is a wondrous person. Man could not create a thing without the power of God working through him.

Man was given a superior brain and the ability to think rationally. He also has a body, soul, and spirit. Each person that God creates is new and different from all of the others created previously down to the minute detail of a fingerprint. Each created person is given the power and freedom by God to think independently of all of the other people around them. Each person is given the power to choose good thoughts or to choose to think evil or ungodly thoughts. Each person can choose to take good care of their body or to allow their body to become decrepit even at a young age. God gave each and every person the correct amount of brains to perform whatever an individual sets his mind to do.

Man is a most wondrous person because God creates them to perform for Him. Some men do perform in the power of God. There are numerous things that have been brought into existence in the last one hundred years which cause peoples of the world to function at near lightning speed. Within those one hundred years, farming techniques moved from the ancient methods to the huge combine that harvests hundreds of acres in one day. The ancient small grain harvesting method used hand labor to bind the grain into sheaves, then place the sheaves into shocks, then gather the sheaves and store them in barns, then bring the sheaves out of the mow and feed them into the thrashing machine. In these last hundred years, man moved from visiting friends and relatives by horse and buggy or train that took hours to move from one county to another or from one state to another, to visiting friends and relatives thousands of miles away within hours of when they left. Man moved from hand carried letters and messages from place to place by horseback that took hours or days, to movement of messages, money, and information within minutes around the world and to distant points into space. Man is using his God-given brainpower to accelerate his way of living to the point where chaos sometimes lifts its ugly head in schools, big business, and government.

4

The Fragility of Man

The first sign of the fragile condition of mankind is given to us in the first chapter of Genesis. Here Adam allowed Eve to do his thinking for him. The result was a complete disaster for all of mankind throughout the world since the beginning of time. In Exodus 14:11, we are given additional evidence of mankind's susceptibility to fragility. It was not long after the Israelites were on their way to the wilderness of Arabia that they imposed upon Moses and Aaron to do their thinking for them. They had soon forgotten who it was and how it happened that they were released from the oppression of slavery at the hands of the Egyptians.

During the time that God used Moses to gather the Israelites together to make their exodus from Egypt, the people witnessed all the miracles and wonders that God performed during their journey. (See Exodus 13:17-22; 14:9-31.) As part of God's revealing of His great love for His people and His mighty power, He had Moses bring the assembly of Israelites before Him at Mt. Sinai. God wanted the people to witness even a greater appearance of Himself on the day the instructions of God were given to Moses. (See Exodus 19 and 20.) All throughout the Word of God, which gives the history of how God's people lived their lives before their maker, is the story (an example) of how mankind fails to see how much God wants mankind to lean on Him for everything.

Mankind's failure to learn this lesson has brought upon themselves a very fragile life. It is a very fragile living because those persons who choose to go through life without the true and living God have brought upon themselves, upon their death, instant eternity without God. If you can imagine what it would be like to be lost in space in a space capsule without the means to return to earth, that is the perfect picture of eternal life without Christ Jesus. The point I am trying to make is that a very high percentage of suffering by mankind would be avoided if man would allow God to be their all in all.

Most of the inhabitants around the world today choose a man-made god instead of the living God. Those persons allow the religious leader of the country they reside in to do their thinking for them. Unless those souls learn about the one true God, they will spend eternity in constant pain and suffering. Without help from people who love and serve God, they will never have the knowledge or strength of spirit to overcome their fragile condition. It is safe to say that most inhabitants of the earth have experienced the almighty power of God. Those experiences can be in the form of surviving a natural disaster, a miraculous escape from the many forms of sickness, accidents, financial calamities, and bodily harm in war and peace. Many people have come through poverty and lack of food and clothing. Governments make well-meaning attempts to provide the needs of its people, but we know they have failed more times than not. Man working by himself or works of governments need to give God the opportunity to be the power at work to meet the needs of fragile man.

We call those persons great who discover or invent near miraculous substances or things. Some examples would be the incandescent light bulb, electricity, the polio vaccine, pasteurization, antibiotics, war machines and equipment, computers, television, radio, radar, x-ray, laser beam, spaceships, etc. The list goes on and on, and mankind's needs go on and on ahead of all the new discoveries and inventions. Man gives credit to man for solving needs. This circle keeps on moving from the need to survive to meeting the need by inventions of the creativeness God provides in mankind. However, wants and needs will never stop in those persons who continue to choose to live outside of the power of God Almighty.

5

The Manifestations of the Sovereign Rule of God

God did not give us, in minute detail, all that God expected from man at the time He created the heavens and earth. However, the sovereign rule of God (His great love for mankind, we can call it the spiritual kingdom of God) is manifested to man at different places, at different times, and in different ways in the Word of God. When God created the heavens and earth, He set out for us, in Genesis, certain rules for man to live by before his Maker, as well as details of His creation. (See Genesis 1:1-31.) This gives us a great deal to think about in retrospect; it reveals to us the awesome power of God. That thought should bring fear and trembling over us, just as we are told that it brought fear and trembling over Moses.

The first part of the creation by God was the heavens and the earth, but it was formless and void. In other words only a sphere. Complete darkness was over the surface of the water. We are told that the Spirit of God moved over the surface of the waters. Then God brought into being light, and God caused the light to be separated from the darkness. The light was called day and the darkness was called night; and when an evening and a morning was completed, God called that one day. Then God created an expanse that separated the waters from the waters and the expanse was called heaven. The end of that work by God was the second day. (See Genesis 1:1-31.)

God gathered the waters into one place and the dry land appeared. The dry land God called earth, and the gathering of the waters God called seas. God caused vegetation to be formed on the earth, many kinds of plants producing seed, fruit trees bearing fruit with seeds all of which were many different kinds, and at the end of this creation was the third day. God created lights in the expanse of the heavens to separate day from the night and to separate the light from the darkness. They were for signs, seasons—days and years. The two larger lights, the brighter one to govern the day and the lesser bright one to govern the night. God made the stars to shine in the heavens. At the end of this creation was the fourth day. God created the living creatures of the waters and the birds of the air, each of their own kind. God said they should be fruitful and multiply and fill the waters of the sea and the birds multiply on the earth. At the end of this creation was the fifth day.

The Beginning of the Sovereign Rule of God on Earth

> Then God said, "Let the earth bring forth living creatures after their kind: cattle and creeping things and beasts of the earth after their kind;" and it was so (Genesis 1:24). Then God said, "Let us make man in Our image, according to Our likeness; and let them rule over the fish of the sea and over the birds of the sky and over the cattle and over all the earth, and over every creeping thing that creeps on the earth." (Genesis 1:26) "God created man in His own image, in the image of God He created

> him; male and female He created them. And God blessed them; and God said to them, "Be fruitful and multiply, and fill the earth, and subdue it; and rule over the fish of the sea and over the birds of the sky, and over every living thing that moves on the earth." (Genesis 1:27, 28)

God gave man dominion over all that God created on earth and He seated man in a very special part of His creation and gave man a very important command: Do not eat of the forbidden fruit of the certain tree. Up until the day man was placed in the special part of the creation by God and man ate of the forbidden fruit of the tree of knowledge of good and evil, God had people to rule over. We can say it was a spiritual relationship between man and God because we are told: The spirit of God moved over the surface of the waters. (See Genesis 1:2.) Also Genesis 3:7-10:

> Then the eyes of both of them were opened, and they knew that they were naked; and they sewed fig leaves together and made themselves loin coverings. They heard the sound of the Lord God walking in the garden in the cool of the day, and the man and his wife hid themselves from the presence of the Lord God among the trees of the garden. Then the Lord God called to the man, and said to him, "Where are you?" He said, "I heard the sound of You in the garden, and I was afraid because I was naked; so I hid myself."

The humans, Adam and Eve, were spiritually pure before they ate of the fruit of the forbidden tree. When they ate of the forbidden tree, they both died in the sense that they could now see they were naked and the spiritual nature left them and they took on the sin nature. They could no longer commune with God through the spiritual nature. Before the spiritual nature left Adam and Eve, God ruled over them through the Holy Spirit, which indwelt them from the time they were made. These humans were different from the other creatures of the earth because they were like God in that they could reason with their superior brain and they could commune with God in the Spirit. The following is from personal correspondence with Glenn M. Wenger, September 16, 2005.[1]

> Although they were originally innocent as babies who can do no right or wrong, now they had received the knowledge of good and evil. They now knew right from wrong, which produced shame of their nakedness. The account goes on to say, "And the Lord God said, Behold, the man is become as one of us, to know good and evil and now, lest he put forth his hand and take also of the tree of life . . . God sent him forth from the Garden of Eden. . . ." (Genesis 3:22, 23) KJV This Scripture brings to light another god-like attribute (God said "the man is become as one of us to know good and evil") that humans have to differ from the animals. It is an attribute that has caused much sorrow because humankind was unwilling to entirely satisfy the responsibility knowledge laid upon us, and humankind fell into sin.
>
> Today we can generally call this the innate moral law. Paul says in Romans 5:12, "Wherefore, as by one man sin entered into the world, and death by sin; and so death passed upon all men, for all have sinned." KJV It is our own sin that condemns us. Adam's sin brought sin and death on all of us,

> because the knowledge of good and evil has been passed down to us from generation to generation from Adam. We sin against that knowledge, and it is our sin that condemns us. If it were not for the knowledge, sin would not be imputed on us. Paul says in the next verse, "Sin is not imputed when there is no law." (Romans 5:13) KJV
>
> Some people believe that we are born as lost sinners, and so they baptize infants with the hope that they will be saved by the baptism. We are not born lost with a debt of sin. But we are born with the nature of Adam. A baby is innocent of any right or wrong. It is interesting to notice specifically how the shame of nakedness (which is our evidence of the knowledge of good and evil in Adam and Eve) develops in a child. As a baby it is obvious that he has no shame. As the child becomes older, he will gradually develop an untaught sense of privacy about his body. He doesn't want his mother to help him with his bath, etc. (See Romans 5:14, 15.)

Not only did spiritual death occur in mankind in the Garden of Eden, but physical death also came upon mankind at the same time. Mankind would have lived forever in complete harmony with God the Father, their Maker. We have a slight hint of that truth in the fact that mankind did live for hundreds of years for a long period of time after the fall. Those years were gradually reduced until longevity leveled off at a very low number of years. Since then longevity began to increase again reaching an attainable age of eighty to one hundred years and more, which is very commonplace today. (See 1 Corinthians 15:20-28.) Christ came also to abolish death.

From this time on, the spiritual kingdom of God was placed

on hold because God could no longer communicate with man through the Holy Spirit. Man brought upon himself the sin nature and, until the sin nature was overcome by the power of God working in and through a man worthy to receive the power of God (the Holy Spirit), God could not restore spiritual communication within man. (See 1 Corinthians 15:21-22.) That man who was worthy to perform for God, sinless and perfect in all respects, is the Son of God/Son of Man. When did Christ become that man God could work through and become the man worthy to receive the Holy Spirit? (See Matthew 3:13-17.) God declared His Son to be worthy to restore the spiritual guidance within mankind. All righteousness, which was removed from mankind in the Garden of Eden, could be restored to mankind through the righteousness of Christ. (See Romans chapters 5 and 6.)

The Interim Sovereign Rule on Earth

One of the least understood manifestations of the sovereign rule of God, which has great bearing on the ultimate outcome of mankind's eternal life with God, is the development of His special people. No other created people group or nation has had continuation of existence like that of the special people of God. The main reason is that the Israelites are the mechanism through which God has worked and is working to bring all mankind, those who answer the call of God unto Himself, in the restored spiritual kingdom. God created a separate people for Himself because mankind in their own will and power failed to live in true love and obedience with one another and with God. God has always projected Himself as the heavenly Father to mankind and He always wanted to be in the Father/

children relationship with His created humans through spiritual guidance. (See Exodus 29:45, 46; 25:8; Leviticus 26:11, 12.) But mankind displayed a rebellious attitude before their Maker and could not of their own will and power restore peace with God.

So, God had to act on behalf of His created humans. God did this for the good of all mankind by choosing out of all the people of the earth a man who would be righteous in the presence of his Maker. So it was, God called Abraham out of the land of the Chaldeans to begin the formation of a special people on the face of the earth that would love, honor, cherish, and give praise and glory to the one and only God. The special people of God are truly very special because they were given, in minute detail, all that God expected from them. However, their failure to live up to all the detailed instructions brought life-giving benefits to the Gentiles.

God used Abraham, Isaac and Jacob as the earthly fathers and leaders to begin His formation of His special people. Within this formation came the twelve tribes of Israel, which provided an accelerated numerical expansion of this special people. Those people were guided through their near constant trials and tribulations to mold them into His people. After God gave them opportunity after opportunity to absorb His teachings and develop understanding of the great love of the only true God, God gave them another earthly leader they could see and follow because it soon became apparent that this special people who were fathered by Abraham, Isaac and Jacob would not allow their heavenly Father to be in the Father/children relationship with them. Thus, the Father had to give them special teachings through Moses, which are set out in the Torah (Pentateuch—first five books of the Old Testament).

The special people now were happy because they had that something they could see and believe in, even though God was in their midst in spiritual form through a pillar of fire by night and a pillar cloud by day. It was not possible for them to live in spiritual guidance from God because the spiritual kingdom of God remained on hold. But God, because of His all-loving and all-powerful manner toward man, had to have a positive and responsible response from His created beings. The teachings given to Moses were the only answer to meet His need and the need of His special people to live in peace and harmony with God by meeting all that the teachings demanded of them.

We read in the Old Testament the historic details of the personal guidance God provided His special people through judges and prophets and how their response to God played out and how it will play out through time. We also know how much the special people of God have sacrificed, unknowingly, to help God bring all mankind unto Himself. With the development of the special people of God, all that we read and study in the Scriptures give us complete guidance for our lives. Everything is laid out for us in complete detail. The ultimate and final act of God will be to bring all peoples of the world to give praise, honor, and glory to their heavenly Father throughout all eternity. (See Revelation 5:13.)

The teachings of Moses, such as the Ten Commandments (Exodus 20:1-17), were given to the special people of God to bring them into a godly relationship. It was a special people God brought into existence to form and develop the Father/children relationship, the relationship God longed to be in with the humans of His creation. When His special people, through their leadership, forsook their position before their heavenly Father and in fact abandoned that place, God returned to His place and He allowed His special people to wander around in their complete disobedience for hundreds of years. After which time, God brought His only begotten Son into the world as the Messiah for His special people.

A New and Different Sovereign Rule of God

Christ Jesus came to earth to make complete all that God desired His special people to be before Him. The Jew's Messiah did provide for the Father all that the teachings of Moses and of the Prophets could not do because it was impossible for them to perform all that God demanded of them. Christ Jesus came to provide the remedy for the weakness of the Torah and the Prophets. (See Hebrews 8-12.)

Christ Jesus' appearance wiped the slate clean for the Jews and Gentiles, only for those who would believe in Him and ushered in the grace of God as the guidance in a renewed sovereign rule of God. The teachings of Moses and the Prophets served God's purposes for guiding His special people until the seed came "to whom the promise was made." (Galatians 3:19)

The following discussion is taken from the Christian Jew Foundation's publication, *The Law of Moses and The Grace of God*, by Charles Halff.[2] Charles Halff said:

> **Beginning of the Law**
>
> When did the law come into being? The answer is found in John 1:17. Notice:
>
> "*For the law was given by Moses, but grace and truth came by Jesus Christ.*"

Could anything be more plainly stated? Could anything be more understandable? The law—all of the law—was given to a specific people, Israel, at a specific time. The law was given to Israel by Moses exactly as he received it from Almighty God.

Does that mean that there was no law before Moses? No, beloved. God commanded Adam to eat freely of every tree in the Garden of Eden except one . . . the tree of the knowledge of good and evil. (Gen. 2:17) God's command to Adam was law—not the law of Moses—but a command from God is law! And if broken, judgment must follow.

However, there was no written law prior to the time of Moses. People were convicted by their consciences whenever they sinned. (Rom. 2:15) But law as a test for man began with Moses just as grace as a test for man began with Jesus Christ.

The Law Was Given Only to the Nation of Israel

However, God's Word makes it plain that the law was never given to any other nation or people but the children of Israel. This is the statement of the Apostle Paul. He says:

"*When the Gentiles, which have not the law, do by nature the things contained in the law, these, having not the law, are a law unto themselves.*" (Rom. 2:14)

This statement admits of no misunderstanding nor quibbling. Speaking by the Holy Spirit, the Apostle Paul authoritatively says:

"*The Gentiles, which have not the law.*"

"*The Gentiles, . . . these, having not the law.*"

This is the Holy Spirit's definite, distinct declaration that in Paul's day the Gentiles did not have the law!

If the Gentiles did not have the law in Paul's day, they did not have it before his day, for there is no record of it having been taken from them at any time previous to his day. If they neither had it in his day nor before his day, they do not have it now in this day. The law was not given to either the Gentiles or the church. The only nation that has ever had the law is Israel. (See Romans 9:4, Nehemiah 9:13-14 and Exodus 20.)

The Law Was Given Not to Keep But to Break

I am going to make a statement which no doubt will be a shock to many of you. Did you know that the law was given to the children of Israel, not to keep but to break? Notice:

"*Wherefore then serveth the law? It was added because of transgressions, till the seed should come to whom the promise was made.*" (Gal. 3:19)

Please notice—the law was added "because of transgressions." In the original it reads like this, "*The law was added FOR THE SAKE OF TRANSGRESSIONS.*" In other words, the law was added to reveal the true nature of unregenerate man. It was given to show the exceeding sinfulness of sin. There's no place in all the Word of God where the purpose of the law is more clearly set forth than in this verse.

God did not give the law to save men. The law has never saved a man and the law never will save men. Why? Simply because Jesus Christ is the only person who ever lived upon the face of this earth who kept God's law. And He kept it perfectly. He kept it for us and died for us because we couldn't keep it.

When Christ died on the cross, He fulfilled the entire law. (Matt. 5:17) He said, "*Not one jot or one tittle shall pass TILL all be fulfilled.*" (Matt. 5:18) Yes, Jesus came to fulfill the law, and He did exactly that. He fulfilled every jot and every tittle of the law. He satisfied the demands of God's holiness and God's purity. In the closing hours of His earthly ministry He said, "*I have glorified Thee on the earth: I HAVE FINISHED THE WORK WHICH THOU GAVEST ME TO DO.*" (John 17:4) Again, just before He bowed His head on His pulseless breast, He cried out from the cross, "*IT IS FINISHED!*" (John 19:30)

Why Then Was the Law Given?

Perhaps you're asking the question, "If the law does not save us or help to save us, what is the purpose of the law?" That's a good question, and the only place to find the right answer is in the Word of God. Notice:

"*By the law is the knowledge of sin.*" (Rom. 3:20)

There it is just as plain and clear as can be. God's Word says, "*By the law is the knowledge of sin.*" It doesn't say, "By the law is the knowledge of grace." It doesn't say, "By the law is the knowledge of salvation." Rather, it says, "*By the law is the knowledge of sin.*"

The law, therefore, is a revealer of sin. Sin was in the world before the coming of the law (Rom. 5:13), but when the law came it helped to expose the awfulness of sin.

The law is like a mirror. When we look in the mirror, we see the dirt on our face. The mirror cannot cleanse your face. It takes soap and water to do that. The same thing is true of the law. The law shows us that we are covered with the rottenness and filth of sin, but it cannot cleanse from sin. It takes the blood of Jesus Christ to do that.

The law was given to one nation to prove to all the world that no one could be saved by the law.

God tried it out on the Jewish nation for 1,500 years and demonstrated that not a single, solitary person on the face of the earth is able to keep the law.

In John 7:19 Jesus said to the Jews, *"NONE OF YOU KEEPETH THE LAW."* What Jesus said to the religious leaders at the Feast of Tabernacles is just as true today. No one really keeps the law. In spite of this, there are great religious denominations that are built on the idea that man can live according to the law and keep the law.

Here is a verse that sums up the whole purpose of the law.

"*Now we know that what things soever the law saith, it saith to them who are under the law: that every mouth may be stopped, and all the world may become guilty before God.*" (Rom. 3: 19)

Paul said that the law was given to stop the mouth of every person who would teach salvation by keeping the law. The law declares every man a sinner.

Notice—the Scripture refers to the law as a mouth-stopper, not a heart-opener. The law of God is the best mouth-stopper on earth. When a man reads the law, it will immediately shut his mouth.

The law says: "*Thou shalt love thy neighbor as thyself.*" (James 2:8) How many of you would say that you love your neighbor like you love yourself? When you buy a new suit for yourself, do you buy a new suit for your neighbor? When you buy a new hat for yourself, do you buy a new hat for your neighbor? When you bake a cake for yourself, do you bake a cake for your neighbor? Do you see how the law tells you to shut your mouth—that you're not nearly as good as you think you are. This is God's mouth-stopper.

Remember the rich young ruler who came

to Jesus inquiring about eternal life? He had the popular idea that somehow he could be saved by keeping the law. But notice how quickly the law stopped his mouth. When he told Jesus that he had kept all the law from his youth up, he seemed to overlook what the law required. It demanded that he love the Lord with all his heart, soul, strength and mind. So Christ put him to the acid test. He told him to go sell all he had, give to the poor and come follow Him. And the young man broke under the test because the Scripture says, "*When the young man heard that saying, he went away sorrowful; for he had great possessions.*" (Matt. 19:22) You see how the law stopped his mouth. It showed him where his treasure was. It showed him that he loved his gold more than his God. He came to Jesus confident; he went away condemned. He came speaking; but he went away silent. The law had done its work. It proved itself to be God's mouth-stopper.

The End of the Law

How long was the law to continue? This question is very plainly answered in God's Word. Notice:

"*Wherefore then serveth the law? It was added because of transgressions, TILL THE SEED SHOULD COME to whom the promise was made.*" (Gal. 3:19)

Now we know that the law was given to the nation of Israel. The Jews asked for it and they got it. (See Ex. 19:8.) For 2,000 years God had been dealing with the human race on a grace basis. Adam lived under grace. Noah lived under grace. Abraham lived under grace. But like so many people today, the Jews preferred law to grace so God let them have it.

Notice that Paul says the law was "*added because of transgressions TILL the seed should come to whom the promise was made.*" Now Paul makes it crystal clear that the law had an end just as it had a beginning. "*IT WAS ADDED . . . TILL THE SEED SHOULD COME.*" When the seed came (the Lord Jesus Christ), the law came to an end.

"*Christ* is *the end of the law for righteousness to everyone that believeth.*" (Rom. 10:4)

What the Law Cannot Do, Jesus Christ Does

In Romans 8:3 we have this enlightening truth. Please notice:

"*For what the law could not do, in that it was weak through the flesh, God sending his own Son in the likeness of sinful flesh, and for sin, condemned sin in the flesh.*" (Rom. 8:3)

Now let us notice that God's saving grace goes further than the law ever did or ever could! Here it is expressly said that there were some things "*the law could not do, in that it was weak through the flesh.*" What were some of the things the law could not do?

FIRST, THE LAW COULD NOT GIVE LIFE. Galatians 3:21 says:

"*If there had been a law given which could have given life, verily righteousness should have been by the law.*"

The law could not give life because it could not be kept. If you think you can keep the law, then you are better than the Jews who tried to keep it for 1,500 years and failed. They broke every law God ever gave them. In fact, Peter said at the church council at Jerusalem when discussing the Christian's relation to the law: "*Now therefore why tempt ye God, to put a yoke upon the neck of the disciples, which NEITHER OUR FATHERS NOR WE WERE ABLE TO BEAR* (keep)?" (Acts 15:10)

No, the law cannot give life, but Jesus came to give us His life. He said, "*I am come that you might have life, and have it more abundantly.*" (John 10:10)

SECONDLY, THE LAW COULD NOT GIVE RIGHTEOUSNESS. It could not give righteousness for the same reason it could not give life—because it could not be kept.

And so Paul says:

"*If righteousness comes by the law, then Christ is dead in vain.*" (Gal. 2:21)

If keeping the law could make us righteous before God, then the death of the cross was the most criminal blunder ever committed, the most useless shedding of blood God ever permitted.

No, the law could not give righteousness; but what the law could not do, Christ did. Christ is the righteousness of God; and when we're saved, His righteousness is imputed to us so that God no longer sees us as the sinners we are by nature—but He sees us through the righteousness of His Son. (See Rom. 3:21.)

THIRDLY, THE LAW COULD NOT GRANT REMISSION OF SINS. Under the law the only blood ever shed was that of animals. But listen to what Paul says regarding such sacrifices: "*For it is NOT POSSIBLE that the blood of bulls and of goats should take away sins.*" (Heb. 10:4) In verse 11 we have this further statement, "*And every priest standeth daily ministering and offering oftentimes the same sacrifices, WHICH CAN NEVER take away sins.*"

Perhaps you are asking the question, "Are all those who died under the law of Moses lost?" No, because when Jesus shed His blood on the cross, it reached in both directions. It reached back to the creation of man and forward to the last man who shall ever be saved within this world. (See Hebrews 9: 15, Galatians 4:4-5 and Romans 3:25.)

Grace Is Our Teacher

Since we are not under law, how does God expect us to live today? The Word of God is very clear on this point. Notice:

"*This I say then, Walk in the Spirit, and ye shall not fulfill the lust of the flesh.*" (Gal. 5:16)

"*For as many as are led by the Spirit of God, they are the sons of God.*" (Rom. 8:14)

According to the New Testament, born again believers are to be led by the Holy Spirit. We are not to be led by the law or by the preacher in the pulpit or by a denominational machine. We now have the Spirit of God indwelling us to convict us of things that are wrong and to comfort us when we are walking in the steps of our Lord and Master.

In Romans 8:2 we are told that the law of the Spirit of life in Christ Jesus has made us free from the law of sin and death. We are now under a higher law, a better law, a greater law—the law of the Spirit.

When we believe on Christ, we receive a new teacher—one who not only can teach us what to do, but one who can give us the strength to do it as well. Listen to these Scriptures:

"*For the grace of God that bringeth salvation hath appeared to all men, TEACHING US that, denying ungodliness and worldly lusts, we should live soberly, righteously, and godly, in this present world.*" (Titus 2:11-12)

Here we are told very plainly that God's grace is now our teacher. It says, "*For the grace of God that*

> *brings salvation teaches us.*" It does't say, "The law of Moses that brings salvation teaches us." No! No! It says, "*THE GRACE OF GOD . . . TEACHES US.*"
>
> The law is not the rule of life for the Christian. The law served until the coming of Christ. When Christ came and was made a curse for us, He redeemed us from the law; so today we have a new teacher—GRACE!
>
> It is the grace of God that teaches us to deny ungodliness and worldly lusts. It is the grace of God that teaches us to live soberly and righteously and godly. The law was Israel's schoolmaster, but "Grace" has become our teacher. Oh, how I praise God for that day when He delivered me from the thunderings of the law and put me under His marvelous, matchless grace.
>
> Beloved, if you want to be saved, don't trust in yourself to keep the law. The Lord Jesus Christ has already kept it to the letter and fulfilled it for you. He cried out at Calvary, "*IT IS FINISHED!*"—and the work of redemption was finished. There is absolutely nothing that you can do except acknowledge your lost condition and ask Him to save you. In His marvelous grace He will save you, for He has said, "*Whosoever will may come.*" Won't you come to Him right now?

The extreme tragedy for the Jewish people, then, has been, when their Messiah came he was rejected by their leadership, the Sanhedrin. They live in rejection by their great God by their own doing. But their unbelief and hardness of heart will not be forever. (See Romans 11.)

The downfall of the Jews was partly due to the fact that their leadership added their own thoughts, ideas, and understanding to what the teachings of Moses and the Prophets taught them. Likewise, today's leadership of some of the "Christian" denominations, independents, and sects has done and is doing the same thing: they interpret, add to, and make changes to the Word of God to suit themselves. They have developed the many denominations, independents, and sects because they do not understand the true way of walking before our Almighty God. They do not adhere to the truths in God's Word to produce true disciples of Jesus and help them become soul-winners for the Kingdom of God. Instead, a great majority of the leadership of the "church system" produces members for the various denominational churches in existence today. It has been said that history repeats itself. This is very true when men do not allow God to do the directing. It seems that man can only learn by making heart-breaking mistakes and by not following the truths in the Holy Word of God.

The Restored Spiritualized Sovereign Rule of God

A second declaration was made by God, later in the book of Matthew that restored the spiritual kingdom of God. The declaration was made to all mankind in Matthew 16:18: "And I also say to you that you are Peter, and upon this rock I will build My church; [called-out ones] and the gates of Hades shall not overpower it." [Clarification added by the author.]

The moment Christ said, as He was dying on the cross, "It is finished," (John 19:30) the sin nature in man could be and is defeated in mankind and spiritual guidance can work again within mankind through the indwelling of the Holy Spirit of God. These two events given to us through the Holy Word of God restored the Holy Spirit to mankind, those who are worthy to receive it, and God restored the spiritual kingdom on earth and in heaven.

The restored spiritual kingdom of God was first occupied by Christ and by the souls who came out of their graves the moment Christ died and by the repentant criminal who died on one of the three crosses. (See Matthew 27:51-53.) Christ became the first fruits, (See 1 Corinthians 15:20-23) of the work of God in restoring the spiritual kingdom of God.

> And one of the criminals who where hanged there was hurling abuse at Him, saying, "Are you not the Christ? Save yourself and us!" But the other answered, and rebuking him said, "Do you not even fear God, since you are under the same sentence of condemnation? "And we indeed are suffering justly, for we are receiving what we deserve for our deeds; but this man has done nothing wrong." And he was saying, "Jesus, remember me when You come in Your Kingdom!" And He said to him, "Truly I say to you, today you shall be with Me in Paradise!" (Luke 23:39-43)

Verse 43 surely can mean nothing other than what it says. Jesus was not speaking in parables; this certainly was a statement holding a sense of urgency and profound truth. This man would be in the restored spiritual kingdom of heaven with Christ which was established by God in His Son in Matthew 16:18 and delineated through the first half of the book of Matthew. The spiritual kingdom is inhabited by those souls Christ released from captivity. (See Ephesians 4:8; Psalms 68:18; Isaiah 61:1; Matthew 27:51-53.) The restored spiritual kingdom of God also includes all who have died in Christ Jesus from the time Christ ascended into heaven and up to the present time. Those persons who are alive today and who have Christ Jesus as Lord and Master of their lives also belong to the restored spiritual kingdom of God. Also, God restored His grace as our teacher.

Captivity Captive

> During those days Christ was on the earth, Scriptures tell us Christ lead captivity captive.
>
> You have ascended on high, You have led captive Your captives; You have received gifts among men, Even among the rebellious also, that the Lord God may dwell there. (See Psalms 68:18)

In Luke 4:18,19, Jesus reads from the book of Isaiah.

> "THE SPIRIT OF THE LORD IS UPON ME, BECAUSE HE ANOINTED ME TO PREACH THE GOSPEL TO THE POOR. HE HAS SENT ME TO PROCLAIM RELEASE TO THE CAPTIVES, AND RECOVERY OF SIGHT TO THE BLIND, TO SET FREE THOSE WHO ARE OPPRESSED, TO PROCLAIM THE FAVORABLE YEAR OF THE LORD."

This same Scripture in Isaiah 61:1 reads,

> The Spirit of the Lord God is upon me; Because the Lord has anointed me To bring good news to the afflicted; He has sent me to bind up the brokenhearted, To proclaim liberty to captives, And freedom to prisoners; (Isaiah 61:1)
>
> And behold, the veil of the temple was torn in two

> from top to bottom; and the earth shook and the rocks were split. The tombs were opened, and many bodies of the saints who had fallen asleep were raised; and coming out of the tombs after His resurrection they entered the holy city and appeared to many. (Matthew 27:51-53)

The very moment that Christ said, "It is finished," those persons who died during the time between Adam and Christ, and who were declared worthy of eternal life with God were released by Christ when He descended into the earth and were, at the time of Christ's ascension, taken to heaven with Him. We are told several times in the Scriptures that only the shed blood of the Son of God could reconcile mankind unto God. The persons (captivity captive) being addressed here were released from the place they were held. We are told in Scriptures that there are two holding places in the earth for persons who died—hell for the evil and ungodly and a second place where those who belonged to God, Christ took captivity captive. They were taken to heaven with Him and were made a part of the spiritual kingdom of heaven.

Sheol

A discussion of the word "Sheol" can shed some light on where those souls were held until the restoration of the spiritual kingdom of heaven. A 1943 printing of *The Holy Bible* by The National Bible Press, distributed by the Goodwill Distributors, Gastonia, North Carolina, gives a detailed description of the word "**Sheol**":

> The place of departed dead. This Hebrew word is

> identical with the Greek word Hades of the New Testament often spoken of as a terminus of human life, the grave (Job 17:13). The natural man may judge from appearances and to him sheol seems no more than a grave (Eccles. 9:10). But Scripture shows it is a place of sorrow (2 Sam. 22:6; Ps. 18:5; 116:3); into which the wicked must pass (Ps. 9:17). In Jonah 2:2 the great fish is to Jonah as sheol is to the dead. But Revelation, while not altering or changing conditions at all, does increase our knowledge of that which before was hidden, and we learn that sheol has two divisions, one for the lost and one for the saved. The latter is known as Abraham's bosom (Luke 16:22) and paradise (Luke 23:43). A great gulf is fixed between these divisions (Luke 16:26). The lost man has his full faculties and memory (Is. 14:9-17; Ezek. 32:21). Since Christ there has been revealed no change in the condition of the lost. At the great white throne scene they pass out to their reward (Rev. 20:13, 14). As to the other division, paradise is now in the presence of God (2 Cor. 12:1-4; Eph. 4:8-10). Both places still await the resurrection (Job 19:25; 1 Cor. 15:52).[3]

The Restoration of the Davidic Throne—Israel's Glorious Reunion with God

The earthly reign of Christ Jesus, we are told, will occur next in the progression of the sovereign rule of God. This rule by Christ Jesus is widely known as the millennial kingdom, but most correctly stated, it is the restored Davidic throne. Christ will rule in person, along with all of the saints. (See Revelation 20:4-6; 2 Timothy 2:10-12.) We are told this continuing kingdom of God will be occupied by all of those who will be raised by God from their graves, and Christ Jesus will bring them with Him to earth at His second appearance. All those who are alive and belong to Christ at the moment Christ appears in the sky are removed from this earth and meet Christ in the air. (See 1 Thessalonians 4:13-18.) However, only those who truly belong to Christ (have Christ Jesus as Lord and Master of their lives) will meet Christ in the air. All of those souls will remain with Christ in safety out of the earth while the last half of the seven years of the tribulation runs its course on earth. Additional souls will come to true salvation in Christ Jesus during the last half of the tribulation and will be added to those souls who meet Christ Jesus in the air. At the end of the seven years of tribulation, Christ Jesus will bring the spiritual kingdom to earth and will reign over the inhabitants of the earth for a thousand years. (See Revelation 20:1-7; Matthew 24; 1 Thessalonians 4:13-18.)

The restoration of the throne of David brings into being Israel's glorious reunion with their God. We are told that great joy is celebrated in heaven when a soul is brought to salvation through the blood of Jesus Christ. We cannot imagine the joy that will be celebrated in heaven and on earth the day the chosen people of God are restored unto God. We could say the joy would be a million times greater and that would not express it adequately, because all of the grief and suffering that the chosen people of God and the saints of the Gentiles experienced will be released all at the same time in heaven. Anyone who cares about the chosen people of God and has studied and thought about the history of the Jewish people will have only a minute understanding of the great joy that will come over our great God the day the leaders of the nation of Israel say, "Blessed is He who comes in the name of the Lord." (Matthew 23:39) At that moment great numbers of the Jewish people will accept their Messiah. At that same moment Christ Jesus makes His second appearance and leads the great victory over the armies of the earth. This happening is similar to the happening that occurred at the first appearance of the Son of God. At that appearance, Christ Jesus restored the spiritual kingdom and all mankind became one again. God's chosen people as a whole are restored unto Himself and the promise made by God concerning the reign by the Son on the Davidic throne is fulfilled.

Why should the people of the "church system" be given understanding concerning the second coming of Jesus Christ? The tables are turned! At the first appearance of our Lord and Savior, the leaders of the Jewish people were living in extreme ignorance of the Word of God. At the second appearance of our Lord and Savior, the "Christian leaders" are living and directing the lives of millions of people in extreme ignorance of the Word of God. The "Christian leaders" tell us that when Christ appears in the sky, He will rapture the church up into the sky with Him. This is where the extreme ignorance has its beginning. The big if is, if all those sitting under the "one-man ministry" have not been discipled into truly belonging to the Lord, they are not ready for the second appearance of the Lord. Just as the Jewish leaders at Christ's first appearance were in extreme disobedience of God, so is the extreme disobedience of the "church system" leadership of today. They serve the church instead of serving God. They are building their own little kingdoms.

It is not the church that God has developed and prepared all His plans and provisions around. Our heavenly Father has been working for the good of all mankind and particularly for His chosen people, the restoration of the Davidic throne (Kingdom of God). It is the throne of David, ruled over by the Blessed Son of God/Son of Man, that brings true justice, true peace, and true government for the people, and will once again be on the earth. This is no little matter that God's chosen people come to the One who had longed to be among them and be their Father. (See 2 Corinthians 6:16.)

The tribulation comes upon mankind for the same reason God brought the great flood upon the earth and wiped out all of the earth's inhabitants except eight people because the people of the earth at that time were corrupt. The great tribulation comes upon the peoples of the earth because mankind does not want God to rule in their life. We witness the rainbow during rain showers. It appears as a reminder of the awesome power and the great love of God. As the end of the tribulation approaches in the form of the gathering of many armies of the nations who do not trust in God and who hate His chosen people, Christ Jesus also appears in the sky with His great army of God. The armies of the earth are gathering against Israel, and in particular the city of Jerusalem, to destroy the Jews. In a lightning quick strike against the forces of Satan's earthly armies, Christ Jesus destroys the entire armies of the earth. The blood of the enemies of God's chosen people runs five feet deep on the battlefield of Armageddon.

Great joy is once again in heaven because the Jews repent of their long-standing sinfulness against God (unrepentful heart and corruption of the bloodline of the people of God—see Ezra 9:2) and they are restored to their heavenly Father. This restoration of God's people to God is the second great work of the Son of God/Son of Man and it happens at the second appearance of Christ Jesus. All of you who read this who are Jews (Israelites) stop grieving God and accept your Messiah before the Son's second appearance and be with the Lord at His appearing.

God has great sorrow over His special people because they refuse to repent of the great sin they committed against God their Father. Many of the Jews, particularly their leadership, do not understand the great all-loving and all-powerful God. The Jews are not alone in the areas of grieving God. Most Gentiles grieve God by following other gods. These gods come in many different forms. Check out the form you follow by asking the true God to show you Christ Jesus and His work of His shed blood. In I Kings 11:1-11 we are told how King Solomon had taken many wives from the forbidden neighboring populations and succumbed to the will of the pagan wives and fell into the worship of idols. Many of the succeeding kings followed the worship of idols and caused the people to follow the king in his sin. The ultimate penalty due to the sin of the chosen people was cause for the kingdom to be divided and ultimately removed from the land. And then God returned to His place. (See Hosea 5:15.) What does this mean, God returned to His place? It simply means He left his place in the temple and returned to heaven awaiting the day His chosen people say, "Blessed is He who comes in the name of the Lord." (Luke 13:35)

The Eternal Kingdom of God

The last manifestation of the sovereign rule of God is the eternal kingdom of God in the new heaven and new earth.

(See Revelation 21.) The eternal kingdom is where God, along with the Son, will reign throughout eternity, visible to all. In 1 Corinthians 15:20-28, we are told that the Son delivers up the spiritual kingdom to God the Father, the kingdom God placed the Son over at Matthew 16:18.

> But now Christ has been raised from the dead, the first fruits of those who are asleep. For since by a man came death, by a man also came the resurrection of the dead. For as in Adam all die, so also in Christ all will be made alive. But each in his own order: Christ the first fruits, after that those who are Christ's at His coming, then comes the end, when He hands over the kingdom to the God and Father, when He has abolished all rule and all authority and power. For He must reign until He has put all His enemies under His feet. The last enemy that will be abolished is death. For He HAS PUT ALL THINGS IN SUBJECTION UNDER HIS FEET. But when He says, "All things are put in subjection," it is evident that He is excepted who put all things in subjection to Him. When all things are subjected to Him, then the Son Himself also will be subjected to the One who subjected all things to Him, that God may be all in all.

Now the kingdom of God will be complete. The Jews have repented of their long-standing sin and are restored to God. The spiritual guidance of man, the spiritual kingdom of God, and the Davidic throne have been restored in and through the Son. God had given the inhabitants of the earth one last chance to repent and come unto the Father during the thousand-year reign by His Son on earth. The original spiritual relationship man had with God in the Garden of Eden is restored. This is one of the mysteries spoken of long ages ago in Scripture. (See Romans 16:25; Matthew 13:35; Titus 1:2.) All this is now available to everyone who has Christ Jesus as Lord and Master of his or her life. The sovereign rule of God that exists since the beginning of time becomes visible to mankind and manifests itself as the eternal kingdom of God. The time has arrived when there is no longer a need for spiritualization between man and God, for God and the Son are sitting on the glorious throne and mankind is worshipping their God in complete truth with great praise, honor, and glory for ever and ever. God is in the midst once again of the people of His creation. Before the eternal kingdom of God comes into being, the great White Throne judgment of those who died and were not part of the spiritual kingdom of God are judged, and their destiny throughout all of eternity is fixed by the final judgment of God upon mankind.

God only has a kingdom to preside over when He has men who are living in harmony and in complete obedience to God through the shed blood of Jesus Christ the Jews' Messiah. God created man in His own image and man began his existence in the power of God. This means that God was able to communicate with man in the power of the Holy Spirit unless God was with man in visible form such as a father rules over his children. But we are told in Genesis that Adam and Eve heard God speak to them and they heard God walk in the Garden of Eden. The assumption is, Holy Spirit relationship existed between God and man in the Garden of Eden before man rejected God by disobedience. That relationship was like the relationship people have with Christ today when they truly belong to God, they are guided by the Holy Spirit. God is not walking around with each soul in the form each and every saved soul can see and converse with God. When man fell away from the all-loving and the all-powerful God, man gave up the Father/child relationship with their maker. Man caused God to set aside the spiritual kingdom of God because man chose not to live under the rule and authority of God. God did not choose to abandon mankind; mankind made that choice. So, the spiritual kingdom of God was set aside because mankind gave up the Father/child relationship. Spiritual death came to man by man and God could only restore the spiritual kingdom through a man. A man who would be obedient to God in all respects and who wanted God to be the all-loving and all-powerful heavenly Father. At the right time Christ died for us. (See Romans 5:6-11.)

6

God Reveals the Restoration of the Spiritual Kingdom

In the book of Matthew, God gives us unmistakable documentation of the primary reason He sent His only begotten Son to earth. God used His Son, Jesus Christ, the Jewish Messiah, and John the Baptist, the preparer of the hearts of the Jewish people, to teach the people the gospel message of Christ. God used Matthew to record the gospel of Jesus Christ and the message that God was restoring the spiritual kingdom of God in the Son, for He is worthy. Throughout the book of Matthew, God sets out for us significant facts and events in the life and ministry of His Son. When those facts and events are looked at collectively and analyzed in light of what we are told in the New Testament concerning Jesus Christ, an amazing truth about the most important reason, among the many reasons, for God to send His Son to earth on behalf of all mankind is revealed. That most important reason had to be for the restoration of the Holy Spirit to humankind and the restoration of the spiritual kingdom of God. Throughout the book of Matthew we read, the kingdom of heaven is near.

In the last half of Matthew, Jesus brought upon the Jewish leaders the wrath of God because, in the first half of Matthew, Jesus, their Messiah, gives them every opportunity, with detailed instructions, to repent. Because of their unrepentant hearts, the Jewish leaders fell into rejection of their Messiah and that opened the way for the Gentiles to be included in the saving power of the shed blood of the Son. If the Jewish leaders had accepted their Messiah, the spiritual kingdom of God would have been restored and the Davidic throne would have been established in the Son of God. For the time being, the Gentiles would have been left out, but God wanted all mankind to be restored unto Himself in the one and only spiritual kingdom of God as first conceived and established by God in the Garden of Eden thousands of years before. (See Ephesians 2; Romans 11:11.)

A Grave Misunderstanding

Many theologians and the very best Bible scholars cling to the thinking that Acts 2:1-18 says God returned the Holy Spirit to earth and that was the day (Day of Pentecost) the church system, as we see it today, had its beginning. God did, in fact, make an appearance on earth that day (a theophany). The Messianic Jewish scholar, David Stern, gives an extended discussion on the subject, the Day of Pentecost, in his *Jewish New Testament Commentary.*[1] Since the day of Pentecost (Shavu´ot) remains a very special day to most Jewish people and in particular to Messianic Jews, we need to become very interested as to the true meaning of what happened on the Day of Pentecost in Acts 2. We need to make certain that we understand the importance of that day to the Gentile follower of the Lord Jesus Christ. We should not want to agree to stealing that day away from the Jews and apply it to or fabricate a new meaning that God did not intend to bring into existence for the application of the Gentile church system only.

We need to look at the wording in Acts 2 concerning the event (the theophany—an appearance of God) through the wisdom and knowledge of Messianic Jewish scholars. At the same time, we need to set aside the popular teachings of the Gentile seminaries on the subject. Acts 2:1, "When the day of Pentecost had come, they were all together in one place." The meaning of the word "they" is given in Acts 1:23-26 and has to refer to the disciples of Jesus. Verses 2 and 3 describes the sudden appearance of God in a violent, rushing wind that filled the whole house where they were sitting. Verse 3, "And there appeared to them tongues as of fire distributing themselves, and they rested on each one of them." Verse 4, "And they [the disciples] were all filled with the Holy Spirit and began to speak with other tongues, as the Spirit was giving them utterance." [Clarification added by the author.]

The next verses give us the reason they spoke in various languages (tongues). We are told that there were believing Jews living in Jerusalem from every nation under heaven. Then we are given the names of those nations. This was the representation, needed by God, of all peoples from all over the world so that God could display His great pleasure in what His Son performed for the Father. The unusualness and uniqueness of this gathering in Jerusalem (God's holy city is similar to Mt. Sinai) on the day of Pentecost should cause us to wonder why the tongues of fire were falling and being distributed upon the disciples; and when they spoke, all who were gathered together heard their message in each one's own language simultaneously. This was one of the wondrous revealings of our heavenly Father, and it was not used to usher in an earthly something to be managed by men of the cloth. The true reason that God made this appearance on the day of Pentecost was that God displayed His great joy over the fact that His Son's birth, ministry, suffering, death, resurrection, and His ascension made it possible for God the Father to restore the spiritual guidance in mankind and the spiritual kingdom of God in heaven and on earth.

The reference above to David Stern's discussion on the day of Pentecost brings out the fact that on the day God gave His people the Law at Mt. Sinai (the Holy Mountain and in that respect is similar to Jerusalem, the Holy City—See Hebrews 12:18-24) through God's servant Moses, a similar theophany occurred. Something with a very great importance to God was revealed to man on the day of Pentecost at Mt. Sinai and in Jerusalem, and God wants us to search His Word to establish human understanding concerning the depth and breadth of the full meaning of what God did for mankind through the birth, life, and death of His only begotten Son, Jesus Christ, the Jews' Messiah.

The Blood of Christ Did It All

And they sang a new song, saying, "Worthy are You to take the book and to break its seals; for You were slain, and purchased for God with Your blood *men* from every tribe and tongue and people and nation. "You have made them to be a kingdom and priests to our God; and they will reign upon the earth." (Revelation 5:9,10) At the moment our Lord and Savior was drawing His last breath, He said, "It is finished." (John 19:30) What was finished? The life and death of the Son of God made several provisions for His father. The most important provision was the restoration of the spiritual kingdom of God.

Matthew 27:50,51, gives us some very good news concerning the provisions the Son of God made for His father: "And Jesus cried out again with a loud voice, and yielded up His spirit. And behold, the veil of the temple was torn in two from top to bottom; and the earth shook and the rocks were split."

The splitting of the veil in the temple symbolized the breaking down of the middle wall of partition between Jew and Gentile (the representatives on the day of Pentecost from every nation), thus making it possible to bring Jew and Gentile back together again as one creation before their maker. But just as important, Christ broke down the middle wall of partition in the temple that stood between God and mankind (See Illustration 1). From that moment on mankind could join the Father in heaven and God the Father restored the spiritual kingdom. This is the reason God showed His great joy on the day of Pentecost. How could God show great joy over the man-made church? In fact the term had not yet been invented by men. (See Part 2, pages 280-313.) The first time the word appeared in a Bible translation was all the way down to 1560 A.D. Back then (16th century) those who were in control of the governments of the nations also controlled religious beliefs and form of worship, not in churches, but that religious thought that was in the minds of the government rulers. We must become educated concerning what was going on throughout the time frame men call the "history of the church!"

The New Testament gives us God's plan (ways and means), first to restore His people unto Himself and, second, to restore the rest of mankind (Gentiles) unto Himself. We must remember that mankind gave God a very grieving heart at the time of the fall. But at the same time, mankind paid a terrible price for the fall. A price that remained for Gentiles until the first appearance of Christ. The price the Jews are paying for their unrepentant heart continues until the second appearance of Christ. However, a number each year are finding peace in salvation in their Messiah. Restoration of mankind unto God was the underlying reason God sent His Son to earth to die on the cross (the most cruel death of all deaths), to suffer the shedding of His blood, to descend into the earth, to be raised from the dead, to ascend into heaven to become the means and head of the spiritual kingdom of God in heaven and on earth.

ILLUSTRATION 1

The Son of God and the Tabernacle/Temple of God[2]

Temple Structure

1. Brazen Altar of Burnt Offering. Lev. 1:3, 10, 14
2. Lavar. Ex. 30:18-20 for Priests to wash.
3. Table of Shewbread. Lev. 24:5-9
4. Seven Golden Candles-Lamp-stand. Ex. 25:31-40
5. Altar of Incense Ex. 30:7, 8
6. Veil. Ex. 26:33
7. Ark of Covenant Ex. 25:10
8. Mercy Seat. Ex. 25:17-22

The Tabernacle/Temple (Schematic)

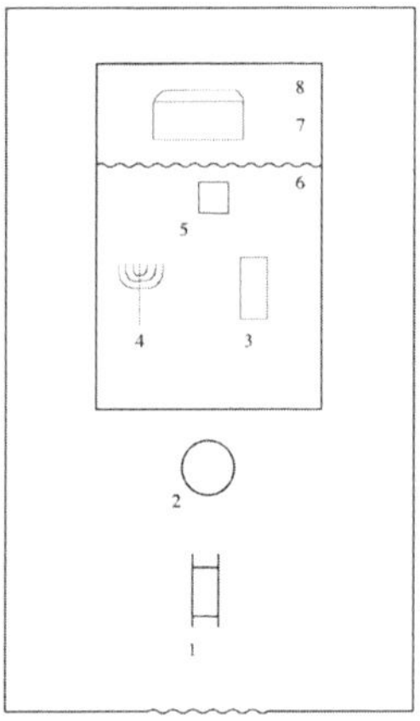

Our Life in Christ Jesus

1. Rom. 12:1 Present your bodies as a living sacrifice. Heb. 10:20 New and living way.
2. Titus 3:5 Washing and regeneration. Eph. 5:26 washing of water by the Word. 1 John 1:7 Cleansed by the blood of Christ.
3. John 6:35 I am the bread of life. John 6:53 Except ye eat My flesh and drink My Blood.
4. John 8:12 I am the light of the world. Matt. 5:14, You are the light of the world.
5. Luke 1:5-10, Zacharias burned incense; people prayed. Ps. 141:2 Prayer as incense. Rev. 8:3 Incense offered with prayer. Eph. 5:2 Christ offered.
6. Heb. 10:20 His flesh. Matt. 27:51, 52 The veil a type of the body of Christ.
7. Heb. 1:1, 2 Spoken by His Son.
8. Heb. 3:1-Our high Priest in the Holy of Holies of heaven. Heb. 9:24, 25 Our High Priest. See Heb. 9:1-28 for additional comparison of the Tabernacle/Temple symbolism of our Lord and Master

Jesus Christ came to earth because this was God's way to give proof to His people, the Jews, concerning His great love for them and also the Gentiles. Christ died on the Jewish Passover and the Feast of Unleavened Bread for the following purposes and provisions of God:

1. Christ fulfilled the symbolic Passover, the Passover Lamb of the first Passover.
2. Christ's shed blood on the cross ratified the New Covenant with the Israelites, but the Jews rejected their Messiah and they would remain in their sin until the great tribulation and until they say, "Blessed is He who comes in the name of the Lord." (Matthew 23:39)
3. Christ's shed blood on the cross redeemed all mankind and, thus, reconciled all mankind unto God.
4. Christ's burial set the captives free—those captives who were being held in God's holding place, Abraham's bosom and paradise, were set free by Christ and ascended into heaven with Christ.
5. Christ's ascension into heaven completed the restoration of the spiritual kingdom of God.
6. Christ established the way we should remember Him and His work. He used the common Jewish custom of blessing the bread before the meal began and the blessing of the wine at the end of the meal. This thanksgiving and remembrance would be acknowledged before our heavenly Father each and every time we eat a meal, by Jews and Gentiles alike.
7. Christ's death, burial, and ascension made all people on the face of the earth one again on the day of Pentecost.

The Kingdom Comes Alive

To initiate these purposes and provisions, God set into motion the creation of a new people through His rule by grace. The return of the Holy Spirit to earth through the Son was an integral part of the plan of God for His chosen people and for all who have His Son as a personal Savior. Remember that God always wanted to be with His created beings. God has projected His relationship with man as Father/children. (See Exodus 25:8.) His creation of His chosen people proves this point. There are four times when God was or is in the direct Father/children relationship:

1. In the Garden of Eden.
2. During the exodus from Egypt and then in the Tabernacle/Temple setting.
3. During Christ's first visit to earth.
4. During the spiritual kingdom and will continue into the restoration of the Davidic throne (thousand-year reign of Christ) and on into the eternal kingdom of God.

As we enter into the study of the kingdom of heaven in the first sixteen chapters, mainly, of the book of Matthew, God causes us to focus our attention immediately upon the Son. From His opening statements concerning the genealogy of His Son, to the command He gave us to fill His kingdom with souls worthy of His eternal care, He gives us the complete knowledge of His kingdom development by those people who become His true disciples. Becoming His true disciple is part of why mankind needs to respond to God's offer to belong to His kingdom. Citing the genealogy of Christ Jesus was most important to the Jewish people. This establishes the fact that God had announced this event of bringing the Messiah to earth in the Scriptures long before the event happened. The Jewish people understood that such an event would happen and they knew the Messiah's lineage. However, the Jewish leadership (ruling body) did not respond to their Messiah.

At the beginning of the second chapter of Matthew, God makes the first of two very important announcements. Matthew 2:2a, "Where is He who has been born King of the Jews?" God projects His Son here as a king. We are reminded also that the Jews wanted Pontius Pilate to kill the King of the Jews. (See Matthew 27:37.) So Christ was declared to be King of the Jews at His birth, and He was declared to be King of the Jews at His death. John the Baptist adds another announcement concerning the King of the Jews. He announces where that kingdom would be established. Matthew 3:2,3, "Repent, for the kingdom of heaven is at hand." For this is the one referred to by Isaiah the prophet when he said, "THE VOICE OF ONE CRYING IN THE WILDERNESS, 'MAKE READY THE WAY OF THE LORD, MAKE HIS PATHS STRAIGHT!'" This is saying, prepare the people to accept what the King is about to do for them. Make them clean so they will be able to receive the gift of the King and can enter the spiritual kingdom. John the Baptist's work with the Jews was to bring them to repentance, for they were still under the condemnation of God at the time He returned to His place. This is the reason John said, "Repent, for the kingdom of heaven is at hand."

The next significant event that broadens our understanding

of the development of the spiritual kingdom is given in Matthew 3:13-17:

> Then Jesus arrived from Galilee at the Jordan coming to John, to be baptized by him. But John tried to prevent Him, saying, "I have need to be baptized by you, and do You come to me?" But Jesus answering said to him, "Permit it at this time; for in this way it is fitting for us to fulfill all righteousness." [The cleaning needed to be done to the Son so that God could declare the Son to be worthy for the basis of the restoration of the spiritual kingdom and that the Son could pass on to those who trust in Him the Holy Spirit, righteousness and eternal life—He is worthy.] Then he permitted Him. After being baptized, Jesus came up immediately from the water; and behold, the heavens were opened, and He saw the Spirit of God descending as a dove and lighting on Him, and behold, a voice out of the heavens said, "This is My beloved Son, in whom I am well-pleased." [Clarification added by the author.]

John the Baptist was created in the likeness of Elijah and was clean before God Almighty so that he could perform the baptism of His Son. The baptism of the Son of God/Son of Man had to be performed by a Godly person. God produced that person at the same time of the birth of His Son. The baby, John the Baptist, was clean. He was filled with the Holy Spirit in the womb of Elizabeth because Elizabeth was filled with the Holy Spirit. (See Luke 1:41.)

It is most interesting to see in Matthew 3:4 that John the Baptist's attire is similar to that of Elijah in 2 Kings 1:8; thus giving us a deeper understanding of Jesus' words in Matthew

11:11-14 and Matthew 17:10-13. Indeed, a type of Elijah did come in the form of John the Baptist to condemn the Jewish leadership's foreknown rejection of their Christ. Elijah, apparently, will make an appearance to the Jews at their Messiah's second coming. John the Baptist was highly critical of the Jewish leadership's attitude and lack of understanding of the prophecies and teachings of the Old Testament. This is the cause of Jesus' rebuke of them and His condemnation of them for having rejected His main reason for coming to establish the kingdom of heaven for them as His special people. He condemns them for attempting to keep the restored spiritual kingdom from happening and for forcing their way into the kingdom of heaven by their traditions of men.

God placed great emphasis on this significant event, the baptism of His Son, because this is the moment, and the day, God returned the Holy Spirit to earth. The Holy Spirit was removed from the earth when Judah was taken into exile (by Nebuchadnezzar) and, at the time of the destruction of the Temple, where God dwelt (586 B.C.). (See Hosea 5:15.) After this, Jesus was immediately led up by the Spirit into the wilderness to be tempted by the devil. (See Matthew 4:1-11.) Jesus proved that He was who He said He was, the King, and He is worthy. In Matthew 4:17b, Christ makes the announcement, "Repent, for the kingdom of heaven is at hand." Now the announcement concerning the coming establishment of the spiritual kingdom of God is complete, Christ's forerunner, John the Baptist, God the Father and Christ make the announcement that the kingdom of God is now in preparation in heaven and God has sent His Son to be the one that will be its king.

Philippians 2:5-11 places emphasis on the kingship of the Son of God:

> Have this attitude in yourselves which was also in Christ Jesus, who, although He existed in the form of God, did not regard equality with God a thing to be grasped, but emptied Himself, taking the form of a bond-servant, and being made in the likeness of men. Being found in appearance as a man, He humbled Himself by becoming obedient to the point of death, even death on a cross. For this reason also, God highly exalted Him, and bestowed on Him the name which is above every name, so that at the name of Jesus EVERY KNEE WILL BOW, of those who are in heaven and on earth and under the earth, and that every tongue will confess that Jesus Christ is Lord, to the glory of God the Father.

Evidence of the Kingdom's Development

Mankind needs to be given instructions on the fact God sent His Son to restore the spiritual kingdom.

In Matthew 4:18, 19 Jesus begins to gather His first followers and helpers to prepare the people for His ministry of the gospel of the kingdom of heaven. Jesus uses His power of healing to bring together great multitudes of people everywhere He went so that He could teach them what they needed to know about being part of the kingdom of God. Jesus used the opportunities to provide food for the great masses of pilgrims on their way to the Passover and Feast of Unleavened Bread at Jerusalem to teach on the subject of the kingdom of heaven. (See Matthew 15:32-39; Luke 9:12-17.) Those groups of people traveling to

Jerusalem could have been as large as 15,000 to 20,000 people each. (See Matthew chapters 5, 6, and 7.)

> Jesus cautions us in Matthew 6:20,21, "But store up for yourselves treasures in heaven, where neither moth nor rust destroys, and where thieves do not break in or steal; for where your treasure is, there your heart will be also. In Matthew 6:26 and 32-34, Christ gives directions on why we need to depend on God for all our needs. "Look at the birds of the air, that they do not sow, nor reap nor gather into barns, and yet your heavenly Father feeds them. Are you not worth much more than they?" For the Gentiles eagerly seek all these things; for your heavenly Father knows that you need all these things. "But seek first His kingdom and His righteousness, and all these things will be added to you." So do not worry about tomorrow; for tomorrow will care for itself. Each day has enough trouble of its own.

It is a most urgent necessity that everyone who darkens a church doorway is certain that they are part of the kingdom of heaven. In Matthew 6:8-15 we are told by Christ how to pray. God knows our needs before we ask Him, and we are to pray that we be worthy to be part of the kingdom. A most important truth to remember. We must be able to forgive others their trespasses against us to be worthy of the kingdom. Those who belong to the spiritual kingdom in Christ have their every need supplied by simply asking.

> Matthew 7:7,8, "Ask, and it shall be given to you; seek, and you will find; knock, and it will be opened to you. "For everyone who asks receives, and he who seeks finds, and to him who knocks it will be opened.

> [Jesus also gives the consequences for those who ignore His teachings.]
>
> Matthew 7:21,24,25, "Not everyone who says to Me, 'Lord, Lord,' will enter the kingdom of heaven, but he who does the will of My Father who is in heaven will enter. "Therefore everyone who hears these words of Mine and acts on them, may be compared to a wise man who built his house on the rock. "And the rain fell, and the floods came, and the winds blew and slammed against that house; and yet it did not fall, for it had been founded on the rock.

Jesus gives us examples of individuals showing great faith after hearing His teachings, which provide guidance for our way to walk before our God. In Matthew 8 there are contrasting examples: the leper and centurion compared to the disciples' experience in the boat during a storm.

In Matthew chapter 10 Christ is giving His twelve disciples their special instructions to go to the house of Israel to preach the gospel of the kingdom of heaven is at hand. The importance of the care of the gospel of the kingdom of heaven has now spread to the disciples of Jesus, but they were limited to take that gospel only to the Jews. Nevertheless, the importance of the gospel of the kingdom is gaining momentum as we approach chapter 13, where the entire chapter is devoted to various explanations by Christ, in parables, what is the kingdom of heaven. In the meantime we are told about how the opposition to Christ's spreading of the gospel of the kingdom, and Christ Himself, is showing its ugly face. (See Matthew chapters 11 and 12.) This opposition brings on the necessity at this time for Christ Jesus to speak to these people in parables. Christ gives those who do not receive His gospel of the kingdom some very difficult teachings to ponder and to discuss among themselves. Included in these groups were the Pharisees who began, at this time, their campaign against Christ to discredit Him and to bring false accusations against Him. This beginning of the Pharisees' uprising against Christ carried into the day the Jewish leadership came out to arrest Jesus. The stage is being set for the struggle between Christ, on the one hand, concerning the reason God sent His Son to earth and the objectors who brought the Sanhedrin into making legal, the rejection of Christ as the Messiah on the Jewish side of the fateful day Christ died on the cross. The people who were against Christ even used the fact that Christ said that He came to establish the kingdom of heaven as evidence in front of Pilate. (See John 19:12.)

In Matthew 11:11-16, Christ tells the people that the time has come when God is making it possible for His people to be reconciled unto Himself. Verse 13: "For all the prophets and the Law prophesied until John." Meaning, John is now telling the people about that prophecy in the Old Testament concerning Jesus Christ. From this point in time, on to the end of time on this earth in its present form, the Law and prophecy is being fulfilled in Christ Jesus. God is fulfilling the Law and prophecy concerning His Son. Something new has been brought to earth that is taking the place of the old and is changing how His people will serve and worship their God. This is part of the reason that the temple in Jerusalem was destroyed in 70 A.D.

The Storm Is Gathering

From this point on in Matthew, God is making the transition from the Old Covenant with His people to the New

Covenant with His people. God is coming up to the time in the book of Matthew when He is making the announcement concerning how the Old Covenant will be replaced. Matthew 11:25-30 is significant for our understanding of the forthcoming announcement in Matthew the sixteenth chapter,

> At that time Jesus said, "I praise You, Father, Lord of heaven and earth, that You have hidden these things from the wise and intelligent and have revealed them to infants. "Yes, Father, for this was well-pleasing in Your sight. "All things have been handed over to Me by My Father; and no one knows the Son except the Father; nor does anyone know the Father except the Son, and anyone to whom the Son wills to reveal Him. "Come to Me, all who are weary and heavy-laden, and I will give you rest. "Take My yoke upon you and learn from Me, for I am gentle and humble in heart, and YOU WILL FIND REST FOR YOUR SOULS. "For My yoke is easy and My load is light."

Christ tells the Jews in plain language that their God has now brought to them their Savior, which was prophesied by the prophets and this good news is made understandable to those kinds of people set out in Matthew 5. Christ tells them about the opportunity that is theirs and how easy it is for them to belong to Him in His soon to come kingdom.

In Matthew chapter 12:20-28, Christ spends time explaining how His kingdom is true and how the people will know it is true. Christ leads us into chapter 13 with the answer to the scribes' and Pharisees' request for a sign. (See Matthew 12:38.) The sign of Jonah is given to them, which is the first time He foretells of His coming death for the sins of the world. Christ lays out for the Pharisees, with very few words, the condition of their very soul because it is their disbelief that Christ was sent to cleanse the hearts and minds of men of sins. Apparently the Pharisees were not able to pray a sinner's prayer and it is evident here they did not go to complete repentance before God and, thus, they remained in their sin. Matthew 12:43-45 explains their condition, and this scripture can apply to those today who only ask Christ into their life without fully confessing their sins and make Christ Lord and Master of their life.

> "Now when the unclean spirit goes out of a man, it passes through waterless places seeking rest, and does not find it. "Then it says, 'I will return to my house from which I came;' and when it comes, it finds it unoccupied, swept, and put in order. "Then it goes and takes along with it seven other spirits more wicked than itself, and they go in and live there; and the last state of that man becomes worst than the first. That is the way it will also be with this evil generation."

Luke 11:24-26 gives the same account of the condition of the Pharisees. In the two verses following verse 26, Christ rebukes the Pharisees: verse 27, while Jesus was saying these things, one of the women in the crowd raised her voice and said to Him, "Blessed is the womb that bore you, and the breasts at which You nursed." But He said, "On the contrary, blessed are those who hear the word of God and observe it." A blistering rebuke to the Pharisees' blasphemous words to our Lord. The author believes the condition of a very high percentage of the church attendees today, is that they have heard the Word of God but they are not given the help (discipled) to make Christ

Jesus Lord and Master of their lives. I beg each and every one who is not actively witnessing to friends, relatives, and strangers who need the Lord, to take inventory to find out why not.

7

The Parables of the Restored Spiritual Kingdom of God

Christ used parables to bring attention to and to cause His people, the Jews, to give greater thought to the teachings of Christ Jesus concerning the "kingdom of heaven," which should have meant everything to them. In fact, Christ used more parables in His teaching on the kingdom of heaven than any other subject in preparing His disciples for establishing the called to the restored spiritual kingdom of God.

Beginning with Matthew 13:3, Christ tells the multitudes standing on the beach of the Sea of Galilee the parable of the sower. The sower's seed fell on four types of soil. The seed of the sower is the Word of God given to four different types of people who hear that Word of God concerning the kingdom. The first type of person hears the Word about the kingdom, but the person pays only a little attention to it and does not respond to God's calling. This person's heart and mind are too full of worldly wants and desires. This person heard the word about the kingdom in the wrong place in a very casual manner. True believers who belong to God need to give more attention to this type of person who hears the Word of God and offer to help him or her to want to seek the truth in the Word of God. The second type of person did receive the gospel of the kingdom of God, but no one paid any attention to him or her to disciple them into truly belonging to Christ and help them become a true disciple. For the kingdom of God to be filled, those who truly belong to God must be helping to disciple their neighbor, friend, or relative.

The third type of person who hears the message about the kingdom is too busy with worldly business and pleasure and does not respond to God's call to him or her. When the fourth type of person hears the word of the kingdom, he or she immediately pays complete attention to it and sets his or her whole mind and soul to study God's word. This person responds to the call of God. He or she becomes a disciple and soul winner in complete obedience to God. Some of these persons win one hundred souls for the Lord, some win sixty souls, and some win thirty souls.

This is a very complete picture of how people respond to the call of God. It shows us how important it is to be alert to those around us and be ready to help those who are too weak to respond to the call of God on their own. We who say we love the Lord Jesus Christ need to be complete disciples. This is the true way of knowing that we belong to the Lord: We are bringing those who need Jesus to the Lord so that He can bring them into the restored spiritual kingdom of God.

The next parable is the Tares among the Wheat given at verses 24-30. This parable tells us of those people who heard the truth of the kingdom of heaven, but they allowed the devil to enter in and contaminate the Word, thus following the lust of the flesh and will suffer loss and those who endured will have eternal life with the Lord.

The parable of the Mustard Seed is in Matthew 13:31,32.

The positive message here is that the Word of the kingdom of heaven grows in the hearts and minds of a very small number of people, but because this remnant is so faithful and true and become disciples and witness to the last, each one of that small group, because they are faithful to God's call, produce a great work for the Lord.

The parable of the Leaven is set out in Matthew 13:33. Those who truly love the Lord and become disciples also truly enlighten many around them to where they too become disciples and this goes on and on. This is what the kingdom of heaven is all about. Those who truly love the Lord are about their Father's business.

The parable of the Hidden Treasure (Matthew 13:44) is the total truth that one finds in knowing Jesus Christ as personal Lord and Master of ones life. That truth then leads the individual to be an active disciple in witnessing to those around him or her who need to know that truth about the kingdom of heaven.

The Costly Pearl is the Lord Jesus Christ. He is and always will be the key to the kingdom of heaven. Anyone who has the Lord has a priceless blessing, an eternal blessing—life eternal. So, man should give up all that stands in the way to obtain that priceless blessing of having the Lord Jesus Christ as Lord and Master of their life. This is the parable of the costly Pearl in Matthew 13:45,46.

The last of the seven parables presented to us for special instruction by the Lord Himself is the parable of a Dragnet in Matthew 13:47-50. The kingdom of heaven is like a dragnet, it reaches all of mankind for the Lord, no one should escape the attention of those persons who truly love the Lord. All people need to be told the saving story of how Christ died for us and that He is calling us unto Himself.

This is the one and only parable of the kingdom of God in heaven that tells of the danger that lies ahead for those without Christ. We need to truly belong to the Lord and that we show fruits to prove it. We are disciples, par excellence, not merely Sunday School teachers, members of the choir, a "Meals on Wheels" participant, altar boy etc.—a thousand different church activities, good deeds experts. We are to be disciples. And woe to the ministers, preachers, and priests who are not producing true disciples.

The parable of the Dragnet comes last in this series of parables of the kingdom of heaven because it is that piece of equipment used in the water that catches everything in its path. Nothing escapes the dragnet. Just like the dragnet searching for something, none will escape the great White Throne judgment. So it behooves all true believers, to show those persons around them who need the truth concerning Jesus Christ, the way to salvation.

In verse 52, those who taste of the truth of the kingdom of God in heaven will now understand both what is said by Christ in Matthew 13 and that which was prophesied about Him in the Old Testament. All is now coming to pass, the kingdom of God is being formed. We who truly believe to the fullest must be part of the chain reaction of passing the truth concerning the kingdom of heaven on to the next whom God has called into the light of the truth. This is the only work we have, all else is extra activity without real purpose in God's eyes.

All of the above parables are presented in the present tense. They speak to the people Christ tried to convince to trust in

Him for eternal life then and they speak to all mankind alive today concerning the very same subject. Many of the people who heard Christ give the definition of the kingdom of heaven with seven illustrations had an excuse for not wanting to trust Jesus for eternal life—their eyes, ears, and heart were closed and hardened because of their distrust. All people on earth today do not have an excuse to miss eternal life for all will have heard the truth of the Gospel of Jesus Christ before the end comes. (See Mark 13:10.)

The parables by Christ are all about filling the spiritual kingdom of God. Christ condemned all the Jews who were within the hearing of Christ because they refused to want Christ and His disciples to take them to repentance at this point in the ministry of Jesus Christ. This period of time in the ministry of our Lord was devoted to opening all the minds of His Jewish brothers and sisters to pass on to them the importance of understanding their position without repentance and accepting Him as their Messiah. In fact, the inhabitants of the earth today stand at the very same crossroad when they hear or read the gospel of Jesus Christ.

8

God Makes the Glorious Declaration

After Christ Jesus established His twelve disciples in Himself and equipped them for the work of adding souls to the restored spiritual kingdom of God, they fulfilled His command. Many individuals and groups of people were established in Christ Jesus by the hard work of the first apostles of Christ and they were called the *edhah* (the Hebrew word used in the earliest writings of the New Testament Scriptures preserved by God and handed down to us through the ages). The true meaning of which is: Community of called-out-ones or an assembly or group of called-out-ones. (See 1 Corinthians 1:1-10.)

The early followers of Jesus lived together as individual households. (See Philemon 1:2.) They worshipped God as individual households. Some households met together in groups in the house of one of the neighbors or a relative. (See Colossians 4:15.) This was the common practice of the early followers of Christ. The way they met together to worship God gives us an insight into the grass-root approach they used to serve God, to make Him known to others around them and to produce disciples for their God throughout the territories under Roman rule at the time of Christ and the early centuries following His death. Christ's apostles began the work of taking the Gospel of Jesus Christ and the kingdom of heaven (one and the same guidance for those who need salvation) to the far corners of the known world. It was those persons who were willing to become a disciple of Jesus who kept the Word of God alive within their areas of influence at home.

There is no mention in Scripture that these new disciples of Christ went to a synagogue to worship God and to make Him known to their neighbors. Christ and Paul used the synagogues in the same way the Jewish teachers used the synagogues for teaching the male Jews. The teachings by Christ and Paul in the synagogues were directed toward bringing the Jews to salvation in Jesus Christ their Messiah and to give them an understanding that Jesus came to restore the spiritual kingdom of God. The Amish use the practice of families meeting in the house of one of the Amish families today. Some Mennonite groups also practice this way of "meeting together" in the "meetinghouse." Isn't that amazing, that over the nearly two thousand years of people making changes and "modernizing" the way we go about serving God, worshipping God, and producing true disciples has not completely disappeared among the God-fearing people! This is a most God-pleasing way to serve and worship God.

The Apostles used hand carried letters to strengthen or correct those who were weak or who were straying away from the truth of the Gospel of Jesus Christ taught them during an earlier visit by an apostle, Paul, and others. The letters were used to praise, teach and admonish the individuals or groups of followers. The letters also provided spiritual understanding to strengthen and sustain them for their walk in the Lord and work for the Lord all over the territories of the Roman Empire.

This work was done in much the same manner as full-time missionaries perform the work of building the kingdom of God today. These letters became the Epistles found in the New Testament today (the books in the New Testament between Acts and 1 Timothy). They were the very first Word of God set down on parchment by the Apostles.

We are to use the Scriptures today the same way. Each and every person who sits in a church pew should be discipled to become a witnessing follower of God. The wording in the letters demonstrated what was given to the Apostles during the teaching sessions by Jesus and teachings given to Paul during the two years he spent with his Lord in Arabia. The Apostles were taught through the power of the Holy Spirit, which came upon each and every one of the Apostles as they became true followers of Christ.

Our Lord and Savior worked long hours over the three years of His ministry on earth, telling the people, instructing and training His Apostles how the Father was about to establish the kingdom in heaven (the restored spiritual kingdom) in His Son, where the Son sat down at the right hand of God pleading mankind's case before God the Father. We need to be working long hours taking the truth concerning our life with Christ Jesus now and when we die to the far corners of our surroundings. (See Revelation 20:6.)

The Precious Blood of the Son of God

In John 2:19-22, Christ Jesus tells us that God the Father will create a temple (restoration of the spiritual kingdom) for mankind in the body of His Son. In John 3:3-13, Christ tells us what we must do to be in that temple of His body. In Matthew 16:18, God made the declaration that He is starting to gather unto Himself the called-out-ones who will be part of the restored spiritual kingdom of God in His Son's body (the flesh and blood of His Son—God sees those who belong to Him in the flesh and blood of His Son). Our body is the temple of God, spiritually. (See 1 Corinthians 3:16,17; 1 Corinthians 6:19,20.) It was stated earlier that this was the relationship Adam and Eve had with God in the Garden of Eden.

It is absolutely essential that each and every soul who sits in a pew of a church be empowered by the Holy Spirit. If the follower of any particular faith or belief is not brought to a saving faith through the blood of Christ Jesus, they do not and cannot have a spiritual tie with God. A spiritual tie with God through His Son is a most important aspect of the very existence of humanity, for that tie and only that tie can give us true direction for our life in this living human form. Our spiritual tie with God comes through our salvation in Christ Jesus. We can only have salvation when we claim our Lord and Savior's shed blood to cover our sin nature. To make that claim, we must confess our sins to God, thank Him for forgiving us, and ask Christ Jesus to come into our life.

We need to follow that confession with making Christ Jesus the Lord and Master of our life. We become His disciple. Christ Jesus comes into our life by Christ giving us the Holy Spirit. We make Christ Jesus the Lord and Master of our life by allowing Christ Jesus to guide us in everything that we do. God shows us all the truths we desire through our daily reading and studying of His Holy Word and through daily faithful prayer. Some of the proof of our salvation in Christ

Jesus will come by godly manifestations of how much we enjoy bringing others who need salvation to where they will want Christ Jesus to come into their life. We cannot serve God fully and completely without the guidance from God through the Holy Spirit. Church-related works, done for the sake of works, are worthless in the eyes of God concerning salvation. Church works that are accomplished by our own human wisdom and knowledge seldom bring anyone to Christ and will not be successful in leading them to trusting in Christ Jesus.

Who Is the Son of God?

Beginning with Matthew 16:13 Christ asks His disciples a very important question:

> Now when Jesus came into the district of Casesarea Phillippi, He began asking His disciples, "Who do people say that the Son of Man is?" And they said, "Some say John the Baptist; and others, Elijah; but still others, Jeremiah, or one of the prophets." He said to them, "But who do you say that I am?" Simon Peter answered, "You are the Christ, the Son of the living God." And Jesus said to him, "Blessed are you, Simon Barjona, because flesh and blood did not reveal this to you, but My Father who is in heaven." (Matthew 16:13-17)

This most important discussion between Christ and His disciples took place about twenty-eight months after Christ began His ministry and about seven to eight months before His death on the cross. It was not long after our Christ Jesus gave training and understanding to His disciples and much of the population of Israel on the subject, the kingdom of heaven, that He gave His life to restore the spiritual kingdom for the Father. In these verses Jesus has established who He is, and who it is that told the witness, Simon Barjona, who He is. Jesus makes it clear that man did not tell Simon Barjona who the Son of Man is, Jesus establishes that it was God through the Holy Spirit who told Simon Barjona who Jesus is.

Jesus had good reason to make sure that Simon Barjona and the other disciples present were following Jesus' line of thought at this time, because Jesus was about to give Simon Barjona a new name and also reveal to them the reason He came to earth. In the next verse, Jesus gave Simon a new name, "I also say to you that you are Peter [in the Greek, Peter is Petros, a little rock] and upon this rock [in the Greek Petra—a big rock] I [God] will build My [God] church; [in the Hebrew, *edhah*, assembly of called-out-ones . . . restored spiritual kingdom of heaven] and the gates of Hades shall not overpower it. (See Matthew 16:18.) [Clarification added by the author.] This is the glorious declaration by God in this Scripture, and it is being used by the enemies of God for ungodly teachings.

Matthew Sixteen and the Eighteenth Verse Is Life to Man

Up to Matthew 16:18, God the Father, Christ, John the Baptist, and the writer of the book of Matthew explain, declare, and record the development of the upcoming restored spiritual kingdom of heaven. There is not a shred of evidence in the book of Matthew that gives credence for switching from the subject "kingdom of heaven" to a totally new subject, the word church. Matthew 16:18 is the pivoting point of our Savior's ministry while on earth and it is the culmination of His ministry. Christ tells His disciples immediately after the declaration in Matthew 16:18 that He must suffer and be killed. (See Matthew 16:21.) And when Peter made the attempt to direct Christ Jesus away from His completion of His mission, Christ Jesus rebuked Peter severely. This rebuke puts great emphasis on what was happening in and through these verses of Matthew 16:18-23. Christ certainly did not establish in all of the chapters preceding Matthew 16:18 that God the Father was going to establish Him as head of an earthly kingdom because that idea was put forward after Matthew 16:18 and never came into existence. Christ dodged the attempt by the people to make Him an earthly king. So any other earthly institution that God would use to bring mankind unto Himself is not given to us in His Word. In fact, He already announced that the kingdom of heaven was at hand and it would be established upon the Rock, Jesus Christ, Messiah to the Jews, His only begotten Son.

We need to take a hard look at the wording of Matthew 16:18. We need to look at that wording in light of who it is that is speaking and who it is that is being spoken of. The author believes Christ spoke as the Son in the first portion of the verse where He gives Simon Barjona the new name Peter. In the second half of the verse, He spoke as God the Father where He makes the glorious declaration; a declaration that only God the Father could make. That declaration established the Messiah (the Rock) where the Father began in the only begotten Son—the restored spiritual kingdom—eternal life—for all mankind who would trust God's only Son and make Him Lord and Master of their life. There are several Scriptures which give support to—Christ spoke as the Son and then also as the Father. (See John 10:37,38; John 14:10,11.)

I also lean very heavily upon David Stern's scholarly wisdom on the subject. Stern wrote:

> "Was Yeshua a prophet like Moshe?" Yes and more. A prophet speaks for God which Yeshua did; but he also spoke as God. He spoke what the Father gave Him to say, as did the prophets; but He and the Father are one (Yn 10:30).[1]

Gentile Bible scholars over the years have presented their understanding and interpretation of the Holy Word of God as if it was given to the Gentiles only. For instance, how could a Jew at the time, 45 A.D., when the book of Matthew was set down on parchment understand the meaning of the word "church"? The people who were being brought to a saving faith in the Lord Jesus Christ, in the early centuries after Christ's first appearance, Jews and Gentiles, knew and understood the Hebrew word *edhah* or *kahal* and the Greek word *ekklesia*. None of those words can be translated to convey or create a concept which the Jews nor the Gentiles, at the time of Christ, could possibly bring into existence the word meaning "church." The Jews (males only)[2] studied and listened to the rabbis' teachings of the Old Testament in the synagogues.

That era of teaching was far removed from the concept of the word "church." The synagogue concept was and still is applied to Judaism. The followers of Christ were not permitted in the synagogues. In fact, the synagogue officials issued orders for the arrest and imprisonment of the believers. The Jews, at the time of Christ, continued to perform their Jewish form of worship and sacrificing in the temple. That form of worship by the Jews continued until the temple was destroyed in 70 A.D.

From that time on, the Jews who practiced Judaism began to convert the synagogues into places of worship by both male and female. When persecution began of the followers of Christ, they were scattered away from Jerusalem, and they continued to meet in houses.

The Word "Rock" in Matthew 16:18

The word "Rock" can only refer to Christ and that God is pointing to the restoration of the spiritual kingdom of heaven in Matthew 16:18, nothing else. Everyone who is seeking the truths in the Word of God must, without fail, come to a complete understanding of Matthew 16:18 so that he or she can make a Godly decision concerning eternal life with God. This is not the first time God hid in His Word, a great truth. Leopold Cohn in teaching about the many names God gave His Son in the Old Testament, which concealed His true identity, wrote, "The Jews' Rock: the Messiah Savior." The author believes it highly significant to give an extended discussion here by Cohn:

> "There are other passages in the Pentateuch which refer to these wonderful revelations concerning the Lord Jesus Christ. For instance, in Exodus 33 Moses pleads with God to show him His face. The answer came, 'Thou canst not see My face, for there shall no man see Me and live.' Then in the succeeding verse we read that God says, 'Behold there is a place by Me, and thou shall stand upon the Rock.' The word rock in the Hebrew is used in connection with the redemption and salvation of the Jewish people. The daily prayer of the Jew is, 'Rock of Israel, rise up to help Israel.' The word 'place' is also used in the Jewish liturgy in a prayer for all the scattered

Jewish brethren, saying 'The Place shall have mercy upon them.' It seems, therefore, that the word rock stands for Jehovah in Jesus as the Redeemer and Savior of Israel.

We are, therefore, justified in seeing in the Word of God to Moses, 'There is a place by Me, thou shall stand upon the Rock,' the wonderful revelation of the indwelling of the Godhead bodily in the Lord Jesus Christ who is the place or locality in which the fullness of the Godhead dwelt and at the same time the Rock of salvation. It was an indication to Moses that some day he would be allowed to see the face of God in that place which means the Lord Jesus Christ and in that Rock. Thus, we find Moses on the Mount of Transfiguration. There he could see the Face of God (Matthew 17). Elijah was specially privileged to accompany Moses to see that glorious Face.

So well did Moses understand this that when he foresaw the Jews' rejection of the Lord Jesus Christ, he refers to Him by the word rock. In his last speech—Deuteronomy 32:15-16—he says, 'He (Jeshurun which means the Jews) will wax fat and will kick . . . he will forsake the God who made him and will esteem lightly the Rock of his salvation.' The Hebrew construction of the words 'his salvation' is such that allows the interpretation 'his Jesus.' Thus it reads, 'They will lightly esteem the Rock, who is their Jesus.' But God gave us the assuring message through Isaiah 12 that the Jew will not abide in that blindness forever but will accept the Lord Jesus Christ 'and in that day thou shalt say . . . Behold, God is my Salvation.' According to the interpretation of the word salvation in Deuteronomy 32:15, this would read 'Behold God is my Jesus.'"[3]

The object of this extended quotation from a very important work by Cohn follows.

> "We have seen so far that the Bible is referring to some wonderful person who is called under many different names, but we have not yet seen plainly who that person is. The Lord foretold through Moses in Deuteronomy 31:17,18, 'Hiding, I will hide My face' (a double expression in the Hebrew) which refers in part to His way of hiding Himself under three different appearance, such as, 'Melchizedek,' 'Angel of Jehovah,' 'Prophet like Moses,' 'Rock of his salvation,' 'Captain of Jehovah's host,' 'Wonderful,' etc. It is because we are not worthy of His direct and sudden manifestation of His glory. He wants us to study His word in order to find out these wonderful manifestations. This is in accordance with God's Word through Hosea 5:15: 'I will go and return to My place till they acknowledge their offense and seek **My Face**.'"
>
> "**The Royal Son Promised to David**—We will now read II Samuel 7:12-17. Here we find an additional name given to that mysterious personality in whom God is hiding Himself, and by this name the identification of the Messiah, the Lord Jesus Christ, will be complete. God gave to David the promise to 'set up thy seed after thee . . . and I will establish the throne of His kingdom forever. I will be His Father and He shall be My Son.' There is here given the new name, 'My Son,' to that mysterious person. Now this name cannot refer exclusively to Solomon, for two reasons. First, we do not find anywhere in the Scriptures that Solomon is called God's Son. Second, that definite expression 'forever' in connection with that Son's kingdom cannot

> apply to any of the kings of Israel who have long ago ceased. But, evidently, without a doubt, it does refer to the seed of David, the promised Messiah, and of Him God says, 'He will be **My Son**.' He, the Lord Jesus, is the everlasting King. He is seated now at the right hand of God. In Psalms 110:1, we find that He is to come the second time and reign visibly over all the world."[4]

Our understanding of what God created in His Son is given some clarity in the preceding quotation from Cohn concerning the word "Rock." This is the key word in Matthew 16:18 where man began the misinterpretation of what God created in His Son. It is this very word "Rock" that indeed has caused man much pain and suffering while the direct opposite was God's plan, He restored the spiritual kingdom of God in heaven and on earth. The Roman and Eastern Orthodox hierarchical leaders are in extreme disobedience of God's Holy Word because of the stand that they have taken on Matthew 16:18 and particularly the words Rock and church—the Pope and the Orthodox leader are in direct succession in their church position and leadership to the Apostle Peter.

9

God Calls—We Answer

Understanding the Call of God

The restored spiritual kingdom of God is added to each and every time a soul answers the call of God and becomes a true follower of Christ Jesus. Everyone who says, "I love You Lord," has to be about their heavenly Father's business, because God is calling thousands, hundreds of thousands, and millions of souls every minute of every day from every corner of this earth. 2 Peter 3:9 says, "The Lord is not slow about His promise, as some count slowness, but is patient toward you, not wishing for any to perish but for all to come to repentance." God needs thousands, hundreds of thousands, and millions of disciples to touch the lives of everyone God is calling. God said in John 4:35-37,

> "Do you not say, 'There are yet four months, and then comes the harvest'? Behold, I say to you, lift up your eyes, and look on the fields, that they are white for harvest. "Already he who reaps is receiving wages and is gathering fruit for life eternal; so that he who sows and he who reaps may rejoice together. "For in this case the saying is true, 'One sows, and another reaps.'"

It is God who gives us the wisdom and knowledge as a disciple to be able to see and understand every opportunity we are given to sow the seed of salvation in Christ Jesus or to bring a searching soul to the Lord so He can bring that soul into His house, the restored spiritual kingdom of God.

Throughout the Word of God, it is an outstanding desire of our heavenly Father, that His chosen people would heed His call and come unto Him in complete love and submission. This call of God has been extended to the Gentiles also throughout the New Testament. However, God has given a grave responsibility to the Gentiles who are true followers of Christ Jesus to cause the Jews to be jealous so that they will answer the call of God.

I say then, they did not stumble so as to fall, did they? May it never be! But by their transgression salvation has come to the Gentiles, to make them jealous. (Romans 11:11)

The call to the chosen people echoes the grief their heavenly Father feels for them:

> "Listen to Me, O Jacob, even Israel whom I called; I am He, I am the first, I am also the Last." (Isaiah 48:12)

> "I am the Lord, I have called you in righteousness, I will also hold you by the hand and watch over you, And I will appoint you as a covenant to the people, As a light to the nations." (Isaiah 42:6)

> "Therefore thus says the Lord, the God of hosts, the God of Israel, 'Behold, I am bringing on Judah and on all the inhabitants of Jerusalem all the disaster that I have pronounced against them; because I spoke to them but they did not listen, and I have called them but they did not answer.'" (Jeremiah 35:17)

We, "Gentiles," should never forget that God's greater attention is on His people not on the Gentiles.

God used various means and modes to call man unto Himself throughout time and those means and modes are everywhere throughout the Scriptures. The most important of the means to call men unto Himself, is, Christ Jesus. The next most important means is His instructions. Parts of His instructions remain a means to call us unto Him today; in particular, the commandments given us by Christ Himself.[1] God also used the prophets and judges to call His people unto Himself. And when all these resources did not produce positive results, God sent His only begotten Son to call His people unto Himself. The following Scriptures will help us understand God's grief over all of unrepentant people of this earth.

> Therefore, holy brethren, partakers of a heavenly calling, consider Jesus, the Apostle and High Priest of our confession; (Hebrews 3:1)

> But we should always give thanks to God for you, brethren beloved by the Lord, because God has chosen you from the beginning for salvation through sanctification by the Spirit and faith in the truth. It was for this He called you through our gospel, that you may gain the glory of our Lord Jesus Christ. (2 Thessalonians 2:13,14)

> "I press on toward the goal for the prize of the upward call of God in Christ Jesus." (Philippians 3:14)

> The Spirit and the bride say, "Come." And let the one who hears say, "Come." And let the one who is thirsty come; let the one who wishes take the water of life without cost. (Revelation 22:17)

The Five Golden Links of God's Redemption of Mankind

God's call to man is the central link in the five golden links of God's redemption of mankind. (See Romans 8:28-30.)

Charles Halff discusses these five golden links in his book of Radio Sermons, *God's Predestination.* Halff said:

> "There are two lines of divine truth that run through the entire Bible. We must understand these two lines of truth or we will never fully understand the Word of God. The two lines of truth are: the sovereignty of God and the responsibility of man. You see, God does the calling—man does the answering. God does the electing—man does the believing."

> "If you will study your Bible carefully, you will find that God is sovereign, that God is on His throne, that God does as He pleases and as He wills. However, man is responsible to God. Man can not reconcile these two lines of divine truth."

The proof that there are two lines of divine truth can be shown by the following questions and answers: Whom does God save? He saves those who believe. And why do they believe? Because they have been called. Why are they called? Because they have been chosen.

> "Since God is sovereign, He has a perfect right to choose or elect those whom He wishes to spend eternity with Him. (See Ephesians 1:4-5.) Now, how can we know we have been elected unto salvation? The answer is—come to Christ. If you want the Lord Jesus Christ, come, and He says, 'Him that cometh unto me, I will in no wise cast out.' (John

> 6:37) That is the sign that we have been elected—if you come to the Lord Jesus and receive Him as your personal Savior. That's the sign that you are one of God's elect."
>
> "In order for a person to be saved, he must have faith to believe because the Scripture says, 'Without faith it is impossible to please God.' (Hebrews 11:6) Now we all agree on this. However, the Lord must give us this faith to believe. The Scripture says, 'By grace are ye saved through faith; and that NOT OF YOURSELVES: IT IS THE GIFT OF GOD.' (Ephesians 2:8) You see, the faith that God requires, He gives."

The above discussion on the sovereignty of God gives the foundation for the study of God's predestination or five golden links in God's plan of redemption. Charles Halff uses Romans 8:28-30 to explain:

> "And we know that all things work together for good to them that love God, to them who are the called according to His purpose. For whom He did Foreknow, he also did Predestinate to be conformed to the image of his Son, that he might be the first born among many brethren. Moreover whom he did predestinate, them he also Called: and whom he called, them he also Justified: and whom he justified, them he also Glorified." (underlining added)

These five golden links begin with eternity past and then tie in our eternity future. Each link magnifies God's glorious and marvelous plan of redemption. The first link, God's foreknowledge, can mean two different things. Halff said,

> "The first meaning is God knows ahead of time everything that is going to take place. He knows the end from the beginning. The Bible says this very plainly and very definitely in many Scriptures. If God didn't know everything ahead of time, then we could not trust Him with our salvation. God could be fooled—He could be surprised by events and happenings that He didn't know would take place. And then God would just be reduced to a being of chance instead of a being of destiny. But God can never be taken by surprise."

> "There are no surprises with God. God is never fooled. See Acts 15:18, Romans 4:17, Isaiah 46:9-10. With man there are a lot of things that are yet to be done. With God they are already done."

Man continues to discover every year a new something of the universe that God put there in eternity past.

> "God has predestinated the salvation of every born-again believer. He has elected His people from the foundation of the world." (See Ephesians 1:4-5.)

The second meaning of God's foreknowledge also comes to us in Romans 8:29. In this verse the word foreknowledge is used in a very special sense. Halff said,

> "It doesn't mean that God looked at us in advance and saw that we would be good or that we would believe or that we would be holy; but when it says that we were foreknown by God, it means that God looked upon us with favor and that He chose us as His own peculiar people."

God chose us in order to make us holy in the Son. (See Ephesians 1:4.) God looked at us (born-again believers) with special favor. Halff again said,

> "'Did you know the Scripture says, that God doesn't know the unsaved? The unsaved are not foreknown by God. (See Matthew 7:23.) Now I think you can understand what the word foreknow means when you look at this verse of Scripture. Jesus is going to say to the unsaved at the great White Throne Judgment, "I never knew you." Now does that mean that the Lord Jesus Christ doesn't know anything about the unsaved, that He's ignorant of the facts of their lives? Does that mean that Christ never knew about their ungodly deeds? Certainly not! It simply means He never knew these people as His own. He never knew them as His own peculiar people. When the Lord Jesus says to the unsaved at the great White Throne Judgment, "Depart from me, I never knew you," He never knew them as His own.'"

The second golden link in God's plan of redemption is predestination. In Romans 8:29, "Whom he did foreknow, he also did predestinate." Halff said,

> "The word predestinate means to determine beforehand. What God predestinated, He decreed or determined what should be done or brought to pass . . . Predestination simply means that God predetermined our salvation and our service ahead of time. And His ultimate purpose is to make us like His Son, the Lord Jesus Christ . . . That's why we have to go through all the trials and testings and heartaches and disappointments of life. That's why God leaves us here in this world to suffer.

> Because through all these testings and trials, He is making us like His Son, the Lord Jesus Christ . . . Throughout the ages, God has always worked on the basis of election. (See John 15:16.) The Bible teaches election from Genesis to Revelation."

The third golden link in God's plan of redemption is God's call to you and me to make us realize our need of salvation. Halff said,

> "You would never have called on the Lord if God had not first called upon you. Throughout the Bible we find that it is God who does the calling. There is not a single person on the face of God's green earth who would have called on the name of the Lord if God in heaven had not first of all called upon him and shown him his need of salvation."

Halff continues,

> "Turn to Acts 2:39 . . . Peter said to the Jews on the day of Pentecost: 'For the promise is unto you, and to your children, and to all that are afar off, even as many as the Lord our God shall call.' Who does the calling, beloved? The Lord God of heaven. The Scripture says, 'As many as the Lord our God shall call.'"

Halff gives another Scripture.

> "II Timothy 1:9. Notice what the Scripture says, 'Who hath saved us, and called us with an holy calling, not according to our works, but according to his own purpose and grace, which was given us in Christ Jesus before the world began.' You see,

> God must do the calling if people are ever to be saved—because no one would ever call upon the Lord if God did not first call upon him."

Halff explains how some preachers say,

> "'Everybody is seeking after God. Everybody wants to know God. Everybody is hungry to know God.' Now beloved, that's not true. The human heart is not seeking after God. Turn to Romans 3:11, 'There is none that seeketh after God.' Now that's plain, isn't it? Nobody wants to know God, nobody wants to be saved, nobody wants to keep out of hell until God Almighty Himself creates a thirst in a person's heart. Man by nature is not interested in the things of the Spirit of God. Men are interested in making money, their homes, their cars and accumulation of material wealth. But no one is really interested in the salvation of his soul until God first convicts him by the power of the Holy Spirit . . . And if man were left alone, he would go to hell of his own free will and accord."

(This is the reason everyone who says, "I am saved" must be an active soul winner—bring the Gospel of the Lord Jesus Christ to the unsaved—they will never seek it by themselves.)

The fourth link in God's plan of redemption—Justification. Halff gives the Biblical meaning of justification by using Romans 3:24,

> "'Being justified freely by his grace through the redemption that is in Christ Jesus.' It doesn't say 'being justified by works.' It doesn't say 'being justified by keeping the law.' It doesn't say 'being justified by being good.'"

Then Halff turns our attention to Romans 5:1 and 8:33.

> "'Therefore being justified by faith, we have peace with God through our Lord Jesus Christ.' It doesn't say 'being justified by works.' It says 'by faith.' Romans 8:33, 'Who shall lay anything to the charge of God's elect? It is God that justifieth.' So one of the first benefits of God's elect is to be justified. Now to be justified means that you can stand before God as if you had never sinned. You can stand before God, beloved, and be declared absolutely righteous."
>
> "Now there is only one kind of people whom God justifies, and I want you to notice this in your Bible. Look at Romans 4:5, 'To him that worketh not, but believeth on him that justifieth the ungodly . . .' Now there it is just as plain, just as simple, just as clear as can be—God justifies only one kind of people, the ungodly. And we are all ungodly because we have all broken God's commandments, we've disobeyed His laws, we've defiled His universe, and we've done those things that have been displeasing in His sight. But the Scripture says that He justifies the ungodly. In other words, He declares the ungodly righteous (in Christ Jesus) so that we can stand before Him as if we have never sinned . . . The Bible says, 'By the deeds of the law shall no flesh be justified in His (God's) sight.'" (Romans 3:20)

Halff points to Acts 13:39 to further clarify,

> "'How then can we be justified?' 'And by him (the Lord Jesus Christ) all that believe are justified from all things, from which ye could not be justified by the law of Moses.' What does it say? It says the law of Moses could not justify anybody. The law only

> points the finger of condemnation. The law says, 'you are condemned because you didn't do this, because you didn't do that.' The law condemns you for your failure. That is the difference between law and grace. The law condemns—but grace forgives. The law says, 'Do or die.' Grace says, 'Believe and live.' The law says, 'Make a new heart and a new spirit.' Grace says, 'A new heart and a new spirit I will put within you' . . . The law speaks of what you must do for God. Grace tells us of what God has done for you."
>
> "Isn't it wonderful to know that our sins have been imputed to Christ and will never be charged against us again? Our sins are cast as far as the east is from the west. They are buried in the sea of God's forgetfulness, never to be remembered again. Now that is justification."

Glorification of the Sinner

Glorification is the fifth and final link in God's plan of redemption. Halff said,

> "To be glorified means that we are going to have the same glory as Christ. We are going to look like Christ—we are going to be like Christ. That's what the Bible says in I John 3:2: 'Beloved, now are we the sons of God, and it doth not yet appear what we shall be: but we know that, when he shall appear, we shall be like him: for we shall see him as he is.' Now that's God's ultimate goal for our lives. That's God's real purpose of salvation. God didn't save us just to keep us out of hell. That's just a mere incidental in the plan of God. God didn't save us just to take us to heaven. God saved us to make us like His Son, the Lord Jesus Christ."

> "Now in order to make us like the Lord Jesus Christ, it's a process of testings, trials, defeats and victories, joys and sorrows. . . . In Romans 8:18, Paul said: 'For I reckon that the sufferings of this present time' (This is suffering time for God's people.) 'are not worthy to be compared with the glory which shall be revealed in us.' . . . This means that this world and its sorrows and sufferings do not compare with the glory which shall ultimately be revealed in us. In other words, this world is not our home. We are going home to glory, beloved! This world is just a temporary dwelling place for God's people."

In summary of this gold link and that of the other links: Halff said,

> "People know a lot about Romans 8:28. They can really rattle this verse off. But they never look at Romans 8:29—the verse of this study. A lot of people know, 'All things work together for good to them that love God, them that are called according to his purpose.' But they never bother to ask, 'What is God's purpose?' What is God's real purpose, beloved? God's real purpose is to make us like the Lord Jesus Christ. That's what the Scripture says: 'Whom he did foreknow, he also did predestinate . . . and whom he did predestinate, them he also called.' But what did he predestinate us for? Look at it: whom he did foreknow, he also did predestinate to be conformed to the image of his Son.' That's God's purpose—to make us like his Son, the Lord Jesus Christ."[2]

The five golden links in God's plan of redemption—God's Foreknowledge, He foreknew us; God's Predestination, He fixed our destiny and predetermined our salvation and service; God's Calling, He called us; God's Justification, He declared us righteous; and finally, Glorification, He makes us like His Son and gives us a glorified resurrection body. The first two are linked together with the last two by God calling us, isn't that an amazing thought, that God calls the sin-riddled wretches, me, you, your uncle, your neighbor, your mother, father, brother, sister, the casual acquaintances. And He uses those who love Him for the glorious work. If we do not respond to God and be the active witnessing disciple, the call of God cannot reach the lost. You see beloved, our salvation started in the mind of God before He ever made this world. Then God called us, He justified us, and to complete our salvation, one of these days He's going to glorify us and we will have glorified, resurrection bodies just like the Lord Jesus Christ . . .

When we are born again, we're saved from the penalty of sin. Halff said,

> "Every day in our lives we are being saved from the habit of sin. But one of these days we are going to be saved from the very presence of sin, and we're going to look like Christ, and we're going to have the same glory as Christ."[3]

The continuing call to man by God to bring man unto Himself is without a doubt a most important aspect of God's Word. The calling is first, for all men to respond personally, become a disciple, and second, become the legs, arms, and voice for God to those around them. We become disciples with a purpose. That purpose is to please God and to cause God and the heavenly host to rejoice over the fruit of our labors. We perform this work for God because we love Him because He first loved us. No greater work hath no man.

10

Halakhah—Way of Walking

Christ followed His declaration concerning the restoration of the spiritual kingdom of heaven in Matthew 16:18 with transferring from the rabbis to His disciples the power to decide what practices should be followed to serve God, to make Him known to others, and to produce disciples—*Halakhah.*

> "I will give you the keys of the kingdom of heaven; and whatever you bind on earth shall have been bound in heaven, and whatever you loose on earth shall have been loosed in heaven." (Matthew 16:19)

Stern's explanation for the words "binding" and "loosing" are translated:

> "'prohibit' and 'permit.' This reflects the first-century Jewish application of these concepts to their leaders, who were understood as having authority from God to decide what practices should be followed by the community, i.e., to determine *halakhah* [a term which dates from a later period]. In verses 18-20 the Messiah transfers this power from the rabbis to his own talmidim [disciples]. This authority was not assumed instantaneously,[51] nor was it assumed

> later when it should have been. But the fact that Messianic Jews and Gentiles have hitherto made little use of Yeshua's [Jesus'] far-reaching grant of authority does not cancel it."[1] Note 51 refers to Mattityahu. (Matthew 23:2) [Clarification added by the author.]

Stern gives an extended discussion on "binding" and "loosing" in his New Testament commentary, p. 57. The Scribes and Pharisees had the power to set the terms and conditions for the people to perform whatever the leaders decided for the people to do. So it was Christ who passed this power to His disciples to determine how the followers of Christ should walk before their heavenly Father.

The weakness, to this very day for much of Christendom, lies in the fact that the theological leadership of the Christian society has not developed the true way of walking in the Lord Jesus Christ. Instead, it holds to a form of godliness which has no power.

The Way of Walking

The way to live before God our heavenly Father has to begin with the very basic truth of the Bible; we need to know and understand how to be sure we belong to God. Second, we need to have Christ Jesus (Messiah) as Lord and Master of our life. Third, we need to become a true disciple of Jesus Christ. Soul-winning and discipling others come next. If we display all of the above traits, we are well on our way to true walking with the Lord.

The question is: How can you be sure we belong to God and

love God with all your heart, and with all your soul, and with all your mind? Until we are walking on a daily basis with the Lord in complete control of our life, we will always lack the power of the Holy Spirit to do His part—provide enlightenment for our life through God's Word.

The utter lack of being sure you belong to God is based on the absence of correct information. Millions of church attendees are unsure of their relationship with God because they have never been told (discipled) how to be sure they are a child of God. Until a person, who wants to become a carpenter so he or she can build a house, they first need to learn how to make a square cut on the lumber they will use and then learn how to place each piece of wood or material plumb or level in relation to each other. So it is with being a true child of God. We need to know that we must have a personal relationship with God as He has made that possible through the shed blood of His Son. The facts concerning the birth, life, crucifixion, burial, resurrection and ascension unto the Father, of His Son, need to mean everything to mankind.

Do you have serious doubts about where you stand with God—even though you have attended a "Christian church" and your parents have sent you off to Sunday school regularly and you believe in God and His Son? Does all that give you assurance that if you were to die today you are sure you would spend **eternity** with God and His Son?

Maybe you have asked Jesus Christ into your life at one time or another or you have gone through that event more than one time. You might be a pastor, a lay leader on the church board or council and one of many other church leadership roles. You might be one of those pastors who have moved into the church system administrative offices, but you really are not sure of your salvation. You might find the following very helpful.

Many who direct and those who participate in the highly-structured church services, programs, and activities are still looking for the real thing—a true relationship with the Lord Jesus Christ. This participation goes on sometimes for many years. Some move on to another denomination, some go on the inactive list, some fall into the rapidly growing "Satan-directed churches," and some pastors and priests just call it quits. Those of you who have never been inside the doors of a church are invited also to take a hard look at the following detailed call of God.

So how do we find peace of mind, turn our life over to the Lord, allow Him to become Master of our life? The details for that answer rest in God's Word. We need to know and fully understand what God did for us in His Son. The following discussion of how to be sure you are a true believer in Christ Jesus was adapted from, *One-to-One Discipling*, by Al and Lorraine Broom[2] and from Bill Bright's, *A Handbook of Concepts for Living.*[3] We begin with a questionaire.

Who is Jesus Christ

		Do You Agree?	
Read:	Answer	(Yes)	(No)
Mark 1:1	Son of God	❑	❑
John 1:1-4, 14	The Word, The light of men, the Word became flesh	❑	❑
John 10:30; 14:6	Jesus is the way, and the truth, and the life, no one comes to the Father, but through Me.	❑	❑
1 Peter 1:1-9	Sure salvation	❑	❑

John 20:30,31	Jesus is the Christ (Messiah) the Son of God	❑	❑

What Has Jesus Christ (Messiah) Done for Us That No One Else Can Do?

Read:	Answer	Do You Agree? (Yes)	(No)
1 Cor. 15:3; Rom. 5:8	Christ died for our sins	❑	❑
1 Peter 2:24	By Christ's wounds we were healed	❑	❑

Why Is the Resurrection of the Son of God so Important to Us?

Read:	Answer	Do You Agree? (Yes)	(No)
Rom. 1:4	Declaration of God's almighty power	❑	❑
1 Cor. 15:17	If Christ did not arise from the dead our faith is worthless	❑	❑
1 Peter 1:3	Born again to a living hope	❑	❑

Our Will Is Involved

How Is a Person's Will Related to His Assurance of the Truth of the Claims of the Bible Concerning Christ?

Read:	Answer	Do You Agree? (Yes)	(No)
John 7:16,17	Our willingness to respond to the will and call of God	❑	❑
Rom. 6:16-22	This is the Holy Spirit working within us, guiding us unto salvation.	❑	❑

A simple "head" knowledge of the above facts is not enough.

What More Is Needed for Christ to Be Your Personal Savior?

Read:	Answer	Do You Agree? (Yes)	(No)
Rom. 10:9,10	Confess with your mouth (witness) Jesus Christ to all who need encouragement and the truth that Christ died for our sins.	❑	❑

Is Salvation the Reward of a Man's Good Works?

Read:	Answer	Do You Agree? (Yes)	(No)
Eph. 2:8,9	No way—How is salvation obtained? It is by the love of God through faith.	❑	❑

We Need to Know and Understand God's Word

What People Are Spiritually Born Into God's Family?

Read:	Answer	Do You Agree? (Yes)	(No)
John 1:12,13	Those who receive Jesus Christ as personal Lord & Savior	❑	❑

What is the Relation Between the Words "Receive" and "Believe" (Trust) in Verse 12?

Read:	Answer	Do You Agree? (Yes)	(No)
John 1:12	Only those who believe (trust) in Jesus Christ can receive Him. This cannot be a game of I believe in Jesus Christ as is played in simple recital of a "creed"		

	or in the simple words of a "confessional."	❑	❑

What is the Result of a Genuine Faith in Jesus Christ?

		Do You Agree?	
Read:	**Answer**	(Yes)	(No)
John 20:30, 31	Eternal Life	❑	❑

*According to Rev. 3:20, if you by faith open the door of your heart and invite Jesus Christ to come into your life to be your Lord and Savior, will He come in?*______________________________________

> Rom. 3:23, "For all have sinned and fall short of the glory of God."
>
> Matt. 20:28, "Just as the Son of Man did not come to be served, but to serve, and to give His life a ransom for many."
>
> Is. 1:18, "Come now, and let us reason together," Says the Lord, "Though your sins are as scarlet, They will be as white as snow; Though they are red like crimson, They will be like wool."
>
> 1 John 1:7, "But if we walk in the light as He Himself is in the light, we have fellowship with one another, and the blood of Jesus His Son cleanses us from all sin."
>
> John 1:12, "But as many as received Him, to them He gave the right to become children of God, even to those who believe in His name."

Being sure you are a Christian (child of God) involves

knowing where we stand before God as a sinful being. Being sure you are a Christian (child of God) involves our emotions. When we come to the realization that we are a sinner before Almighty God, we will feel sorrowful and even guilty. These are the emotions brought upon us as we truly feel sorrowful for the type of life we have lived. At the same time the sorrowfulness leads us to repentance which is part of giving up the past life and entering into the new life as a child of God.

We Need to Know the Why and How to Ask Christ Into Our Life

Being sure we are a Christian (child of God) involves becoming willing to agree with God that we are a sinner and we need to claim the shed blood of His Son for our sin.

When the call of God through His Word reaches our heart and mind and we recognize we need His Son as personal Lord and Master we are ready to pray to God concerning our condition and our relationship with Him.

That prayer needs to include the following:

1. Confess you are a sinner—agree with God that you have sinned.
2. Repent of that sin.
3. Claim the shed blood of Jesus to cover your sin.
4. Thank God for forgiving you.
5. Ask Jesus Christ into your life as your personal Savior, Lord and Master.

Have you received Christ into your life in this way? __________

____

If so, where is Jesus Christ in relation to you? ________________

____

*On the basis of Rev. 3:20, how do you know?*________________

____

According to 1 John 5:9-13, where is **eternal life** *to be found?* __

____

> "If we receive the testimony of men, the testimony of God is greater; for the testimony of God is this, that He has testified concerning His Son. The one who believes (trusts)* in the Son of God has the testimony in himself; the one who does not believe (trust) God has made Him a liar, because he has not believed (trusted) in the testimony that God has given concerning His Son. And the testimony is this, that God has given us eternal life, and this life is in His Son. He who has the Son has the life; he who does not have the Son of God does not have the life. These things I have written to you who believe (trust)* in the name of the Son of God, so that you may know that you have eternal life." (I John 5:9-13) [Emphasis added by the author.]

How Do We Know That Christ Is in Our Life?

If a person has Christ in his life, and that person allows Christ to be Lord and Master, what else does he have? ________________

____

Can a person know that he or she has **eternal life***?*____________

____

* In this case, and many others, the word trust is more true for the deeper meaning. The author's personal view and that of some Bible versions.

Do you know that you have **eternal life***?* ____________________

____

On what basis? ________________________________

____

Assuming at this point all of you who have read and can answer affirmatively the question: "How can we be sure we belong to God?"—you now know you are a child of God and you now know with certainty that you will go to heaven when you die—the very next thing you need to do is to be baptized by immersion.

Why by Immersion?

Like some of the other important words of God's Holy Word, man in his wisdom in producing the many Bible versions made some very peculiar changes from the Greek, in the case of the New Testament, to English. The word *Baptizo* in Greek meaning immersion was changed to *baptize.* Jewish scholars, both Orthodox and Messianic, will very quickly confirm that an error can be made in the application of ritual cleansing by water according to the whole Bible. One danger that exists in using the term *baptize* instead of *immerse,* baptize provides a very broad latitude in application, therein lies the error by not following the truth intended by God in the original writing and making a very arbitrary change to the true meaning. As it has been stated before, God wants us to search out the Scriptures for the truth that He has for those who love Him. In the case of immersion, it is a picture of a death, burial, and resurrection—the symbolical death, burial, and resurrection of our Lord and Savior Jesus Christ (Messiah). When we are immersed we go from dead in sin to the new life in Christ our propitiation (See 1 Peter 1:18,19; Colossians 2:12; Romans 6:3,4.) and just as the participation in the Passover and Festival of Unleavened Bread—reminds us that Christ has passed us over from death to **eternal life** in Him, raising of our body in the rite of immersion is representative of a resurrected body, a new person in Christ Jesus. Baptism has nothing to do with salvation. We are baptized because we are saved through the blood of Christ Jesus.

Christ was immersed and by that symbolized burial, washing of that body of a man (for He was man, a sinless man) and resurrection and immediately the symbol of the Holy Spirit ascended upon Him a clean man in the sight of God. Therefore, we need to follow that well-established plan set out for us by God. It is most important to be submissive and obedient to God's great love for us. Man's way will end in destruction, always!

If perchance you have already been baptized as an infant, you would do well to go through a water washing by immersion for the reasons stated above. The author went through two baptisms by sprinkling, one as an infant that I did not have a record of until later in life. The second as an adult when joining the Lutheran Church in America. A third time was by immersion after I found the truth concerning true salvation.

Does the above discussion give you good understanding that baptism by sprinkling has no meaning to God?
(See Romans 6:3-9.)

Personal Prayer and Bible Study

Personal prayer and Bible study will provide the direction, power, and joy for the life of those souls who truly belong to and are walking with the Lord. It is the promise of God that He will supply all of our needs and that He will care for us, no matter what comes our way. God is faithful in all of His promises. We need to hunger for the guidance of God through the Holy Spirit. We need to develop a prayerful attitude to be able to see and hear the Holy Spirit's directions in our life. Bible study should begin our day and end our day, each and every day. The following Scriptures are helpful for a better understanding of the depth and breadth of our great God.

> "FOR THE EYES OF THE LORD ARE TOWARD THE RIGHTEOUS, AND HIS EARS ATTEND TO THEIR PRAYER, BUT THE FACE OF THE LORD IS AGAINST THOSE WHO DO EVIL." (1 Peter 3:12)

> "Every good thing given and every perfect gift is from above, coming down from the Father of lights, with whom there is no variation or shifting shadow." (James 1:17)

> "Many, O Lord my God, are the wonders which You have done, And Your thoughts toward us; There is none to compare with You. If I would declare and speak of them, They would be too numerous to count." (Psalms 40:5)

> "We have come to know and have believed the love which God has for us. God is love, and the one who

> abides in love abides in God, and God abides in him." (1 John 4:16)
>
> "Blessed be the God and Father of our Lord Jesus Christ, the Father of mercies and God of all comfort, who comforts us in all our affliction so that we will be able to comfort those who are in any affliction with the comfort with which we ourselves are comforted by God." (2 Corinthians 1:3,4)

As we learn to lean more and more on Jesus Christ for all our needs, He will give us deeper and deeper understanding of His Word and of the desires of our heart.

Witnessing

The next thing you need to begin to do after you are sure you are a Christian (child of God)—practice witnessing as God gives you the opportunity to a family member, friend, or even a stranger each of whom needs to be sure they are a Christian (child of God) and that they have **eternal life** in Christ Jesus. This is called, soul-winning. This is not the easy to do thing, like giving an invitation to attend church. This is the Holy Spirit directed and empowered work of one who is truly saved and is now part of the restored spiritual kingdom of heaven. (See Romans 10:14,17,18; Psalms 126:6; Acts 20:20.)

There are many, many good booklets available everywhere to use as a follow-up of your witness. Make sure the booklet you choose has been written by people like: *Moody Bible Institute; the Navigators; Chosen People Ministries; Jews for Jesus; Radio Bible Broadcast; Back to the Bible Broadcast; Stonecroft*

Ministries, Kansas City, MO; the *Gospel Hour, Inc.*, Greenville, SC; *Ariel Ministries* and the *Christian Jew Foundation.* If per chance you do not feel comfortable to witness by yourself, invite a saved friend to join you.

Spiritual Buddy

Here is the next thing you need to practice after the salvation experience. Each and every person who is truly walking with the Lord (the Lord is Master of their life) needs a spiritual buddy. This person can be the husband, the wife, the close friend, grandma, grandpa, mother, father, sister, or brother. You definitely need a spiritual buddy. In the workplace it is imperative to have a secret spiritual buddy for emergency prayer and uplifting conversations. God gives us many people to pray for nearly constantly. Example, that person who likes to tailgate. Do you hit the brake light to cause he or she to back off? Do you speed up to increase to a safe distance? No, God gave you that person to pray for. All other irritating instances in our life, God put them there for a reason—**PRAYER**—and to show our love for God. (See Romans 12:10-13.)

Ministry

The term *ministry* is usually associated with the "men of the cloth," "those with the turn-around collar," or simply, "minister, preacher, reverend, and today, senior pastor." The application of the term in this writing is directed toward all who have the true relationship with the Lord Jesus Christ. The emphasis here is not on becoming a minister or a missionary in some other place other than your own area of residence. It does not apply to being involved with discipling, Sunday school teacher, or any of the commonplace "church work." This ministry is above and beyond witnessing and soul-winning. In fact, it is because you are witnessing, discipling, and soul-winning that you will also be involved in caring for the elderly, homeless, underprivileged children, teenage problem people, poor people, people with handicaps including temporary illness and many many more caring areas on a voluntary basis as God gives opportunities. We perform any one of these ministries because we love our neighbor. I challenge all of you who love the Lord to pick up on one of this type of ministry. They are available everywhere you turn today. We cannot expect the government to do it or to legislate it. This must be done by those who truly have Christ as Lord and Master.

Beyond beginning by being sure we belong to God, we need to make the development of right spiritual leadership in each and every family a very high priority. Fathers are to be the head of the family. (See 1 Corinthians 11:3-7; Ephesians 6:4; Genesis 18:19.) As head of the family, it behooves all fathers to become a true disciple of the Lord Jesus Christ. Each father has the responsibility to disciple all of the other family members. Fathers in the leadership role of the family is in serious decline in the United States as well as worldwide. Family leadership is adrift in the morass of secular humanism and the feminist movement of women liberationism and Satan is exploiting this weakness of the family to the fullest.

What, then, should we do to turn this disease that is more serious than cancer or AIDS away from overcoming our children's future family development capabilities? The following discussion on how to implement Godly direction is the best remedy in a high percentage of cases.

Directions for Establishing Godly Management of Our Lives and Pureness of Worship

The following is an introduction to that which the Apostles set out for Godly management (not organizational structuring) for our lives to worship God and service to God. The Mennonites at one time followed the New Testament directions outlined here as evidenced in many Mennonite congregations today. But as liberal thinkers of the Mennonite hierarchy took over control, many congregations succumbed to the new and "modern" way and now very "liberal" directions are commonplace throughout Mennonite gatherings. The better explanation would be, they have fallen away from God also. The Mennonites not too many years ago used the term "meetinghouse" instead of church. They used "elders" for teaching and instructing instead of the "one man minister." They cleansed sin from the gathering by bringing the guilty person before the elders and finally before the gathering instead of allowing the sinful person to remain undisciplined, to mention only a few of their Godly practices in former years.

The directions and pattern for establishing Godly management of our lives are set out in the New Testament. The instructions are applicable to a single family and also to multiple families gathered for worship of God and for service before God to those around them. The directions for management of our lives are summarizations from Manuscript No. 106, *The Local Church*, A. G. Fruchtenbaum.[4]

Using households as the fundamental unit God is dealing with to explain the New Testament directions for establishing Godly worship and management of our lives we look to the head of each household to become a disciple of Jesus Christ. Under Biblical direction the head of the household would be the authority charged by God to disciple all household members of each family. The wife would be under that God given and directed authority. When a grouping of households living as disciples would form in any given area, elders would be appointed as the ruling body of the gathered households. The elders would have the responsibility of general overseers. (See Acts 20:17,28; Philippians 1:1; 1 Timothy 3:1,2; Titus 1:7.)

The concept of elder originated from the concept of the elders of Israel who had authority within the body of Israel. There would be a plurality of elders since more than one function requires oversight (ruling function and teaching function). There would be more than one elder for each function for checks and balances within the group of disciples to maintain rightness before God Almighty.

The duties of the elders:

- To rule. (See 1 Timothy 3:4,5; 5:17; 1 Thessalonians 5:12.)
- To oversee. (See 1 Timothy 3:1; 5:1-3.)
- To feed the flock. (See Acts 20:28; 1 Peter 5:2.)
- To guard right doctrine. (See Titus 1:9; Acts 15:1-6; 15:22-29; 16:4; Hebrews 13:17.)
- To anoint the sick. (See James 5:14,15.)
- To supervise financial matters. (See Acts 11:27-30.)

The qualifications for an elder are given in 1 Timothy 3:1-7; Titus 1:6-9. Elders are to be appointed for service, they are not brought into service by a democratic election. The person who is to be an elder is qualified by another elder and after the determination the person is qualified and he desires to be an elder he can be appointed as an elder. A thorough investigation is made to determine the person to be qualified under the Scriptures.

The second type of office among the disciples is the deacon. Deacons are servants of the elders to help the elders perform their function. There would be more than one deacon in the group of disciples. (See Acts 6:1-16; Philippians 1:1.) They perform the physical functions—caring for the needy (health, food, clothing, shelter).

The qualifications for a deacon are given in 1 Timothy 3:8-10. The qualifications for a deacon are not in the leadership, they are a servant. Deacons come into office by the same method as elders, investigation of qualifications and laying on of hands. Those who are part of the groups of households and have become disciples under the rule and teaching of elders and are being cared for by deacons have the following responsibilities:

- Be subject to leaders and servants. (See 1 Corinthians 16:15,16.)
- Get to know and esteem the leaders and servants. (See 1 Thessalonians 5: 12,13.)
- Honor your elders. (See 1 Timothy 5:17-19.)
- Be subject to your elders. (See 1 Peter 5:5,6.)
- Consider those who rule over: remember them, obey them, imitate them. (See Hebrews 13:7, 17,24.)

The last of biblical guidance for those who group together and live for God are: measures which bring discipline to those who stray from the Word of God.

Discipline is needed to:

- Correct difficulties between two parties of the group.
- To avoid divisions.
- To maintain purity of the group.
- To bring offenders to repentance.
- To avoid disorderly conduct.
- To correct false teaching.
- To avoid crass sins.

The procedure for discipline. (See Matthew 18:15-20.)

Four specific steps:

- Private confrontation between the two parties involved (if settlement is not reached)
- The offended confronts the offender again but with two or three witnesses (if settlement is not reached)
- The offended brings the matter before the gathering of the groups (if the offender fails to respond to the admonishment of the gathering)
- The offender is expelled from the gathering

The forms of discipline—there are three different forms:

- Admonishment. (See 1 Thessalonians 5:12,13.)
- Exclusion from fellowship. (See 2 Thessalonians 3:6,14.)
- Excommunication. (See 1 Corinthians 5:5.)

Application of discipline—examples in Scripture:

- For immorality. (See 1 Corinthians 5:1-5.)
- For blasphemy. (See 1 Timothy 1:18-20.)

Attitudes and effects of applying discipline in the gathered saints (those who truly follow their Almighty God):

- Discipline is to be done in meekness. (See Galatians 6:1.)

- Discipline is to be done with the spirit of being willing to forgive if the person finally responds. (See 2 Corinthians 2:5-11; 7:10-13.)
- The effects of discipline will be felt by the offender and the gathering of the saints.
  - The offender will be sorrowful and will feel shame.
  - The people of the gathering will be protected from any further decay, they will feel godly fear and they will have the attitude that restoration is the goal of discipline.

While this outline gives only a glimpse of the way to establish godly management of our lives as families, the outline is intended to cause you to think about how wonderful it would be to have peace within our worship of God. On the other hand some could say, what an opportunity for a fanatical and egotistical leader, but that which is begun in the power of God cannot be directed by Satan. For a very long time during the writing of this book the author struggled with the question, what will I tell the people concerning that which is the correct way for man to fellowship with God in small as well as large gatherings, such as what is commonly perceived as "the church?" The answer is in the Word of God, not in the seminary. Just as God has ordered our very being, He has ordered all direction for our lives whether it be civil government, scientific investigation or physical care of our body. We cannot leave God out of what we do!

Worship in Spirit and Truth

In John, chapter 4, Jesus uses His discussion with the

Samaritan woman at the well to teach us the true form of worship of our God. We pick up the discussion at verse 19.

> "The woman said to Him, 'Sir, I perceive that you are a prophet. Our fathers worshiped in this mountain, and you people say that in Jerusalem is the place where men ought to worship.' Jesus said to her, "Woman, believe Me, an hour is coming when neither in this mountain nor in Jerusalem will you worship the Father. You worship what you do not know; we worship what we know, for salvation is from the Jews. But an hour is coming, and now is, when the true worshipers will worship the Father in spirit and truth; for such people the Father seeks to be His worshipers. God is spirit, and those who worship Him must worship in spirit and truth.' The woman said to Him, 'I know that Messiah is coming (He who is called Christ); when that One comes, He will declare all things to us.' Jesus said to her, 'I who speak to you am He.'" (John 4:19-26)

Jesus was explaining to the Samaritan woman that the well-known temple worship of the Jews and that worship by the descendants of Ephraim in the hills referred to by the Samaritan woman were going to be removed and replaced by spiritualized worship. The worship as practiced at that time would cease because of the death of Christ, and worship of all those who love God would be different. The true worshipers, those who trust in Christ and allow him to be Lord and Master, will worship in spirit and truth. Why? Because they are indwelt by the Holy Spirit. This Scripture then brings full meaning to the restoration of the "spiritual kingdom" and helps to give the basis for clearer thinking for that which God created in His Son.

We need to be thinking in terms of our heavenly home and not in terms of the worldly institution, the church and all that man has made it out to be. This worship in spirit and truth is not the out-of-control highly emotional worship as is demonstrated in some of the denominations that had their beginning at the turn of the 20th century. This is true Holy Spirit led worship without leadership induced emotionalism. This, then, we might say, is the end product of what God created for mankind in His Son—the true form of worship of our God. It is also part of our true way of walking. Those words, "worship in spirit and truth" need to become part of our very being and Godly management of our lives. (See Colossians 3:16.)

Religious Excitement

Glenn Wenger in his publication, *The Way of Truth*, aptly discusses, "Religious Excitement," [that worship which is induced by a worship leader]. [Clarification added by the author.]

> "In the battle against spiritual lukewarmness and lethargy, one solution that is commonly tried is to promote religious excitement. The excitement is often understood as spirituality. Excitement is an emotional response, and should not be confused with Christian spirituality. The divine truths of God's Word and the recognition that our weight of sin has been taken away and the presence of Holy Spirit power in our lives will naturally excite us to an extent and this is good. However, excitement should

not be thought of as a way to promote spirituality, as this will lead into the error of confusing emotion with spirituality and relying on emotion rather than truth. Below we quote part of a letter written by Charles Finney, possibly the most successful evangelist of the 1800s. His success could be measured by the fact that the revivals he started endured the test of time. The following was taken from his letter entitled "Unhealthy Revival Excitement":

> "Another error, which has prevailed to a considerable extent in promoting revivals of religion, I apprehend, is that of encouraging an unhealthy degree of excitement. Some degree of excitement is inevitable. The truths that must be seen and duly appreciated to induce the sinner to turn to God, will of necessity produce a considerable degree of excitement; but it should always be understood that excitement, especially where it exists to a high degree exposes the sinner to great delusions. Religion consists of the heart's obedience to the law of intelligence as distinguished from its being influenced by emotion or fear. When the feelings are greatly excited, the will yields to them almost of necessity. I do not mean that it does absolutely by necessity, but an excited state of feeling has so much power over the will that it almost certainly controls it. Now the mind is never religious when it is actuated by feelings, for this is following impulse. Whatever the feelings are, if the soul gives itself up to be controlled by feelings rather than by the law and gospel of God, as truth lies revealed in the intelligence, it is not a religious state of

> mind. Now the real difficulty in obeying the law of intelligence is in proportion to the amount of excitement. Just in proportion as the feelings are strongly excited, they tend to govern the will, and in so far as they do govern the will, there is and can be no religion in the soul whatever these feelings are.
>
> Now just so much excitement is important in revivals as is requisite to secure the fixed and thorough attention of the mind to the truth, and no more. When excitement goes beyond this, it is always dangerous. When excitement is very great, so as to carry the will, the subjects of this excitement invariably deceive themselves. They get the idea that they are religious in proportion as they are governed by their feelings. They are conscious of feeling deeply, and of acting accordingly, and because they do feel. They are conscious of being sincerely actuated by their feelings. This they regard as being true religion. Whereas, if they are governed by their feelings as distinguished from their intelligence, they are not religious at all."

Charles Finney put this knowledge to work in his own revivals. Frequently, the excitement and conviction became so intense in his revivals, that he would dismiss the people, telling them to walk quietly to their own homes and not raise their voices or talk to others. He felt that the truths of the gospel could not be as well grasped when the people were in such emotional excitement, so he would dismiss them for another day. Genuine spiritual excitement is the result of the great truths of God being impressed on the soul."[5]

Part Two

Errors of the Ways of Men

11

Knowing Right From Wrong

Johnny came into mommy one day with a big problem—"Mikey pushed me, mommy, and I lost my candy. So I beat up Mikey and sent him home to his mommy with a black eye. Now I feel worse than when I lost my candy, because Mikey was my best friend."

"Johnny," mother asked, "what is the lesson you learned from this?"

Johnny told his mother, "Friends are more important than a little piece of candy anyday!"

"Thanks Johnny for seeing your mistake. I know you can mend your friendship with Mike and I am sure you will be able to apply this lesson many, many times as you grow up—two wrongs never make a right, Johnny."

Traditions of Men in the Church Institution Most Harmful to Mankind

Much of "church doctrine" as practiced by the individual denominations is highly interspersed with the traditions of men. Christ condemned the Pharisees for following traditions of men instead of the truth given His chosen people in the instructions given to Moses. (See Matthew 15:9; Mark 7:9.) The average church attendee is at the mercy of those they follow as someone who would lead them in all truth. Some of the most dangerous traditions of men which remain today without being detected or exposed follow.

Creedal Recital

Reciting any one of the creeds developed by man can only be looked upon as saying, I believe in you, God, to that extent stated in the creed. Reciting the creed does not do anything for the individual's salvation. Until one has Christ as Lord and Master of his or her life you can recite a creed a hundred times a day (or the rosary) but that person is no closer to salvation than the day before. This is tradition of men without any meaning to God.

Christmas/Easter

People say: "Isn't it wonderful to have a Santa Claus and an Easter Bunny for the children!" Some of those same people also say, "I love you Lord." That is impossible, because the Easter Bunny and the Santa Claus are pagan representatives of events brought to man by God concerning man's redemption, and they are in fact forms of gods that we put ahead of the only one true God—our heavenly Father. Those people share a pagan worship ritual with their worship of God and God is a jealous God. He does not want us to have any other god before Him. Whether we want to admit it or not, for those who worship God and also participate in the two pagan activities are in fact committing sin before God.

I realize we were all brought into this by "family traditions," it is now time to be awakened to the truth. We need to bring into true focus what our celebration should be for the time of year when we recognize the birth of our Lord and Savior and His death and resurrection. Begin by weeding out all ungodly overtones such as attention on "Santa" and the "Bunny" instead of heart and mind on Jesus. Concentrate on the Lord for a two-week period during the season of His birth and the season of His death and resurrection. Give adoration, praise and glory truly to Jesus without mixing in the existing traditions of men.

Church Membership

To declare before man that you belong to God, because you trust in the shed blood of His Son Christ Jesus on the cross for your sins and that you have asked Him to come into your life is one thing, but for man to require formal membership so that your name can be on the rolls of a specific church is not a requirement of God. Membership anywhere is a commitment to man and church membership is a commitment to man. Those who truly have Christ as personal Lord and Master have the only truth that counts—**eternal life**. Our heart and mind need to be focused on heaven as our home not church membership.

Reformationism

The works of the men who put their life on the line to expose the evil and inhumanities being carried out by men carrying and making the sign of the cross, performing pseudo-

Christian acts and at the same time proclaiming to be the representative of God on earth, fell way short of the mark. While they did succeed in exposing some of the errors inherent in the system, most remain to this day because they fought to reform the men of the system instead of guiding the men of the system to conform to God's plan for man.

Many of the theologians over the past 450 years gave praise to the reformationist and even up to the present time theologians still remain in the dark concerning the evil being spread by reformationism. Conformity to God's plan for man has been passed by for the plan by those who desire to spread ecumenicalism. Godliness in the world and particularly in the United States is disappearing at a rapid rate. Inroads into this nation by ungodly people who are at the root of causing the falling away from God is very simple to confirm when we look at what 200,000 strong Unitarians led by Madeleine Murray O'Hare did while 140,000,000 "Christians" looked on with complete apathy. Now we are beginning to pay the price; juvenile delinquents are now the complete criminal without a moral conscience, AIDS is spreading like an uncontrolled cancer, everyone, even our government leaders, are doing drugs. Government leaders push to expand gambling. Drunkenness is not even paid attention to unless it happens to be a celebrity in the sports world. Same sex marriages are being heralded by those who say they love America!

Statues and Other Idols

Stained glass windows placed in memory of, the bust of a famous seminary professor or a president of the seminary, a statue of Christ, Mary His mother, Peter, Joseph, biblical saints or earthly saints—idols or are they simply works of art to be enjoyed? God's Word says these things are idols. The dictionary defines an idol as being, "any person or thing devotedly or excessively admired." God says "thou shalt have no other gods before Me." (Exodus 20:3)

Church Constitution and Bylaws

Does the Bible direct man to live by a constitution and bylaws in managing our affairs in the church? The answer is a resounding no. These documents set out in the church to guide the affairs of the church are at best one big foot of Satan in the doorway of that church and you can be sure the crack will become wider in a very short time. If the people forming a particular church have so little faith in God that He cannot order the affairs of that church then all who are about to join together in that church better first become a believer in Christ Jesus and have Him as personal Lord and Master, then join in a fellowship group who meets together to give praise, honor, and glory to God only—without praise and adoration to the pastor or one another. For, if a gathering of people needs a constitution and bylaws to order its affairs, God cannot honor those affairs because complete trust is not in God. God requires complete trust in Him—nothing short of complete trust will do.

Church Hierarchical Systems

As the Roman Empire spread its deadly poisonous government system over the then-known world, particularly Western

Europe, they spread with it a religious poison and gave it the name Catholicism. The two poisons were combined into one huge force that ruled both government and religion wherever it conquered. The influence of the combination of civil government, civil and criminal justice and religious beliefs wrapped up in one small group of men held sway over the civilized world until the days of the Reformation. The civil government and justice systems were cast off but the powerful influence of the Eastern and Western pseudo-Christianity systems remain today.

Robert Brow in his book, *The Church,*[1] gives a scathing summary of how the hierarchical systems came into being and an indication of the harm inflicted upon church attendees who have no way of knowing what affect the systems have on their lives.

Not only did those powerful religious systems help to conquer nations, they forced their deadly misinterpretations of the Holy Word of God on the people wherever they went. Thus the hierarchial systems we have in our churches today have been copied from those original systems. For instance, our one-man ministry idea of today came from the lord of the manor during the Middle Ages when he hired a priest to care for the religion of his subjects.[2]

There is a very subtle danger in following along with hierarchical powers. The ritualistic liturgy of the service developed by those called, "heads of the church," becomes the routine of the worship which makes it difficult for the Holy Spirit to work within individual worshipers to have a part in the worship of God. It is the worship of rituals instead of pure praise and glory to God. The evangelicals say their worship of God is

Bible based, but the minister does nearly all of the worshiping. As long as the attendees of churches are comfortable with heads of the denominations orchestrating their form and methods of worship of God, men will continue to receive the glory and not God. Eyes are on the Pope, priest, senior pastor or the TV minister. Hero worship is a very insidious thing. I was told by a friend some time ago, she was sure her pastor could be the CEO of a large corporation! We need to be most careful who we follow when our **eternal life** is at stake!

Denominationalism

Denominationalism is one of Satan's most potent poisons, divide and conquer, keep everyone guessing, what is the truth of God's Word concerning salvation for the souls of men, and theologians oblige him. Because of denominationalism, Satan can and did bring into existence many false teachings including: Jehovah Witnesses, Mormons, Moonies, Unitarians, and Christian Science. For details of these and other cults see *Handbook of Today's Religions,* Josh McDowell and Don Stewart, 1983. All of these have a small amount of truth mixed in with a very large amount of untruth. This is very easy for Satan to do.

Clergy and Laymen

Again Satan has put division in the midst of those who trust God. Eyes of men are on an earthly man not God our heavenly Father. No matter how much one attempts to explain away the problem (we should have) with the statement—we need a leader, all explanations will bring you back to—eyes are on man in the "one-man ministry" system. All true believers are preachers to the lost world with the proper instructions. All true believers are soul winners with the proper instructions. All true believers are teachers of Scripture with the proper training. We cannot find anywhere in the New Testament Scriptures "clergy" and "laymen." These terms have come to us by those who would elevate themselves above other men and that is a sin.

Church Doctrine

Choosing parts of the Holy Word of God to develop church doctrine and adding to it religious traditions of men can never be relied upon as the guide for those who want to belong to God; to know they will be with Him when they die. The true believer's guide is the entire Word of God, not just parts of His Word. This is the evil that has been devised by the various leaders of the "church system" and it is the basis of church denominationalism and sects. Using the entire Word of God to produce disciples (soul winners) is the true way of walking before God Almighty. God shows us in His Word that man can-not by himself come to depend on God through church doctrines alone. God has a true mediator between Himself and man, the Holy Spirit. Everyone who yearns for Godly direction for their life has to understand that it is God's guidance through the interaction of the Holy Spirit with their spirit that gives a person true guidance for their life. This interaction comes to man by diligent study of and hearing the Holy Word of God. However, reading the Word of God is the most powerful interaction because there is but one mediator, the Holy Spirit of God.

A Glimpse of the "History of the Church"

Sometimes the facts given in this writing were very difficult for the author because the very heart of all that meant so much had to be set aside—prayed over—scrutinized, weighed very cautiously, verified, and looked at to determine what was truly based on God's Word and what was based on traditions of men and what was downright untrue. Everyone sitting under the teaching of the church system needs to have a deeper understanding of where those teachings are taking them. Are those teachings giving them all they need to reach the most important goal of their life, not on this earth, but **<u>their life in all eternity</u>**? If anyone never gives any thought to that question they are either a fool or have no brain at all, so they must be a fool.

The Scriptures which help the reader to focus on that thought with very penetrating and sobering effect are given in Luke 16:19-31; Jesus is speaking to His disciples and the Pharisees standing by heard these words:

> "Now there was a certain rich man, and he habitually dressed in purple and fine linen, joyously living in splendor every day. And a poor man named Lazarus was laid at his gate, covered with sores, and longing to be fed with the crumbs which were falling from the rich man's table; besides, even the dogs were coming and licking his sores. Now the poor man died and was carried away by the angels to Abraham's bosom; and the rich man

> also died and was buried. In Hades he lifted up his eyes, being in torment, and saw Abraham far away, and Lazarus in his bosom. And he cried out and said, 'Father Abraham, have mercy on me, and send Lazarus so that he may dip the tip of his finger in water and cool off my tongue, for I am in agony in this flame.' But Abraham said, 'Child, remember that during your life you received your good things, and likewise Lazarus bad things; but now he is being comforted here, and you are in agony. And besides all this, between us and you there is a great chasm fixed, in order that those who wish to come over from here to you will not be able, and that none may cross over from there to us.' And he said, 'Then I beg you, Father, that you send him to my father's house—for I have five brothers—in order that he may warn them, so that they will not also come to this place of torment.' But Abraham said, 'They have Moses and the Prophets; let them hear them.' But he said, 'No, father Abraham, but if someone goes to them from the dead, they will repent!' But he said to him, 'If they do not listen to Moses and the Prophets, they will not be persuaded even if someone rises from the dead.'" (Luke 16:19-31)

The persuasion needed for mankind is in God's Word, and it rests in the truth of the shed blood of God's only begotten Son on the cross. Every man, woman and child needs to know and understand completely what eternal life with God in His Son means on an individual basis. Many people have been exposed to the Gospel of salvation in the Lord Jesus Christ in many different forms, but very few of the denominations and independent faiths that were a direct result of the Reformers work present it in its fullest and truest God-redeeming and salvation in Christ Jesus form. In plain, simple language, if the teachers of fifth grade arithmetic taught their students with the same level of competence as the leaders of the many denominations and independent sects teach God's Word, fifth graders could not find that 14.42 ÷ 0.013 to two decimals should be 1109.23. Nor would the student know that 0.013 is the divisor, 14.42 is the dividend, and 1109.23 is the quotient. Examples of the poorest instruction by denominational teaching of how one becomes a child of the kingdom of heaven are: one, by confirmation after intensive instruction on denominational beliefs, participation in communion on a regular basis and infant baptism; Two, the simple confession of believing on the Lord Jesus Christ without confessing sin and without discipling.

Many denominations are guilty of these errors and lack total discipling. Much of the material used to instruct individuals in the church system was developed many centuries ago and is directed toward church membership instead of winning souls for eternal life with God. The simple David and Goliath and other "Bible stories" type of instruction in the church school or Sunday school system have tremendous room for improvement when one takes a hard look at the examples set out by Christ.

In the book of Matthew, Christ in very rapid succession began to explain and teach His disciples, with very vivid illustrations, the purpose of His very being. He zeroed in on establishing with His disciples all that they would need to know and understand who He was and to prepare them for teaching, discipling and to establish these truths with all the people wherever they went after His death and resurrection. The training missions became more and more intense, more and more in-depth. His healing of bodily deformities, of the mind, and healing of those overcome by sin increased at a rapid rate. He entered Jerusalem as a humble being. The teaching of the kingdom of heaven prophecy increased with greater and greater intensity and emphasis.

All of the book of Matthew is directed toward a deep understanding and enlightenment for us as to what God did for mankind as a whole, but in Matthew 16:18-21, in particular, He told us He would establish our life with Him in heaven in His Son. Then, in the remaining chapters the Son lived out that promise in detail. God gave us, at the end of the book, the very simple short instructions that we should not miss, He gave us what our responsibility is in order to thank God for all that He made possible for us. Just being a church member is not what God tells us!

Chapter 16 comes near to the middle of a most important book in God's Word. Much of what God gives us in the rest of the books of the New Testament except for the Revelation and Hebrews gives detailed explanations of what is said in Matthew and certainly the spiritual kingdom and kingdom of heaven blessing are at the heart of His message. The keystone chapter and the keystone verse of all of the book of Matthew is Chapter 16 and verse 18. All other thought of the book revolves around that great verse. Reason enough that Satan would use it to his advantage.

However, this important message is not recognized by most men of the church and we might say that Satan blinded most of mankind concerning the depth of the teachings of Christ. We need to be reminded that mankind paid the price for remaining in blindness, for the Holocaust devastation is the ultimate example of what man can do when directed by Satan and this should bring to our mind how Satan has devastated all of mankind—where hundreds of millions are in jeopardy and stand at the threshold of destruction due to blind leaders leading the blind. Some will say, chalk it up to apostasy. That answer will never please God. Those who teach need to take inventory of what is true and what is false—what is complete and what is incomplete discipling.

The history of the world is embedded in the hand of God working in man to bring mankind unto Himself. We see in our history how man has resisted the loving efforts of God to reach his finest part of His creation. Since history cannot lie, it is to history we must go to help establish truth on the subject, church history, what is true and what is false in the documentation of the historical past. That subject carries with it the greatest disagreement of all subjects including Judaism and American politics. This is because the adversary also has been reaching out to mankind with his lethal venom by injecting mankind with lies. Table 1 gives in contrasting form some truths but mostly lies conveyed to us from the early years of "Christian history."

This discussion is leading up to the fact, people need to come to the realization that not all that has been written and spoken by theologians can be trusted as coming from someone who loves God. To bring my point into focus we need to look into the historical facts as recorded near the beginning of "Christianity" and onward. In outline form we review some of the events and developments which are recorded in history that has been passed off as "history of the church." Certain parts of the world accepted "Christianity" and certain parts did not. Those people who did not, for the most part, remain in darkness, that is, they remain in their paganistic lifestyle. This was their choice to reject the one true God. Therefore, those people now serve a god manufactured by man with the help of Satan. The man-manufactured god comes in many forms depending on the whims of man in a particular country and even a particular section of a given country. Those people of the world without the truth of Jesus Christ are at the heart of the objective of those who say they follow the one true God. They have the living Lord on their side to perform that work. Indeed God has performed miraculous works in taking the Gospel message of the saving power of the Lord Jesus Christ to a lost world.

Since Christ entered and exited this world, those men who came to know about Christ, some developed a true relationship with Him, some learned the truth but then did not do anything about it, some listened to the words and did not respond at all. This is the scene in the world today. People living in that part of the world we term "Christianized" are living in the various stages of "Christianization" as defined above. It is this condition of mankind that produced the following pseudo-Christian events in the history of the church—the tares have indeed lived and are living among the wheat. Each of us needs to recognize the historic facts for what they are, remembering there can only be two kinds of facts, there cannot be any in between, they are Godly or they are ungodly even in the so-called "Christianized" world.

TABLE 1

Selected Statements From Christian History

		Godly	Ungodly
1.	The disciples of Jesus Christ were the first and that is the very truest form of winning the lost for the Lord.	■	❑
2.	The very earliest persecution of the true followers of Jesus Christ by the Roman Emperors from 64 A.D. to 250 A.D.	❑	■
3.	The writings of Clement of Rome, Ignatius of Antioch, Polycarp of Smyrna and Hermes of Rome which are considered part of church history were legalistic and ascetic (a person who practices extreme self-denial or self-mortification for religious reasons)**	❑	❑
4.	Ecclesiastical judgement (judgement by the church is);	❑	■
5.	The process used by man to select the books of the Bible included in the New Testament	■	❑
6.	Christians think of Jesus more as the founder of the Church than as God's disclosure of His nature, the Word	❑	■
7.	Creation of the station for a man as Bishop of Constantinople, Rome, England, etc.	❑	■
8.	The presbyters advised the bishops, performed the preaching and administration of the sacraments in the congregation with the bishop's permission	❑	■
9.	Baptismal regeneration (baptism is a new birth—forgiveness of sin)	❑	■
10.	Excommunication for nonconformance to "church practices"	❑	■
11.	Councils or synods called to settle differences in the church	❑	■
12.	Development of the several Creeds*	❑	■

	Godly	Ungodly
13. Constantine's action of establishing by edict everyone has an equal opportunity to become a Christian	❑	■
14. Use of torture and fear to make Christians worship the Roman gods	❑	■
15. Suffer martyrdom at the hands of the "Roman Christians"	■	❑
16. The early Church as defined by what we know of its early development during the 4th-6th centuries	❑	■
17. The statement—the "church leadership" can have some inconsistencies with the Word of God	❑	■
18. In the "Lord's Supper"—the teaching of transubstantiation	❑	■
19. Confession of sin to a man (priest or pastor) or the forgiveness of sin by a man	❑	■
20. Infallibility of a man as applied to what is truth in the Holy Word of God	❑	■
21. Celibacy practice	❑	■
22. The Christian church is the true heir of the promise	❑	■
23. The Crusades promoted by the church*	❑	■
24. The inquiry by the church of all those accused of heresy (known in history as the Inquisition). The church abhorred the shedding of blood so it was decided that those who were found guilty of heresy were burned to death.*	❑	■

---

* We have been led to believe by many writers of the "history of the church" that the items marked with an asterisk were carried out by "the church" and therefore we are to assume that those acts are Godly events, but in fact, are no different than other events of history, i.e., the Boston Tea Party, the signing of the Declaration of Independence, the Cuban Missile Crisis. It is very simple to prove by Scriptures that all of those so marked above are just events in the history of the pseudo-Christianity not events and practices put forth by Godly human beings.

** The jury is still out on this item. Scholars remain in a tie as to how true these men were to God.

Theologians need to sort out the causes of the conflict which exists between the forces of truth and the forces of evil and who it is that perpetrated the conflict and the consequences to be levied against those who are guilty. Because man has been more of a follower than a leader, there are very few leaders, so, due to this inherent flaw in the makeup of the human being, it is very easy for evil forces to become the strong leaders in the areas of great power; i.e., government, religion, law and commerce. History proves this point over and over again.

The sources looked to by the author for proof concerning this dilemma of mankind and particularly the conflict within the realm of Christian religion (the church) are:

- *Jews, God and History*[3]
- *Augustus*[4]
- *Columbia History of the World*[5]

In these books the important events of history are given in succinct language which makes it possible to see the conflict that rages between Godliness and ungodliness. The books make it possible to see more clearly which forces are on the side of God and who it was that consistently carried on the work against God and who that organization is that continues the work against God and the people of God. It would be nice to say and it would be very easy to say that it is Satan. But that would not help mankind one iota, would it? Learning comes about by recognizing we have a problem. Set the problem down on paper. Analyze all the knowns. Then state the cause and effects of each known. Pinpoint who or what it is that is behind the problem. Lastly, set out a plan to counteract the problem in such a way that the problem and solution will be recognized by all mankind and those whose heart and mind have been penetrated by the importance of the solution will act to escape the negative consequences. The problem is the church, for the most part, with all its organization and resources is a failure before God Almighty in the area of producing true disciples. This very brief discussion on the subject, "church history" is intended to enlighten and make the reader aware of the shortcomings of the majority of the leadership of most of the church system.

12

Traveling Companions

All the people who attend "church services" and participate in the various church educational programs across America are traveling companions, taking the many different paths, that each hope will take them to heaven. Everyone traveling the path of his or her choosing, needs to know without a shadow of a doubt, where the pathway is taking them—**will I have eternal life with Jesus Christ?**

In sharp contrast to Christ's direction for following Him is the theologically-guided way handed down through the centuries and adhered to by many of the different denominations. Within that theologically-guided church system today, there are 14 kinds of religious groups in America according to the *Handbook of Denominations in the United States*. Those 14 are further divided into more than 200 variations of the way each individual entity directs its followers to walk before God.[1] Those hundreds of denominations show almost as many different approaches to worshipping and serving God. The denominations make known and declare to the world their own individuality compared to their fellow Americans' faith across the street or across town or in a different town or city. So when we say, "I worship God as a Lutheran" or "I am a Methodist" or

"I am a Presbyterian" or "I am a Catholic" and on down through the hundreds of different denominations, independents, and sects, what are we really saying? When that question is fully and completely addressed, we can say, Satan is divisive! The doctrine which a church declares to the world concerning the nature of that church, why it belongs to a certain denomination, or why it is a church, is a true measurement of where they stand before God.

Your Neighbor's Faith

A representation of the mass of data collected from a large number of churches contacted across the United States follows: The statements of faith from 151 churches who responded to a survey of over 300 churches from all parts of the United States was used to arrive at, "What is the church?", from the church perspective. There are many similarities, yet different in one or more doctrinal beliefs, even near duplication of wording, but I believe the results are effective and valid. The church denominations are presented in alphabetical order. The name of the church and location, the source of the information within the particular church that the reply came from, and the number of churches of that denomination responding from various parts of the country is given. Each statement that defines the word "church" by the various churches herein represented is highlighted by underlining. It is not to say, because I did not include, in some cases, more than one church from the same denomination, in this listing, that all of them presented identical doctrine and statement of faith data. Most churches act independent of one another, particularly where strong, hierarchical powers are not looking over their shoulders.

Anglican Church in America, West Des Moines, IA, Episcopal (The Saint Louis Affirmation) (1)

"PRINCIPLES OF DOCTRINE

THE NATURE OF THE CHURCH

We gather as people called by God to be faithful and obedient to Him. As the Royal Priestly People of God, the Church is called to be, in fact, the manifestation of Christ in and to the world. True religion is revealed to man by God. We cannot decide what is truth, but rather (in obedience) ought to receive, accept, cherish, defend and teach what God has given us. The Church is created by God, and is beyond the ultimate control of man.

The Church is the Body of Christ at work in the world. She is the society of the baptized called out from the world: In it, but not of it. As Christ's faithful Bride, she is different from the world and must not be influenced by it."

Lakeview Assembly, Stockton, CA, (Assemblies of God) (The General Council) (18)

"10. The Church and Its Mission—The Church is the Body of Christ, the habitation of God through the Spirit, with divine appointments for the fulfillment of her great commission. Each believer, born of the Spirit, is an integral part of the General Assembly and Church of the Firstborn, which are written in heaven. (Ephesians 1:22,23; 2:22; Hebrews 12:23)

Since God's purpose concerning man is to seek and to save that which is lost, to be worshiped by man, and to build a body of believers in the image of His Son, the priority reason-for-being of the

Assemblies of God as part of the church is:

a. To be an agency of God for evangelizing the world. (Acts 1:8; Matthew 28:19,20; Mark 16:15,16)

b. To be a corporate body in which man may worship God. (1 Corinthians 12:13)

c. To be a channel of God's purpose to build a body of saints being perfected in the image of His Son. (Ephesians 4:11-16; 1 Corinthians 12:28; 1 Corinthians 14:12)

The Assemblies of God exist expressly to give continuing emphasis to this reason-for-being in the New Testament apostolic pattern by teaching and encouraging believers to be baptized in the Holy Spirit. This experience:

a. Enables them to evangelize in the power of the Spirit with accompanying supernatural signs. (Mark 16:15-20; Acts 4:29-31; Hebrews 2:3,4)

b. Adds a necessary dimension to worshipful relationship with God. (1 Corinthians 2:10-16; 1 Corinthians 12,13,14)

c. Enables them to respond to the full working of the Holy Spirit in expressions of fruit and gifts and ministries as in New Testament times for the edifying of the body of Christ. (Galatians 5:22-26; 1 Corinthians 14:12; Ephesians 4:11,12; 1 Corinthians 12:28; Colossians 1:29)"

Trinity Church, Scottsdale, AZ, (Assemblies of God) (Assemblies of God Information Series) (18)

"Why Church—A Model for Christians—<u>The concept of church was God's idea. He created it to encourage and help Christians, in order that</u>

they might serve Him and accomplish His work on earth. In the Assemblies of God we believe the local church is the vital core for effective ministry. Not to be confused with a building or facility, the local church is a network of people committed to fulfilling the work of God.

We believe the Church has three obvious purposes: (1) to introduce the lost to Christ; (2) to provide an environment for fellowshipping with others who hold similar values and love for God; and (3) to effectively train and nurture believers.

We feel if we as Christians are to maintain our walk with God, we must submit ourselves to His Word and other Christians who are firmly rooted in the faith. These goals can best be accomplished through a warm and caring body of believers—the local church."(Acts 20:28; Philippians 2:15; 1 Thessalonians 5:11)

Westland Baptist Church, Lakewood, CO, (Baptist) (Articles of Faith) (26)

"We believe that a Baptist Church is a congregation of baptized believers associated by a covenant of faith and fellowship of the gospel, said church being understood to be the citadel and propagator of the Divine and Eternal Grace; observing the ordinances of Christ; governed by His laws; exercising the gifts, rights, and privileges invested in them by His Word; that its officers of ordination are pastors or elders whose qualifications, claims, and duties are clearly defined in the scriptures; we believe the true mission of the church is found in the Great Commission: First, to make individual disciples; Second, to build up the church;

Third, to teach and instruct as He has commanded. We do not believe in the reversal of this order; we hold that the local church has the absolute right of self government, free from the interference of any hierarchy of individuals or organizations; and that the one and only superintendent is Christ through the Holy Spirit; that it is scriptural for true churches to cooperate with each other in contending for the faith and for the furtherance of the Gospel; that every church is the sole and only judge of the measure and method of its cooperation; on all matters of membership, of policy, of government, of discipline, of benevolence, the will of the local church is final.

(Acts 2:41,42; I Cor. 11:2; Eph. 1:22,23; Eph. 4:11; I Cor. 12:4, 8-11; Acts 14:23; Acts 6:5, 6; Acts 15:23; Acts 20:17-28; I Tim. 3:1-13; Matt. 28:19,20; Col. 1:18; Eph. 5:23,24; I Pet. 5:1-4; Acts 15:22; Jude 3,4; II Cor. 8:23,24; I Cor. 16:1; Mal. 3:10; Lev. 27:32; I Cor. 16:2; I Cor. 6:1-3; I Cor. 5:11-13)"

Taylors First Baptist Church, Taylors, SC, (Baptist) (The Baptist Faith & Message) (26)

"A New Testament church of the Lord Jesus Christ is a local body of baptized believers who are associated by covenant in the faith and fellowship of the gospel, observing the two ordinances of Christ, committed to His teachings, exercising the gifts, rights, and privileges invested in them by His Word, and seeking to extend the Gospel to the ends of the earth.

This church is an autonomous body, operating through democratic processes under the Lordship of Jesus Christ. In such a congregation members are equally responsible. Its Scriptural officers are pastors and deacons.

The New Testament speaks also of the church as the body of Christ which includes all of the redeemed of all the ages.

(Matt. 16:15-19; 18:15-20; Acts 2:41,42,47; 5:11-14; 6:3-6; 13:1-3; 14:23,27; 15:1-30; 16:5; 20:28; Rom. 1:7; 1 Cor. 1:2; 3:16; 5:4,5; 7:17; 9:13,14; 12; Eph. 1:22,23; 2:19-22; 3:8-11,21; 5:22-32; Phil. 1:1; Col. 1:18; 1 Tim. 3:1-15; 4:14; 1 Peter 5:1-4; Rev. 2-3; 21:2,3)"

The Orchard, Modesto, CA, (Baptist) (Statement of Beliefs of the North American Baptist Conference) (26)

"We believe the Church is the body of which Christ is the head and all who believe in Him are members. (Ephesians 1:22,23; Romans 12:4,5) Christians are commanded to be baptized upon profession of faith and to unite with a local church for mutual encouragement and growth in discipleship through worship, nurture, service and the proclamation of the Gospel of Jesus Christ to the world (Acts 2:41,42,47; Luke 24:45-48). Each church is a self-governing body under the lordship of Christ with all members sharing responsibility (Acts 13:1-3; 14:26-28). The form of government is understood to be congregational (Matthew 18:17; Acts 6:3-6; 15:22,23). The ordinances of the church are baptism and the Lord's Supper. Baptism is the immersion of a believer in water in the name of the Father, and of the Son, and of the Holy Spirit. (Matthew 28:18-20) It is an act of obedience symbolizing the believer's identification with the death, burial and resurrection of the Savior Jesus

Christ. (Romans 6:3-5) The Lord's Supper is the partaking of the bread and of the cup by believers together as a continuing memorial of the broken body and shed blood of Christ. It is an act of thankful dedication to Him and serves to unite His people until He returns. (I Corinthians 11:23-26)

To express unity in Christ, local churches form associations and a conference for mutual counsel, fellowship and a more effective fulfillment of Christ's commission. (Acts 15; I Corinthians 6:1-3)"

Brethren in Christ Church, Hanover, PA, (Manual of Doctrine and Government) (1)

"NATURE OF THE CHURCH

Through the Holy Spirit, Jesus Christ established the church to be God's new community, which has its roots in the people of God in the Old Testament and testifies to the presence of the kingdom of God on earth. Jesus Christ is the Head of the church, the redeemed community. His Word and will are authoritative among us.

The church consists of all those who trust Jesus as Savior and follow him as Lord. We become part of God's family, loving the Lord Jesus and learning to love and care for one another. We are a covenant community vowing before God and fellow members to live a holy life, to remain loyal to the church, and to foster oneness within the body of Christ. Our understanding of this covenant is expressed in a commitment to the local congregation, where the integrity of our discipleship is lived; to the denomination, where relationships with a wider fellowship of God's people are realized; and to the body of Christ throughout the world, by which we fulfill the prayer of Jesus that we all may be one.

The essential functions of the church are worship, fellowship, discipleship, and mission. In worship, we bring our whole-hearted devotion to the Lord God. In fellowship, we live out our deep commitment to love one another. In discipleship, we follow the call of the Lord Jesus to obey and to teach all things commanded by him. In mission, we proclaim the gospel to all people and minister to human need as Jesus did.

As a covenant community we practice mutual accountability among our members. We accept the steps outlined by Jesus: first going privately to the one who sins against us; then, if necessary, returning with one or more witnesses; and finally, if needed, involving the congregation. When the church deals with sin, we seek to respond with compassion and concern. The objective of church discipline is to restore the erring church member and to maintain the integrity and purity of the church's fellowship and witness.

LIFE OF THE CHURCH: PRACTICES

Practices which are important aspects of life and worship in the Christian community:

We regard the practice of washing one another's feet as modeled and taught by Jesus to be a demonstration of love, humility, and service to one another, pointing beyond itself to a way of life. In the life of the church, the feetwashing service is an occasion for reconciliation, affirmation of one another, and testimony of God's grace.

The Christian marriage ceremony witnesses to God's order and design for the union of a man and a woman in a lifelong commitment of love and fidelity. Vows are affirmed and the marriage is celebrated in the context of the congregation, which is called to support the couple in their life together. Christ's covenantal, self-sacrificing love for the church and the church's loving response is the model that husband and wife are to follow.

The practice of dedicating children affirms their place in the midst of the congregation. The service of dedication provides an opportunity for parents to commit themselves to the Lord in the care and training of their children. Members of the congregation join with the parents in pledging to pray for and to nurture the children.

The gospel includes healing for the ill and deliverance for the oppressed. The church follows scriptural practices in praying for the sick, laying on hands, and anointing with oil in the name of the Lord. The service of divine healing affirms that God responds to the brokenness of the human condition with healing or with grace to endure suffering.

When death comes to the community of believers, the funeral provides an opportunity to focus on the risen Lord. The congregation responds compassionately with the bereaved. Death reminds us of our mortality and the hope of the resurrection.

MISSION OF THE CHURCH: IN RELATION TO THE WORLD

Jesus Christ commissions the church to make disciples of all the world's peoples. The church is called to share the gospel in every culture and strata of society. Evangelism includes bringing people to a saving faith in Christ and to responsible membership in the church. The people of God are also called to be a redemptive influence in the world, confronting corporate sin and seeking to overcome evil with good. They are to be a voice for righteousness, peace, and justice.

The church recognizes the place God ordains for government in society. As Christians, we pray for the state and those who are in authority. At the same time, we believe loyalty to Christ and the church, which is trans-national, takes precedence over loyalty to the state. Selective involvements in the affairs of government are appropriate for believers if loyalty to Christ and the principles of his kingdom are carefully guarded, and if such participation will enhance one's Christian witness and service.

Christ loved his enemies and he calls us as his disciples to love our enemies. We follow our Lord in being a people of peace and reconciliation, called to suffer and not to fight. Preparation for or participation in war is inconsistent with the teachings of Christ. Similarly, we reject all other acts of violence which devalue human life. Rather, we affirm active peacemaking, sacrificial service to others, as well as the pursuit of justice for the poor and the oppressed in the name of Christ.

Those who follow Christ are strangers and pilgrims in the world, called to share the light of Christ. In the renewing of our minds by God's grace, we resist conformity to our fallen, broken world. Nonconformity calls us to reject the world's unrestrained materialism, its sensualism, and its self-centeredness. Rather we seek to express the values of God's kingdom by a lifestyle of modesty and simplicity."

Christian Fellowship of the Rockies, Denver, CO, (Doctrinal Statement) (9)

"The church is the *Body of Christ* and in relation as His Bride, dedicated to the worship and service of God, the observance of the ordinances of Baptism and the Lord's Supper, and the practice of good words. The primary tasks of the church are to *teach all nations,* establishing disciples, bringing forth the Gospel to every aspect of life and thought, with the ultimate mission of the church being to answer the cry of a lost and dying world, leading the world to the one and only Redeemer.

(Matthew 28:19) Therefore go and make disciples of all nations, baptizing them in the name of the Father and of the Son and of the Holy Spirit.

(Romans 12:4) Just as each of us has one body with many members, and these members do not all have the same function.

(1 Peter 2:5-10) You also, like living stones, are being built into a spiritual house to be a holy priesthood, offering spiritual sacrifices acceptable to God through Jesus Christ. 6 For in Scripture it says: 'See, I lay a stone in Zion, a chosen and precious cornerstone, and the one who trusts in him will never be put to shame. 7 Now to you who believe, this stone is precious. But to those who do not believe, 'The stone the builders rejected has become the capstone,' 8 and 'A stone that causes men to stumble and a rock that makes them fall.' They stumble because they disobey the message—which is also what they were destined for. 9 But you are a chosen people, a royal priesthood, a holy nation, a people belonging to God, that you may declare the praises of him who called you out of darkness into his wonderful light. 10 Once you were not a people, but now you are the people of God; once you had not received mercy, but now you have received mercy."

Christian and Missionary Alliance, Wooster, MA, (Statement of Faith) (4)

"The Church consists of all those who believe in the Lord Jesus Christ, are redeemed through His blood and are born again of the Holy Spirit. Christ is the Head of the Body, the Church, which has been commissioned by Him to go into all the world as a witness, preaching the gospel to all nations.

The local church is a body of believers in Christ who are joined together for the worship of God, edification through the Word of God, prayer, fellowship, the proclamation of the gospel and observance of the ordinances of baptism and the Lord's Supper."

Des Moines Christian Reformed Church, Des Moines, IA, (What Do We Believe) (4)

"Christian Reformed people regard the church very highly. That's because of the way the Bible describes the church.

The church is the bride of Christ, the bride He loves.

The church is the branches growing from Christ, the vine; His life flows in and through the church.

The church is the body of Christ. He is the Head; we are His hands, feet, voice, and heart to do His work in the world.

The Christian Reformed Church Order translates into practical life our thinking about the church. The first section is about *The Offices of the Church*. Christ is the chief officer of the church. He rules it by His Word and Spirit. Although every believer holds the office of 'Christian,' we believe that Christ has instituted four special offices for the good ordering of His church: ministers to care for spiritual needs, elders to exercise supervision, deacons to help the poor, and evangelists to call unbelievers to the Christian faith.

The second section of the Church Order is about *The Assemblies of the Church.* Under our so-called Presbyterian system, the primary governing body of the church is the *consistory* (or council) in the local church. Representatives from consistories meet at an area *classis,* and representatives from various *classis* at an annual *synod.*

The third section of the Church Order deals with *The Task and Activities of the Church.* The most obvious activity is worship. We can't demonstrate that it's a scriptural requirement, but we have agreed to worship at least twice each Sunday. That's one of our distinguishing features."

Church of Christ, Fort Des Moines, IA, (What This Church Believes) (6)

"We are an undenominational family of believers who are attempting to live by the teachings of the Scriptures. We are not a building, but a fellowship of believers with diverse background that respond to building each other up through God's love. We have placed our faith in Jesus Christ, the Son of the living God.

(Matthew 16:13-18), being obedient to Him according to what is recorded in God's Holy Word, the Bible.

. . . that the church is the body of Christ on earth and exists to save the lost and edify the saved. (Ephesians 4:1-16)."

Central Church of Christ, Spartanburg, SC, (Jesus & His Church) (6)

"In the New Testament, the church is compared

to a human body with Christ as its head. The head supplies the body with its life. The head unifies and coordinates the different organs of the body. At the same time, the head depends on the body to carry out its functions. My brothers and sisters and I are the hands, the feet, and the voices by which Jesus continues His work in the world today.

One of the most exciting characteristics of the church family is the fact that we each have a part to play. There are no free rides and no part-time memberships in the church that Jesus established. Just as the members of a human body carry out complimentary functions, the members of the church's body have different strengths and talents. One may teach. Another may serve. Another's gift may be in giving . . . or encouraging . . . or in spreading the gospel to those who have yet to hear."

Lafayette Church of the Nazarene, Lafayette, CO, (The Church of the Nazarene) (7)

"WHAT IS THE CHURCH OF THE NAZARENE?

It could be defined as the Living Bread of which St. John speaks in the Bible. The Bread of Life that can be divided endlessly and still nourish, like the miracle of the five loaves and two fishes in the small boy's lunch. Only love can be divided endlessly and still not diminish. God's love. We partake of God's love when we love each other. In the church, it is ours for the taking . . . for the giving. In His love, one is never alone.

WHAT IS THE CHURCH OF THE NAZARENE?

It might be defined as a community of believers who face life in interdependence as children in the universal family of God. In such interdependence, one is never alone.

In the church, of all places, you should never experience human aloneness. Paul, in his letter to the church at Ephesus, said: 'Now therefore ye are no more strangers and foreigners, but *fellowcitizens* with the saints, and of the *household of God;* and are built upon the foundation of the apostles and prophets, Jesus Christ himself being the chief corner stone; in whom all the building fitly framed *together* groweth unto an holy temple in the Lord: in whom ye also are builded *together* for an habitation of God through the Spirit.' (Ephesians 2:19-22) This is the goal of the Church of the Nazarene."

Church of the Nazarene, Sanford, FL, (The Articles of Faith) (7)

"We believe in the Church, the community that confesses Jesus Christ as Lord, the covenant people of God made new in Christ, the Body of Christ called together by the Holy Spirit through the Word.

God calls the Church to express its life in the unity and fellowship of the Spirit; in worship through the preaching of the Word, observance of the sacraments, and ministry in His name; by obedience to Christ and mutual accountability.

The mission of the Church in the world is to continue the redemptive work of Christ in the power of the Spirit through holy living, evangelism, discipleship, and service.

The Church is a historical reality, which organizes itself in culturally conditioned forms; exists both as local congregations and as a universal body; sets apart persons called of God for specific ministries. God calls the Church to live under His rule in anticipation of the consummation at the coming of our Lord Jesus Christ.

[Exodus 19:3; Jeremiah 31:33; Matthew 8:11; 10:7; 16:13-19,24; 18:15-20; 28:19,20; John 17:14-26; 20:21-23; Acts 1:7,8; 2:32-47; 6:1,2; 13:1; 14-23; Romans 2:28,29; 4:16; 10:9-15; 11:13-32; 12:1-8; 15:1-3; 1 Corinthians 3:5-9; 7:17; 11:1,17-33; 12:3,12-31; 14:26-40; 2 Corinthians 5:11-6:1; Galatians 5:6,13,14; 6:1-5,15; Ephesians 4:1-17; 5:25-27; Philippians 2:1-16; 1 Thessalonians 4:1-12; 1 Timothy 4:13; Hebrews 10:19-25; 1 Peter 1:1,2,13; 2:4-12, 21; 4:1,2,10-11; 1 John 4:17; Jude 24; Revelation 5:9,10]"

Abundant Life Community Church, Pasedena, CA, (Statement of Faith) (10)

"THE CHURCH

God by His Word and Spirit creates the Church, calling sinful men out of the whole human race into the fellowship of Christ's body. By the same Word and Spirit He guides and preserves that new, redeemed humanity. The Church is not a religious institution or denomination. Rather, the Church universal is made up of those who have become genuine followers of Christ and have personally appropriated the gospel. The Church exists to worship and glorify God as Father, Son, and Holy Spirit. It also exists to serve Him by faithfully doing His will in the earth. This involves a commitment to see the gospel preached in all the world for a testimony. The ultimate mission of the Church is the redemption of souls. When God transforms human nature, this then becomes the chief means of society's transformation.

All members of the Church universal are to be a vital and committed part of a local church. In this context they are called to walk out the New Covenant as the people of God and demonstrate the reality of the kingdom of God. The ascended Christ has given gift ministries to the church (apostles, prophets, evangelists, pastors and teachers) for the equipping of Christ's body that it might mature and grow. Through the gift ministries all members of the Church are to be nurtured and equipped for the work of ministry. In the context of the local church, God's people receive pastoral care and leadership and opportunity to employ their God-given gifts in His service in relation to one another and to the world."

First Covenant Church, St Paul, MN, (Covenant Affirmations—a brief form) (4)

"**The Church as a fellowship of believers,** characterized by mutual participation in and sharing of the new life in Christ. Membership is by confession of personal faith in Jesus Christ as Savior and Lord. It is open to *all* believers. Considerations of class or race, education or pedigree, wealth or prestige do not enter. Uniformity in creedal details is not expected. What is required is that one be 'born anew to a living hope through the resurrection of Jesus Christ from the dead.' (1 Peter 1:3) 'The doors of the church are wide enough to admit all who believe and narrow enough to exclude those who do not,' said our forebears. We affirm no less today.

The ministry of the Holy Spirit, who with the Father and the Son calls the Church into being, empowers its witness, guides its mission, and supplies the gifts needed by the Church and its members to exalt Christ.

The reality of freedom in Christ, who delivers us from the power of sin and moves us by his grace into a whole new experience of obedience and life. This freedom creates an ecclesiastical climate which allows for differences of opinion in matters of interpretation, doctrine, and practice within the context of biblical guidelines and historical Christianity. Such freedom 'is to be distinguished from the individualism that disregards the centrality of the Word of God and the mutual responsibilities and disciplines of the spiritual community' (*Preamble to the Constitution*). Affirmations like these are not to be taken as creedal statements. They are rather to be understood as true and valid descriptions of what Covenanters believe and cherish as they continue to grow in the grace and knowledge of God, awaiting that day when 'the kingdom of this world has become the kingdom of our Lord and of His Christ, and He shall reign for ever and ever.' (Revelation 11:15)"

Trinity Episcopal Church, Whitinsville, MA, (39 Articles of the Church of England) (3)

"XIX. Of the Church.

The visible Church of Christ is a congregation of faithful men, in which the pure Word of God is preached, and the Sacraments be duly ministered according to Christ's ordinance, in all those things that of necessity are requisite to the same.

As the Church of Jerusalem, Alexandria, and Antioch, have erred; so also the Church of Rome hath erred, not only in their living and manner of Ceremonies, but also in matters of Faith.

XX. Of the Authority of the Church.

The Church hath power to decree Rites or Ceremonies, and authority in Controversies of Faith: and yet it is not lawful for the Church to ordain any thing that is contrary to God's Word written, neither may it so expound one place of Scripture, that it be repugnant to another. Wherefore, although the Church be a witness and a keeper of Holy Writ, yet, as it ought not to decree any thing against the same, so besides the same ought it not to enforce any thing to be believed for necessity of Salvation."

Evangelical Free Church of Tracy, CA, (The Statement of Faith) (2)

"8. That the true Church is composed of all such persons who through saving faith in Jesus Christ have been regenerated by the Holy Spirit and are united together in the Body of Christ of which He is the Head.

9. That only those who are, thus, members of the true Church shall be eligible for membership in the local church.

10. That Jesus Christ is the Lord and Head of the Church and that every local church has the right under Christ to decide and govern its own affairs."

Epiphany Lutheran Church, Chandler, AZ, (About Being Lutheran) (23)

"What is a Lutheran Church? It's part of the Christian Church—a means through which the Holy Spirit works to help Christians grow in grace.

A Lutheran Church Is:

A Confessional Church—that acknowledges Jesus as Lord and Savior, and the Bible as revealing God's will.

An Ecumenical Church—(in most cases) that works for the unity of ALL Christians.

A Visible Church—where Christians gather together to hear God's Word.

An Invisible Church—made up of all those people together who are saved by faith in Christ as Savior.

Lutherans affirm the original Apostolic Faith."

Crown of Glory Evangelical Lutheran Church, Orlando, FL, (This We Believe) (23)

"THE CHURCH AND ITS MINISTRY.

1. We believe that there is one holy Christian church, which is the temple of God (1 Cor. 3:16), the body of Christ. (Eph. 1:23; 4:12) The members of this one church are all those who are 'the sons of God through faith in Christ Jesus.' (Gal. 3:26) Whoever believes that Jesus died for his sin and rose again for his justification (Rom. 4:25) belongs to Christ's church. The church, then, consists only of believers, or saints, whom God accepts as holy for the sake of Jesus' imputed righteousness. (2 Cor. 5:21) These saints are scattered throughout the world. Every true believer, regardless of the nation or race or church body to which he belongs, is a member of the holy Christian church.

2. We believe that the holy Christian church is a reality, although it is not an external, visible organization. Because 'man looks at the outward appearance, but the Lord looks at the heart' (1 Sam. 16:7), only the Lord knows 'those who are his.' (2 Tim. 2:19) The members of the holy Christian

church are known only to God; we cannot distinguish between true believers and hypocrites. The holy Christian church is therefore invisible and cannot be identified with any one church body or the sum total of all church bodies.

3. We believe that the presence of the holy Christian church nevertheless can be recognized. Wherever the gospel is preached and the sacraments are administered, the holy Christian church is present, for through the means of grace true faith is produced and preserved. (Isa. 55:10,11) Moreover, where these means are in use, we are confident that the church is present, for the Lord has entrusted them only to his church of believers. (Matt. 28:19,20) The means of grace are therefore called the marks of the church.

4. We believe that it is the Lord's will that Christians gather together for mutual edification and spiritual growth. (Heb. 10:24,25) and for carrying out the whole of the Lord's commission. (Mark 16:15) Since these visible gatherings (for example, congregations, synods) confess themselves to the marks of the church and make use of them, they are called churches. They bear this name, however, only because of the true believers present in them. (1 Cor. 1:2)

5. We believe that the holy Christian church is one, united by a common faith, for all true believers have 'one Lord, one faith, one baptism, one God and Father of all.' (Eph. 4:5,6) Since this is a unity of faith in the heart, it is seen only by God.

6. We believe that God bids us on our part to acknowledge oneness in faith among God's saints on earth only as they by word and deed reveal (confess) the faith of their hearts. Their unity becomes evident when they agree in their confession to the doctrine revealed in Scripture. We believe, furthermore, that

the individual through his membership in a church body confesses himself to the doctrine and practice of that body. To assert that unity exists where there is no agreement in confession is to presume to look into man's heart. This only God can do. It is not necessary that all agree on matters of church ritual or organization. About these the New Testament gives no commands.

7. We believe that those who have become evident as united in faith will give recognition to their fellowship in Christ and seek to express it as occasion permits. They may express their fellowship by joint worship, by joint proclamation of the gospel, by joining in Holy Communion, by joint prayer, by joint church work. We believe that we cannot practice religious fellowship with those whose confession reveals that error is taught or tolerated, supported or defended. The Lord bids us keep away from persistent errorists. (Rom. 16:17,18)

8. We believe that every Christian is a priest and king before God. (1 Pet. 2:9) All believers have direct and equal access to the throne of grace through Christ, our Mediator. (Eph. 2:17,18) To all believers God has given the means of grace to use. All Christians are to declare the praises of him who called us out of darkness into his wonderful light. (1 Pet. 2:9) In this sense all Christians are ministers of the gospel.

9. We believe that it is the will of God that the church in accordance with good order (1 Cor. 14:40) call qualified men (1 Tim. 3) into the public ministry. They are to preach the Word and administer the sacraments publicly, that is, not merely as individuals who possess the universal priesthood, but by order and in the name of fellow Christians. These men are the called servants of Christ, ministers of the gospel, and not lords over

God's heritage, his believers. (1 Pet. 5:3) Through its call the church in Christian liberty designates the place, form and scope of service. We believe that when the church calls men into this public ministry, it is the Lord himself acting through the church. (Acts 20:28)

10. We reject any attempt to identify the holy Christian church with an outward organization, and likewise any claim that the church must function in the world through specific organizational forms.

11. We reject any views that see in the church, as the body of Christ, an extension of Christ's incarnation.

12. We reject as false ecumenicity any views that look for the true unity of the church in some form of external or organizational union, and we oppose all movements toward such union made at the expense of confessional integrity.

13. We reject the contention that religious fellowship may be practiced without confessional agreement.

This is what Scripture teaches about the church and its ministry. This we believe, teach and confess."

First Mennonite Church, Phoenix, AZ, (Who are the Mennonites) (3)

"WHO ARE THE MENNONITES?

Mennonite groups had their beginning during the sixteenth-century Reformation time. A small group of Swiss Brethren led by Conrad Grebel, Felix Manz, and George Blaurock felt that the existing church did not meet God's standards and the needs of the people. They wanted to go further than other reformers did. They argued for a free church, one not established by and connected with the government. They believed that all persons should voluntarily choose whether or not they wished to join a church—ideas which were considered revolutionary at that time.

These early Swiss Brethren, later called Anabaptists, practiced adult believers' baptism instead of infant baptism. Those who voluntarily joined their group were expected to live a life of discipleship, committing themselves to obey the words of Christ. (Mt. 18:15-22) The Bible was their guide and source book for their conduct. They also believed that their relationships to others were to be governed by love and truth. For them, fighting and killing were contrary to the law of love, by which they felt the Bible taught they must live.

Both recognized church and state of that time joined hands to destroy this new Christian movement which dared to teach separation of church and state, believers' baptism, and the way of the cross in unjust suffering. Despite the martyrdom of over five thousand members within a few generations after its beginning, Anabaptism quickly spread throughout Switzerland, South Germany, and into the Netherlands and France. Using the Bible as their guide and norm, these early Anabaptists took seriously Christ's command to go into the world to witness to all people everywhere, even across national boundaries. Those who voluntarily accepted the gospel were baptized and received into the church.

The person who did the most for the early Anabaptists was a man named Menno Simons. After his conversion in 1536 in Witmarsum, he went around northwestern Europe encouraging and strengthening these persecuted people by preaching and writing tracts to defend their faith and way of life. Because Menno Simons was such an outstanding leader, the Anabaptists came to be called Mennonites. They are still known by that name today.

Persecution and hardship continued to scatter the increasing number of Mennonites across Europe and into the New World. While some trekked across Europe into Russia at the invitation of Catherine the Great in 1789, others were migrating from Europe to America. All were looking for a place where they could establish homes and churches and practice their Christian faith as they believed.

The migration of Mennonites from one nation to another and from one continent to another has continued through the more than 450 years of their history. From 1683 Mennonites continued to come to America in large numbers, ever moving westward with the frontier. In the late nineteenth century over twenty thousand Russian Mennonites immigrated to the United States and Canada, helping to make the midwest section of the North American continent the breadbasket of the world with their Turkey Red winter wheat. Prior to and after World War II, many European Mennonites found new homes in Paraguay, Brazil, Canada, and the United States. Even today some Mennonites from Russia are finding new homes in Germany. Mennonites in more prosperous countries have always been instrumental in helping oppressed Mennonites in other areas find new homes.

While Mennonites have migrated to frontier lands to be true to their faith, it is true that many Mennonites at various times and places have grown rich and become insensitive to God and His leading. While Mennonites have sought to represent Christ's kingdom in the world, they have also at times lost sight of what Christ's kingdom really is and how being part of it determines actions toward others.

Present-day Mennonites are scattered all over the world. There are over 500,000 persons who identify themselves with the Christian faith as practiced by the Mennonites. They are divided into different groups because of their beliefs, church practices, or national and cultural backgrounds. However, there is a common biblical Mennonite faith which unites them around the world.

CHARACTERISTICS OF MENNONITE FAITH

A believers' faith. The outstanding characteristic of Mennonite groups continues to be today, as it was in its beginning, a voluntary church made up of believers who have placed their faith and trust in Jesus Christ. Only those who are old enough to decide carefully and prayerfully that Jesus Christ is their Savior and Lord are baptized and received into membership in a Mennonite church. This is called believers' baptism.

A living faith. Even though the Mennonites have voluntary membership, they are a disciplined community. Mennonites believe that those who sincerely desire to be part of the church will live out their faith daily in a way that will set them apart from those who do not profess Christ as Lord. 'Therefore, the Mennonites believe that the church is a people not a building, and that members of the church are identifiable by their lifestyle and connection with the peoplehood of Jesus Christ.'

A caring faith. The early Anabaptists looked upon their fellowship as the body of Christ. They felt that the only way people could find fellowship was in caring for each other both physically and spiritually. With Christ as Lord of their lives,

Mennonites still feel it is possible to share their material possessions with each other, particularly with those in need. This interdependence of persons within the church gives life and salvation a new meaning, making real community possible.

A sharing faith. Because those who are joined together in Mennonite churches have experienced love and forgiveness from God and each other, they seek to be a community which will draw those who are not Christians into a fellowship in which they also can experience love and forgiveness with God and others. Mennonites take the Great Commission of Jesus (Mt. 28:19,20) seriously, actively seeking to make disciples among all nations and races. Mission programs which minister both to the spiritual and physical needs of people are a dynamic part of Mennonite groups. Mission work is carried on all over the world.

A serving faith. Members of the Mennonite churches, believing that faith and action are inseparable, bond together to serve the needy in the name of Christ. The Mennonite Central Committee, which is made up of many Mennonite denominations and the Brethren in Christ, does many acts of service for a needy world. Their work includes programs to feed the hungry and help the hungry to feed themselves, rehabilitation of refugees, and disaster service in areas flooded or shattered by storms. It is an organization known both nationally and internationally. Since its founding in 1920, thousands of people, most of them volunteers, have served under its auspices. In addition, millions of dollars are being contributed every year to aid needy people all over the world.

A loving faith. As Christians who take the teachings of the Bible seriously, Mennonites seek to practice the way of love. Through his life Jesus taught that persons should not only help their friends and neighbors, but also their enemies. Mennonites seek to practice this by helping people and nations to find peaceful resolutions to their problems rather than to go to war. During wartime many Mennonites have voluntarily chosen alternative service instead of military service. But voluntary service is also a vital part of the peacetime witness of Mennonites."

New Covenant Bible Fellowship, Hudson, MA, (Articles of Faith) (4)

"Article 12. We believe each Christian is called and chosen in God to be a priest unto God to offer up the sacrifice of praise (the fruit of His lips), to give his time, strength, and material possessions to the service of the Lord. All believers have been purchased with the blood of Jesus and are no longer their own, but belong to the Father to be used for His glory, and, as possessions of the Lord, must give themselves to serving Him, finding their place in the Church, His Body, and making themselves available by being present when the Church comes together, that they might be able to minister their gifts and talents for the building up of the Body of Christ. (John 15:16; Ephesians 1:4,5; I Corinthians 6:20; 12:18; Hebrews 13:15; I Peter 2:5,9)"

St. Basil Greek Orthodox Church, Stockton, CA, (Introducing The Orthodox Church) (1)

The leaders of the Eastern Orthodox Christians proclaim their Church is the Body through which Jesus is present and active in the world today. That church had its beginning by Christ and its clergy of today are connected to Christ's Apostles. Thus the clergy are connected to Christ by what the Eastern Orthodox Church calls apostolic succession. This claim makes the Eastern Orthodox Church the original church with Christ as its head. The Eastern Orthodox Church is changeless.

Faith Presbyterian Church, Aurora, CO, (Who We Are—Distinctives of the EPC) (9)

"5. The true Church is composed of all persons who through saving faith in Jesus Christ and the sanctifying work of the Holy Spirit are united together in the body of Christ. The Church finds her visible, yet imperfect, expression in local congregations where the Word of God is preached in its purity and the sacraments are administered in their integrity; where scriptural discipline is practiced, and where loving fellowship is maintained. For her perfecting, she awaits the return of her Lord."

Catholic Church of Jesus, Our Risen Saviour, Spartanburg, SC, (Handbook For Today's Catholic) (6)

The Roman Catholic Church is the universal church. It is in the form of a mystical body and is a mystery; it has a visible form and an invisible form, the Eucharistic body. The Roman Catholic Church has a representative of God on earth, the Roman Pontiff (Holy See). The Roman Catholic Church is a visible sign of Christ in the world; it is organized for this world.

Victory United Brethren in Christ Church, Burbank, CA, (United in Christ) (1)

"HISTORICAL STANCE

People sometimes want to know where the Church of the United Brethren in Christ fits into the religious spectrum of society. Usually such inquirers desire to know our historical stance among the religions of the world and our denominational heritage within the Protestant sector of the Christian faith. Here, we will isolate our common distinctives with other Christian groups.

Christian

First of all, we are *part of the Christian religion.* As such we have no equals, because Christianity is superior to all other religions: it is the revealed religion and it gets its name from the central figure, Jesus Christ. To understand Christianity's true nature, to study its influence on mankind, and to experience its transforming powers is to be convinced beyond doubt of the superiority of Christianity over all other religions. The Christian faith stands far above Hinduism, Buddhism, Confucianism, Shintoism, Mohammedanism, Bahaism, and all other religions.

Christianity is revealed through Christ, the central figure mentioned earlier, and He is revealed through Scriptures, which in turn have been inspired by the Holy Spirit. According to 2 Timothy 3:16, 'All Scripture is God-breathed' (NIV). The Scriptures tell of Jesus' virgin birth, His ministry, suffering, death, resurrection, and ascension. As Christians, we believe in one God, not many gods as taught by certain other religions.

Our denomination, The Church of the United

Brethren of Christ, includes the name of Christ in its official name. We believe—

> 'That He is very God and man: that He became incarnate by the power of the Holy Spirit in the Virgin Mary and was born of her: that He is the Savior and Mediator of the whole human race, if they with full faith in Him accept the grace proffered in Jesus: that this Jesus suffered and died on the cross for us, was buried, arose again on the third day, ascended into heaven, and sitteth on the right hand of God to intercede for us: and that He shall come again at the last day to judge the quick and the dead.' (Confession of Faith)

Thus, our first distinctive is that we are part of the Christian religion.

Orthodox

Our second distinctive is that we are an *orthodox* church rather than a heretical cult. There are many active cults today. Many of them do not accept Christ as the head of the Church; rather, some will acknowledge Him only as one of their leaders.

Others deny the basic orthodox beliefs. For example, The Way International denies the doctrine of the Trinity. Sung Moon of the Unification Church professes to be the 'Third Adam' (Messiah) claiming that the first Adam and the second Adam (Christ) failed, and he, Sung Moon, will accomplish what they failed to do for the world.

We are orthodox in that we adhere to traditional and established beliefs and practices. We hold to the fundamentals of the faith, including the virgin birth of Jesus, the death and resurrection of Jesus, the second coming of our Lord, the necessity of forgiveness from our sins, justification by faith, and the reality of heaven and hell. We believe that those who are orthodox hold to these fundamentals.

Protestant

A third distinctive is that the United Brethren Church is *Protestant.* The Christian faith, of course, is divided into two religious views—Roman Catholicism and Protestantism. We are distinctively Protestant in that we believe in the priesthood of all believers, the authority of the Scripture above tradition, and in justification by faith.

As a denomination, we do not regard church tradition as equal to Scriptural authority. Our Confession of Faith states:

> 'We believe that the Holy Bible, Old and New Testaments, is the Word of God; that it contains the only true way of our salvation; that every true Christian is bound to acknowledge and receive it with the influence of the Spirit of God as the only rule and guide; and that without faith in Jesus Christ, true repentance, forgiveness of sins and following after Christ, no one can be a true Christian.'

Evangelical

One other distinctive is that we are *evangelical.* Within the Protestant tradition there is danger of placing labels on particular groups. However, it ought to be noted that there are extreme fundamentalists and liberals.

We consider ourselves to be distinctively evangelical—different from the liberals who are more interested in relationships rather than doctrine, and yet different from the extreme fundamentalists whose interest in doctrine over relationships leads to their separatist attitudes. We hold the same doctrinal views as the fundamentalists, yet we are not separatists. On the other hand, we do not hold to an ecumenical concept of one organized world Church.

As a part of the National Association of Evangelicals, we are distinctive in that we hold to the orthodox fundamentals and beliefs. We are compelled by Scripture to cooperate as one with all who hold similarly orthodox beliefs, but to avoid sacrificing doctrine in an effort to become an organized body driven by common fear or a desire for power.

Summarizing briefly . . . Among the religions of the world, we are part of Christianity. We are different from many other churches of Christianity in that we are orthodox. There are two types of orthodox churches, Catholic and Protestant, and we are the latter. And we differ from other Protestant churches in that we are evangelical.

Trinity United Methodist Church, Denver, CO, (A United Methodist Is . . .) (9)

"A UNITED METHODIST IS . . .

- A person who has made a covenant together with God and members of a local church.
- A person who has acknowledged Jesus Christ as Savior and pledged allegiance to his kingdom, professed the Christian faith as contained in the Old and New Testaments, promised to live a Christian life and to remain a faithful member of the church, pledged to be loyal to The United Methodist Church and support it with prayers, presence, gifts and service. (Adapted from *The Discipline,* ¶211)

These simple vows can lead to a life of service and

> joy, sustained by the courage and wisdom God grants to those who seek to live as disciples of Jesus Christ.
>
> A WORLD CHURCH
>
> Affirming their historic stand that 'the world is our parish,' United Methodists are bound in faith and tradition with Methodist Christians around the world. A half million—in Africa, Europe and the Philippines—are members of central conferences that are organically part of United Methodism as are the 73 annual conferences within the United States and Puerto Rico.
>
> Methodists in a number of other countries, most notably those of Latin America, have historic ties with Methodists or Evangelical United Brethren in the United States, but now have become affiliated autonomous churches. Still other churches of the world Methodist family grew from different beginnings, including the original Wesleyan movement in Great Britain. Methodist-related bodies in 90 countries maintain their family ties through the World Methodist Council.
>
> The ministry of United Methodism extends to many of those 90 nations and to others as well through cooperative endeavors with other Christians. Besides supporting missionaries in medical, educational, agricultural, technical, evangelical and other forms of ministry, the church also acts as an enabler by helping nationals who are committed to God's service in their own lands."

"The church is the Body of Christ," seems to be the most commonly accepted answer to the question, "What is the church?" from the church perspective. To simply say, "the church is the Body of Christ," is not correct. However, fourteen of the twenty-five churches used to illustrate the perspective of the church, included, "Body of Christ," in their statement. Four used lengthy statements of their beliefs to define, "What is the church?" One said it is a community of believers. Two said it is part of God's family. Others said it is a fellowship of Christ's Body; a congregation of faithful men; the church is a mystery; a human body with Christ as head; a local body of baptized believers and one did not give a discerning answer. I can only say these answers are typical of how pastors and church attendees perceive what it is that they direct their attention to on Sunday morning or some other chosen time of a given week.

It is not my intention to enter into a detailed critique of each and every one of the denominations and independent churches represented here. The purpose of presenting the statements of faith is to show how people of the church perceive "What is the church?" I believe that objective has been accomplished.

The lengthy statements of individual church bodies such as the Mennonites, Lutherans, Baptists, Brethren in Christ, and United Brethren in Christ included here do provide some very deep insight into how the hierarchy of each perceives it is serving God.

The Body of Christ—the Fullness of Christ Jesus

When we refer to the term 'Body of Christ'—what does that mean? In 1 Corinthians 10:16 Paul wrote, "Is not the cup of blessing which we bless a sharing in the blood of Christ?" (See Discussion on page 202.) And then 16b, "is not the bread which we break a sharing in the body of Christ?" Verse 17, "Since there is one bread, [Christ Jesus' body. See John 6:26-

65.] we who are many are one body; for we all partake of the one bread." Romans 12:5, "so we, who are many, are one body in Christ, [spiritual form, for God sees us in the flesh and blood of His Son] and individually members one of another."

Ephesians 1:22,23 "And He [God] put all things in subjection under His feet, [Christ] and gave Him [Christ] as head over all things to the church, [called-out-ones] which is His body, [Christ's body, literally–spiritual form] the fullness of Him [all that Christ could give—His flesh and blood] who fills all in all." Christ became the propitiation for every man, woman, and child-reconciliation of man unto God-restored spiritual kingdom-only for those who have Christ Jesus as Lord and Master of their life. Symbolism here is—Christ's flesh given for us. He suffered and died for our sins. It was the sacrifice of the animals, their flesh and blood that was given for the chosen people of God that met the requirement of God for the remission of the sins of the people, a mere shadow of things to come. All that God performed for the good of mankind over the millennia was provided as a prelude and example of the real event to come, (the mystery of long ages ago) performed by the Son of God/Son of Man, i.e. the animal sacrifices, the tabernacle, the Sabbath, the Passover, the Day of Atonement, and the Feast of First Fruits, etc. All were played-out and fulfilled by Christ Jesus for the Father for the good of mankind. [Clarification added by the author.]

In the book of Hebrews, the writer explains that Christ fulfilled for the Father, through the ultimate sacrifice; the Son's flesh and blood, Christ Jesus paid the penalty of sin. Christ Jesus' blood covered once and for all the sins of man-kind. (See Hebrews 10:1-39.)

Colossians 1:9-28 beginning with verse 18,

"He is also head of the body, the church; [those who belong to Christ Jesus, called-out-ones] and He [Christ] is the beginning, the firstborn from the dead, [fullness of God] so that He Himself will come to have first place in everything. For it was the Father's good pleasure for all the fullness to dwell in Him" . . . Verses 22-28, "yet He has now reconciled you in His fleshly body through death, [blood of Christ] in order to present you before Him [God] holy and blameless and beyond reproach—if indeed you continue in the faith firmly established [a true disciple] and steadfast, [a soul winner] and not moved away from the hope of the gospel that you have heard, which was proclaimed in all creation under heaven, and of which I, Paul, was made a minister. Now I rejoice in my sufferings for your sake, and in my flesh I do my share on behalf of His body, which is the church, [those who are in Christ Jesus] in filling up what is lacking in Christ's afflictions. [Christ suffered for the sinner on the cross.] Of *this church I was made a minister* according to the stewardship from God bestowed on me for your benefit, so that I might fully carry out the preaching of the word of God, that is, the mystery which has been hidden from the past ages and generations; but has now been manifested to His saints, to whom God willed to make known what is the riches of the glory of this mystery among the Gentiles, which is Christ in you, the hope of glory. We proclaim Him, admonishing every man and teaching every man with all wisdom, so that we may present every man complete in Christ." [A disciple.] [Clarification added by the author.]

Colossians 2:6-14, "Therefore as you have received Christ Jesus the Lord, so walk in Him, having been firmly rooted and now being built up in Him and established in your faith, [discipled] just as you were instructed, and overflowing with gratitude. See to it that no one takes you captive through philosophy and empty deception, according to the tradition of men, according to the elementary principles of the world, rather than according to Christ. For in Him all the fullness of Deity dwells in bodily form, and in Him you have been made complete, and He is the head over all rule and authority; and in Him you were also circumcised with a circumcision made without hands, in the removal of the body of the flesh by the circumcision of Christ; [cleansed of sins] having been buried with Him in baptism, in which you were also raised up with Him through faith in the working of God, who raised Him from the dead. When you were dead in your transgressions and the uncircumcision of your flesh, He made you alive together with Him, having forgiven us all our transgressions, having canceled out the certificate of debt consisting of decrees against us, which was hostile to us; and He has taken it out of the way, having nailed it to the cross." [Clarification added by the author.]

Colossians 3:1-3, "Therefore if you have been raised up with Christ, keep seeking the things above, where Christ is, seated at the right hand of God. Set your mind on the things above, not on the things that are on earth. For you have died and your life is hidden with Christ in God." . . . Verses 12-17, "So, as those who have been chosen of God, holy and beloved, put on a heart of compassion, kindness, humility, gentleness and patience; bearing with one another, and forgiving each other, whoever has a

> complaint against anyone; just as the Lord forgave you, so also should you. Beyond all these things put on love, which is the perfect bond of unity. Let the peace of Christ rule in your hearts, to which indeed you were called in one body; and be thankful. Let the word of Christ richly dwell within you, with all wisdom teaching and admonishing one another with psalms and hymns and spiritual songs, singing with thankfulness in your hearts to God. Whatever you do in word or deed, do all in the name of the Lord Jesus, giving thanks through Him to God the Father.
>
> 1 Thessalonians 4:7,15-18, "For God has not called us for the purpose of impurity, but in sanctification." . . . "For this we say to you by the word of the Lord, that we who are alive and remain until the coming of the Lord, will not precede those who have fallen asleep. For the Lord Himself will descend from heaven with a shout, with the voice of the archangel and with the trumpet of God, and the dead in Christ will rise first. Then we who are alive and remain will be caught up together with them in the clouds to meet the Lord in the air, and so we shall always be with the Lord. Therefore comfort one another with these words."

These Scriptures give the full and complete description of the fullness of our life in Christ Jesus. They put great emphasis on the urgency that each and every man, woman and child should understand concerning their need to become a disciple of our Lord Jesus Christ, not mere "church members." Most theologians, Bible scholars, and church leadership cause us to believe that the church is the body of Christ, a group of persons that gather at a building at preset times to worship God. A very worldly concept with worldly organizational guidance, mixed in with doctrine and traditions of men, interspersed with the Word of God. It is impossible for the church to be the body of Christ. When a person says the church is the body of Christ, that includes every man, woman, and child who regularly attends the church services held there.

The preceding Scriptures and accompanying discussions make it very clear that only those who truly belong to Christ are in the body of Christ (literally in the Spirit in His body). Unless the leadership of the church you attend takes each and every soul who attends that church on a regular basis to discipleship, one cannot say that church is the body of Christ. On the other hand, when and where the leadership of a gathering of souls, in fact, have in place, discipleship training as the very basic training and purpose for existence, God is adding souls to the body of His Son (God sees each and every soul in the flesh and blood of His Son). Each and every soul has the very basic need of becoming a disciple of the Lord Jesus Christ. (Also see 2 Corinthians 5:1; Ephesians 4:4-7,15,17,30; John 17:21-23; 1 Corinthians 6:14-17; 1 Corinthians 12:11-14,18-20; Ephesians 2.)

Church Practices That Help to Determine—What Is the Church?

Liturgy/Mannerisms

The formality of fixed events in a worship service gives honor and glory to men rather than to God. The repetition of following the same pattern Sunday service after Sunday service becomes a "we just follow the leader," we really don't know why. We think it is a good idea, mom and dad did it, grandpa and grandma did it, it has been our tradition. Worship of God needs to be alive, heart-felt, thanks and glory to God for all He has given us. If we do not think in those terms it becomes a rigid ritual with no meaning whatsoever except, "that is the way its done." So half of the praise and glory to God is lost in a ritualistic repetition and God is not served, man is served.

Programs/Activities

Church programs today are the big (cool) thing. It is used to attract new people, hold the people we have, and make them happy. "Church-busy people" are happy "church-going people." It is used to hold the attention of the membership. Church programs have become the substituted substance of what church life is all about. "This is what God wants us to do for Him" attitude; "I feel good about it;" "it keeps me close to all of the other believers;" "we are fellowshipping."

The study of 151 churches across the United States, shows that Programs/Activities seem to be a very high priority for most denominations and independent churches. The most recent program is clubs for children. The object is if you get the children to church then you have a chance to attract the parents. Some of the programs considered to be in line with God's Word and meet the needs of the downtrodden are: seniors' groups, health centers, counseling, singles' groups, family camps, help to the homeless, MOPS (Mothers of Preschoolers), food distribution, home school, Christian peacemakers, comfort to those involved in divorce, cell groups and C.I.A. (caring, information, assistance). These Programs/Activities are more in line with the teachings of Christ. The Programs/Activities of a Godly gathering should be part of the ongoing ministry of each saved soul. The activities would reflect the true condition of our life with Christ.

TABLE 2
Church Programs/Activities

Socials/Gatherings	Church Library	Church Cookbook
Seasonal Plays	AWANA	Short Term Foreign Missions
Vacation Bible School	Musical Ministry (When Worship teams do all the praising)	Church-Sponsored Education (does not include Christian schools)
Girl Scouts	Aerobics	Sports/Sports Leagues
Boy Scouts	Pioneer Clubs	

Table 2 gives a listing of general programs/activities of churches which the author includes under a main heading of "Busy Work" in many churches.

Evangelism

True evangelism is most difficult to pinpoint as a high priority in churches in general. True evangelism-preaching and teaching the Gospel of the saving power of the shed blood of Jesus Christ is very rare in the Eastern, Western, Episcopal, and Church of England of the U.S. churches. True evangelism is most constant and with effectiveness in Baptist,

Nazarene, Mennonite, Evangelical Free, and Assemblies of God churches. The mainline churches fall in between as to the regular effectiveness of true evangelism preaching and teaching. Examples are: Methodist, Lutheran, Presbyterian, Reformed, Church of Christ, and Church of God. There are certainly exceptions in each and every one of these groupings of churches. Independents can vary widely as to their trueness to God also. To go into detail would not be possible and the author chooses to deal in generalities on this particular subject even at the risk of being called biased, nevertheless, my point is made with extreme confidence.

Discipling

Discipling as our Lord taught it to His twelve Apostles within the church system is virtually non-existent. This is the most important work of the church but is given the least attention. The author takes this view because of the lack of training and emphasis given the subject in the many seminaries from the greatest to the least. The author's evidence for this conclusion is given in the subject, Seminary Practices That Help to Determine—What Is the Church? (See p. 246). Generally the pastors of churches turn this aspect of the church over to the Sunday church school program where a series of Bible knowledge study intensifies much like the public school system (i.e., mathematics is increasingly more difficult as progress is made toward graduation day). The student learns much about God but they never get the instruction that helps them know God. Some students might be led to Christ, but few become disciples. The reason the author can say this is that the parachurch is the strongest source of producing disciples. The parachurch is the institution that came into being over the last fifty years to fill the gap made by the church system. They are giving help to those persons having one of many different societal difficulties, i.e., marital problems, single parent problems, drug-related problems, and a host of others. It is my belief that a high percentage of these problems exist because the "church system" has failed God in two main areas; **Discipling** and **Evangelism Follow-up** (discipling).

Men and women involved in numerous types of Christian radio and television ministries are frantically attempting to fill the gaping void left by the "church system" in the areas of mending people's lives, developing ways and means to overcome a sin-filled life and bringing people some relief from the unscriptural teaching of the "church syndrome." These same ministries feed on the void left by the "church syndrome" by offering book after book which I must admit, will provide the purchaser some relief and some will find a true walk with the Lord, but there is absolutely no substitute for one-on-one discipleship training. Whatever the intentions might be of the producers of many of these books mentioned above, Christ-centered discipleship as set out by Christ in the New Testament is the only way to guide people after finding peace with God through His Son. All other means and methods will only prolong the agony of searching for the truth. The disease of the "church syndrome" has been recognized, but the cure is still being searched for by the "church system." I find it highly ironic that many of the so called "born again" congregations are the very ones who have fallen prey to this lethal phenomenon.

Missions

Supporting missions is nearly everything in most mainline denominations and is everything in the Assemblies of God, Baptist (all), Nazarene, Christian Missionary Alliance and many non-denominational churches, all to the near neglect of discipling at home and in the mission field. Many people are exposed to the preached Word of God but the production of disciplers is very weak here at home and on foreign mission fields. All of those who support this vast church program will tell you, "this is what God tells us to do," and I am the first to admit that, but all of God's will as set out in Scripture needs our attention to fulfill the Great Commission. To carry the Word of God to the mission fields without producing reproducers is working against the will of God. There are of course some exceptions to this broadly covering statement, China, South Korea and the former Soviet Union countries, India, Japan, and Central America. For the volume of dollars expended, only the Word is being spread with very little discipling because missionaries trained in the seminaries or elsewhere have not been prepared.

13

Soul-searching by Pastors

Soul-searching by pastors presents a witness to the fact that the church system as we know it today lacks the power of God and it certainly does not enlighten men's hearts. The pastors first set out what is wrong in the church and then they give the solution for the change in the leadership's thinking and teaching which will then bring about the change in congregational membership. The main problem cited, clergy fail to follow the guidance set out in God's Word and therefore the church is failing to produce spirit-filled believers who then become the ministers spreading the kingdom into all places and people who need to know the great love of God's redemption message. This spreading of the kingdom message in fact would develop the members of congregations into the true assembly of the called-out-ones.

The clergy of today are struggling for identity concerning their purpose and "who am I serving?," how do I find peace of mind? Some call it the parish pastor "burn out." While the mega church seems to flourish, many ministers of lesser churches have second thoughts about what they are doing. Great numbers of pastors have written books which give details of their concern for the church. These men, it seems, are searching for the real purpose of the church, a winning system, if you will, within the church system.

Pastor Thomas S. Goslin, II

Donald McGavarn in his Foreword to Thomas S. Goslin's book, *The Church Without Walls*[1] makes a most profound statement:

> "In the affluent society of America the church is popularly seen as a building in which church members assemble. Founding a new church means buying five acres to assure ample parking space and building an imposing edifice. Consequently, the discipling of the more than 150 million in the United States who almost never go to church and the multiplication of congregations among them have been tied to raising enough money to erect adequate buildings.
>
> This modern American concept finds no support in the Bible. In the entire New Testament we do not find a single incidence of the Church of Jesus Christ buying one square foot of land or building any kind of a building. In New Testament time every church was a church without walls. Congregations met in homes, in upper rooms, in patios, in gardens.
>
> The great multiplication of Christians which went on in China since 1968 has taken place in churches without walls. The tremendous multiplication of Methodist societies in John Wesley's time took place in homes. One might almost say that every great expansion of the church has taken place by a liberated body of Christ reproducing its congregations quite freely in homes,

> rented halls, school buildings and other convenient meeting places."[2]

While this book advocates the principal of house churches it also gives some insight as to what God did establish in His Son for mankind to follow. Goslin wrote:

> "When the early church founders spoke of churches, ekklesias, they were referring to gathered communities of believers, not buildings. The followers of the way gathered for worship principally, we believe, in each other's dwellings. Opposition from government developed almost instantly and believers had to meet furtively, often outdoors.
>
> The successive great waves of persecution rolling over the church literally drove the early Christians underground. Visiting the catacombs, in the environs of Rome, we see powerful testimony to the faith of our forebears, who would not allow any emperor to stop them from gathering to worship the risen Lord, even if it meant martyrdom.
>
> In the early church, the evangelism and mission task was carried on by communities which met in homes. They shared bread, worshiped and hosted travelers and strangers. Their firm commitment to Jesus Christ and their understanding of the church as a living organism of brothers made this loose knit collection of households a powerful missionary force.[3]
>
> Yet this finest hour of the church happened without a single building. Imagine! No sanctuaries. No pulpits. No pews. No pipe organ. No stained glass windows. The church consisted only of people, gathered together by the power of the Holy Spirit."

Goslin now quotes the German theologian, Moltmann as saying:

> "'Our state churches know only the charisma of the preacher [who] is hired specifically as the one with the charisma, the one who has the Spirit. The others should listen to what [this one] says and believe what [this one] preaches. I find this attitude to be extremely narrow. The New Testament pictures the body of Christ as composed of many members, but in our state churches the body of Christ consists of one big mouth and many little ears.'"[4]

Pastor A. W. Tozer

In the book, *Rut, Rot or Revival—The Condition of the Church*[5], James L. Snyder put together a compilation of messages by A. W. Tozer, which brings to light a very penetrating image of what man should be doing for the heavenly Father.

Tozer begins his onslaught by saying:

> **Dictatorship of the Routine**
>
> "The treacherous enemy facing the church of Jesus Christ today is the dictatorship of the routine, when the routine becomes 'lord' in the life of the church. Programs are organized and the prevailing conditions are accepted as normal. Anyone can predict next Sunday's service and what will happen. This seems to be the most deadly threat in the church today. When we come to the place where everything can be predicted and nobody expects anything unusual from God, we are in a rut. The

> routine dictates, and we can tell not only what will happen next Sunday, but what will occur next month and, if things do not improve, what will take place next year. Then we have reached the place where what has been determines what is, and what is determines what will be.
>
> That would be perfectly all right and proper for a cemetery. Nobody expects a cemetery to do anything but conform. . . . God's people are supposed to grow.
>
> As long as there is growth, there is an air of unpredictability. Certainly we cannot predict exactly, but in many churches you just about can. Everybody knows just what will happen, and this has become our deadliest enemy. We blame the devil, the 'last days' and anything else we can think of, but the greatest enemy is not outside of us. It is within—it is an attitude of accepting things as they are. We believe that what was must always determine what will be, and as a result we are not growing in expectation."

Tozer wrote that there are progressive stages toward the goal of reaching the condition of the church today: The first stage:

> "I begin with what I will call the rote. This is repetition without feeling. If someday someone would read the Scripture and believe it and would believe what is sung in the great Christian hymns, there would be a blessed spiritual revolution underway in a short time. But too many are caught up in the rote, repeating without feeling, without meaning, without wonder and without any happy surprises or expectations. In our services God cannot get in because we have it all fixed up for Him. We

say, 'Lord, we are going to have it this way. Now kindly bless our plans.' We repeat without feeling, we repeat without meaning, we sing without wonder, and we listen without surprise. That is my description of the rote.

We go one step further and come to what I will call the rut, which is bondage to the rote. When we are unable to see and sense bondage to the rote, we are in a rut. For example, a man can be sick and not even know it. The doctors may have confided in the man's wife and said, 'We don't want to frighten your husband, but he could drop any minute. He is critically ill, so just expect it at any moment.' But the man himself does not know he is seriously ill. He goes about his business as though nothing is wrong. He may play golf or tennis, maybe even go on a hunting trip. He is sick, and yet he does not know how sick he really is. This may in fact hasten his end. Not knowing is risky business and full of danger. Spiritually speaking, the rut is bondage to the rote, and the greatest danger lies in our inability to sense or feel this bondage.

There is a third word, and I do not particularly like to use it, but the history of the church is filled with it. The word is rot. The church is afflicted by dry rot. This is best explained when the psychology of nonexpectation takes over and spiritual rigidity sets in, which is an inability to visualize anything better, a lack of desire for improvement.

There are many who respond by arguing, 'I know lots of evangelical churches that would like to grow, and they do their best to get the crowds in. They want to grow and have contests to make their Sunday school larger.' That is true, but they are trying to get people to come and share their rut. They want people to help them celebrate the rote and finally join in the rot. Because the Holy Spirit is not given a chance to work in our services, nobody is repenting, nobody is seeking God, nobody is spending a day in quiet waiting on God with open Bible seeking to mend his or her ways. Nobody is doing it—we just want more people. But more people for what? More people to come and repeat our dead services without feeling, without meaning, without wonder, without surprise? More people to join us in the bondage to the rote? For the most part, spiritual rigidity that cannot bend is too weak to know just how weak it is.

When people in the church only point to others for improvement and not to themselves, it is sure evidence that the church has come to dry rot. It is proof of three sins: the sin of self-righteousness, the sin of judgment and the sin of complacency.

Self-righteousness is terrible among God's people. If we feel that we are what we ought to be, then we will remain what we are. We will not look for any change or improvement in our lives. This will quite naturally lead us to judge everyone by what we are. This is the judgment of which we must be careful. To judge others by ourselves is to create havoc in the local assembly.

Self-righteousness also leads to complacency. Complacency is a great sin and covers just about everything I have said about the rote and the rut. Some have the attitude, 'Lord, I'm satisfied with my spiritual condition. I hope one of these days You will come, I will be taken up to meet You in the air and I will rule over five cities.' These people cannot rule over their own house and families, but they expect to rule over five cities. They pray spottily and sparsely, rarely attending prayer meeting, but they read their Bibles and expect to go zooming off into the blue yonder and join the Lord in the triumph of the victorious saints.

> If we call Him Lord, how dare we sit any longer in the rut!"

Tozer suggests the reason we stay in the rut:

> "We may not be converted at all. I am convinced that many evangelicals are not truly and soundly converted. Among the evangelicals it is entirely possible to come into membership, to ooze in by osmosis, to leak through the cells of the church and never know what it means to be born of the Spirit and washed in the blood. A great deal that passes for the deeper life is nothing more or less than basic Christianity. There is nothing deeper about it, and it is where we should have been from the start. We should have been happy, joyous, victorious Christians walking in the Holy Spirit and not fulfilling the lusts of the flesh. Instead we have been chasing each other around the perpetual mountain.
>
> What we need is what the old Methodists called a sound conversion. There is a difference between conversion and a sound conversion. People who have never been soundly converted do not have the Spirit to enlighten them. When they read the Sermon on the Mount or the teaching passages of the epistles that tell them how to live or the doctrinal passages that tell how they can live, they are unaffected. The Spirit who wrote them is not witnessing in their hearts because they have not been born of the Spirit. That often happens.
>
> How did we get into this fix that we are in? Well evangelicals usually follow a trend. It is dangerous to follow a trend unless your eyes are open and you know where the trend is going. This trend began in the last decades of the 20th century and carried on

with some big names promoting it. In their zeal to make converts and adherents, they oversimplified the Christian faith. That is our difficulty today. We oversimplified it, and yet we never get simple. Isn't that odd? We oversimplified the truth, and yet we have the most complex, mixed up beliefs. . . .

We have simplified so Christianity amounts to this:

God is love; Jesus died for you; believe, accept, be jolly, have fun and tell others. And away we go—that is the Christianity of our day. I would not give a plug nickel for the whole business of it. . . .

You will find a few of God's people here and there even in that kind of atmosphere. Whole generations of Christians have grown up believing that this is the faith of our fathers living still, in spite of dungeons, fire and sword. The devil would not be caught dead trying to kill anybody for acting like that. It does not bother him . . .

The devil does not mind if you are not a bother to him, and most of us are not. The devil looks at us, smiles and says, 'That poor little emancipated weakling can't do my kingdom any harm.' A whole generation has thought this to be Christianity. That is the faith of our fathers, living still, in spite of dungeon fire and sword. Nobody ever put people like that in a dungeon—they are already there. They were born into it. Nobody ever threw them to the flames, because they are harmless."

Tozer wrote:

"There must come a reformation, a revival that will result in a fresh emphasis on neglected truth. I do not preach any new truth. I do not have a new doctrine, and if anybody would come here

> preaching a new doctrine, I would say, 'I'm sorry, but we already have our doctrine.' I would not allow that preacher in the pulpit. We do not want new doctrine—we want fresh emphasis on doctrine already well known by all of us."

Tozer wrote:

> "We must have a revival that will mean purity of heart as a normal standard for everybody. . . . Purity of heart is taken for granted, yet we must have it to be clean people."

If the words of these pastors causes you to want more of the truth from the authors cited in these pages of this section, please read for yourself the exciting direction for hope for our increasing lost condition in this nation. From the deep concern these pastors have for where the church is today and its lack of true direction (members of the spiritual kingdom), only Christ could give a more clear condemnation of the church institution. He does so in the book of Revelation.

> The list of titles in seminary and Bible college libraries on the subject "The Church" goes on and on. Most do nothing to reveal the truth concerning the conditions of that which is the result of misguided men.

14

The Great Soul Robbery

Of the traditions of men in the church institution most harmful to mankind, Communion/Mass has to be the most devastating. The pseudo-Christianity and nearly all of the denominational hierarchy and the leadership of most independent churches are responsible for leading the people following God to believe that a ritualistic public display for remembering our Lord and Master is a Godly practice, when in fact, those who participate are being driven to the brink of destruction by Satan. The instructions God gave to man do not have to be exercised in a church, cathedral, etc. by a priest, pastor, minister, preacher, reverend, etc. God gave the instructions to all mankind. To proclaim a narrow thought that remembering our Lord and Master has to be tendered by "men of the cloth" is sacrilege. Those who love the Lord and have Him as Lord and Master of their lives are guided by the Holy Spirit, they do not have to have a special ordained someone for their spiritual well being. (See Judges Ch. 17.) There is too strong an emphasis placed on making Holy Communion/ Mass, etc. and baptism as "sacraments of the altar."

We, those who truly love the Lord are the temple of the living God. (See 1 Corinthians 3:17; 2 Corinthians 6:16.)

There is no plain easy way to understand the Word of God in all of Scripture for man to place such strong emphasis on these two subjects (Holy Communion/Mass and baptism). The two are practices developed and nourished by weak men at the expense of downplaying the real power of the living God. The real power of God working in man is man living a life by every Word of the Scriptures bringing mankind to a complete trust in the pierced body and the shed blood of Christ Jesus to the Gentiles, the Messiah to the Jews. Further, repeating the Lord's prayer, repeating a creed, confession of sins to a man or enmasse and being baptized as an infant does nothing for the participant's eternal soul. These practices cause mankind to look at the Word of God very shallowly and cause mankind to forget the depth and breadth of our heavenly Father. This was one of Luther's battles with the Roman Catholics.

Included in the Lutheran order for confession and forgiveness during their Communion Service and near the end of that ceremony, pastors make the claim to forgive sins.[1] I sat under that extreme disobedience of God by the men of the cloth of the Lutheran church for many years. Every time I participated in the Lutheran "Holy Communion" I could feel the power of God nudging me to move away from such a treacherous and paganistic practice—only God can forgive us of our sins.

Sacrament of the Altar (Communion/Mass) vs. Passover*

---

*A study which leads those who love God to the true way to remember how our Lord and Master made it possible for us to dwell with Him throughout eternity. This is not a time or place to confess our sins as practiced by some churches. We confess our sins to God at the very moment sin is committed. This is the reason this part of this writing is called "The Great Soul Robbery."

This complex and difficult subject of Scriptures has been misinterpreted by most Gentile Bible scholars. The Scriptures involved are those of the Old Testament where God gave a command to the Israelites, which, when followed exactly as directed, God delivered them from bondage in Egypt because of their obedience to God. It was also the beginning of His special people. The other Scriptures involved are those of the several books of the New Testament where Christ gathered His disciples to celebrate the Passover (Lord's Supper—Last Passover to some who divorce themselves from those who hold to Communion/Mass) on the night in which He was betrayed, which, when that Passover was completed by Christ, He provided the way to deliver all mankind, Jew and Gentile, from eternal death due to sin. Christ fulfilled the symbolical Passover in His suffering, death and resurrection.

To understand the true meaning of the Scriptures concerning the Passover of the Old Testament and that Passover Christ celebrated the last night He spent on earth, we need to look at and have a deep understanding of what the Jewish people do on their days of preparation and participation in the Passover and the Festival of Unleavened Bread (two distinct Jewish festivals). We also need to understand how God's people give the blessing at each meal and how Israelitic covenants were ratified.

Table 3 shows, in outline form, the Passover and Feast of Unleavened Bread and the corresponding Passover events Christ shared with His disciples on the night He was betrayed. The presentation gives the reader a clear picture of each part of

---

** It should be noted here, the Old Testament reveals periods of time when the masses of Israelites failed to celebrate these festivals. One such period is related in 2 Chronicles 30:13-26.

the Jewish Passover celebrated for 3440 years** in contrast to those parts of the Passover described in the New Testament as participated in by Christ and His disciples. The instructions God gave to His people in Exodus and the Scriptures of the New Testament relate the events of the very same Passover celebration in which Christ ratified the New Covenant between God and His people. The Christ to the Gentiles and the Messiah to the Jews (Israelites) also provided redemption unto God for both Jew and Gentile, **the most important statement of this discussion.**

TABLE 3

Events of the Passover and Feast of Unleavened Bread (Brief Outline Form)

Passover	**Passover Lamb Exodus 12**				**Feast of Unleavened Bread Exodus 12**										
Covenant from God	1. Select the lamb on 10th day of the first month (Nisan). 2. Hold to the 14th day of first month (Nisan). 3. Slaughter the Passover Lamb. 4. Collect blood. 5. Sprinkle on door posts and lintel. 6. Roast the Passover Lamb that same night eat with family (Seder)				Eat Unleavened Bread 7 days from the 14th (Nisan) to the 21st (Nisan). Eat it with the Passover Lamb (Seder)										
As celebrated by Messianic Hebrews (Abbreviated form)[2]	Kindling of the Candles	The Cup of Sancti-fication 1st Cup	Washing of the Hands	Dipping of the Parsley	Breaking of the Middle Matzah	The Story of the Pass-over	The Four Questions	The Cup of Plagues 2nd Cup Thanks-giving	Eating of the Bitter Herbs Recline	The Pass-over Supper	Eating of the Afikomen	The Cup of Blessing and Redemption 3rd Cup	Hallel	The Cup of Completion 4th Cup
The corre-sponding parts of the Passover as recorded in the New Testament and cele-brated by Christ and His disciples				Dipping of the Hyssop Recorded in:[Mark 14:18-20; Matt. 26:23; John 13.26]	Breaking of Bread Recorded in: [Luke 22:19, Matt. 26:26, Mark 14:22]*			2nd Cup Thanks-giving Recorded in: [Luke 22:17]	Recline Recorded in: [Luke 22:14; Mark 14:18]			3rd Cup Cup of Blessing and Redemption Recorded in: [Luke 22:20; Matt. 26:27; Mark 14:23;]*	Hallel Recorded in:[Matt. 26:30; Mark 14:26]	4th Cup of Completion Recorded in: [Matt. 27:48; John19:28-30; Mark 16:36]

*Note: The two parts of the Passover celebrated by our Lord on the night He was betrayed as practiced in the Gentile "Holy Communion" are noted by an asterisk and highlighted by darkened outline. These are the same two events singled out by denominations, independents and catholic churches for celebration of communion/mass. Theologians and church leaders lead everyone to believe that this is "The Last Supper," "The Lord's Supper," "Holy Communion," "Mass," and one of the "Sacraments of the Altar." If this was to be a new something to be celebrated by those who belong to God through the shed blood of His Son, the author believes, God would have made such important instructions so plain man would not misunderstand the intentions of God just as He did for the Israelites at the first Passover. Under the shed blood of Jesus Christ all mankind is now a very special people before Almighty God, both Jew and Gentile. Satan has suppressed that truth by causing man to institute an ungodly ritual in place of the Godly celebration of remembering what Christ (Messiah) did for mankind. This is the ungodly tradition of men brought into being by pseudo-Christianity. The New Testament account of Christ's participation in the Passover with His Apostles on the night in which He was betrayed does not say this is an ordinance set out by God for those who trust in Jesus Christ or a sacrement of the altar.

How mankind interprets the New Testament Scriptures concerning this act by God is all important to the salvation of those who sit under the interpretations. First of all, the Jews need to know and understand that God consummated another Covenant with His people at that time. Many of God's people performed their part—they accepted their Messiah. If those Jews had not accepted their Messiah there would not have been anyone to spread the Gospel (Good News) to the Gentiles. On the other hand, if the Jewish religious leaders of that day had not rejected their Messiah, the Gentiles could not have been included in the redemptive power of the shed blood of Jesus. That the Jews would be a blessing unto the Gentiles someday was told to Abraham as part of the Abrahamic Covenant (Genesis 12:3; Galatians 3:8 and Acts 3:25). This is a very important thought to all who have heard the message of Jesus Christ. Satan's people (both Jew and Greek) have worked very hard on that point to negate its power (explained in detail herein).

Just because Christ died at the time of the Jewish Passover celebrations and that Christ spoke of the events of that Passover in the New Testament in symbolic terms (the reason Christ died for us on the Passover is covered later) does not give Gentiles the reason to isolate and use two of the several God-given directions Christ followed in the Passover and turn them into an ungodly ritual such as was done by pseudo-Christianity. I must point out that not all churches use the Scripture that describes the Jewish Passover. Some church denominations use 1 Corinthians 11:23-30 and John 13:1-20 with the wrong application. I have to ask all theologians, how many other ungodly practices have you allowed the pseudo-Christianity to misguide you and all people who follow your leading blindly?

What God wanted all true followers who put their complete trust in His Son's shed blood to understand was, each and every time you break bread, every meal time, remember with thanksgiving not just the food, but more importantly remember what His one and only Son did for mankind. It has to be highly significant to us that God in His wisdom highlighted for us the breaking and blessing of bread and the cup of wine three times in His Word (See Table 3), because when we know and understand that the Jews (some, not all) practice this blessing at each and every meal there can be no better way nor time to remember our Lord and Savior. It would be an everyday occurrence to remember our Lord and an everyday reminder of who we are and who we belong to.

Before Christ, the Israelites celebrated the Passover and Feast of Unleavened Bread as commanded by God in Exodus 12. The form that celebration followed, the exact wording used, is not completely verifiable, but because the Israelites celebrated the Passover every year for 3440* years they would not have become very mixed up concerning how to go about celebrating two of their most important festivals set out by God. It is said that the format of the Passover has many versions (1200) due to individual interpretations, legends and traditions.[3] One thing we can be certain of, the practice of "spring house cleaning" came from the Jewish Passover and Feast of Unleavened Bread. Some Jewish Haggadahs relate how the entire house was searched and swept clean to be absolutely certain there was no leaven in the house before the Jewish celebrations began.

"The Last Passover"—"The Lord's Supper Instituted"—nowhere in all of Scripture are these terms substantiated to have been given by God. The two are man-made subheadings inserted at the beginning of those Scriptures where God gave man the description of those events which occurred on the days His Son was arrested, tried, crucified, suffered and died for the sin of mankind. God did not give us those terms. Man added them to the various translations of God's Holy Word.

To understand what happened when Christ told His Apostles to go and prepare the Passover (Matthew 26:17-19) we need to look at Exodus 12 where God put into effect His Covenant with His people to deliver them from the Egyptian bondage. The Israelites were told to select a lamb on the 10th day of the first month (Nisan), the first month of the Jewish Calendar year. They were to hold the lambs until the 14th day of the first month (Nisan) and then the lambs were slaughtered. The lambs became the Passover Lambs, because, when the Israelites collected the blood from the lambs and placed it on the lentil and doorposts of each house of the Israelites, the destroyer passed over that house. Because the Israelites were to celebrate the Passover each and every year on the very same day of the year as the first Passover, it was very important to determine the exact day the new moon occurred which began the Jewish New Year and the countdown to the 10th day of the first month (Nisan). All the Jews (over 2 million) who made the pilgrimage to Jerusalem that year to celebrate the Passover had their lambs sacrificed at the Temple by the Priests and assistants. Good reason to study through these Scriptures again.

In three of the four gospels; Matthew, Mark and John, we are told, "the leaders of the Jews plotted together to seize Jesus by stealth and kill Him, But they were saying, "Not during the festival, otherwise a riot might occur among the people."

(Matthew 26:4,5) When we consider the above Scripture, the betrayal, arrest, trial, and crucifixion of Jesus Christ had to occur before or after the feasts of Passover and Unleavened Bread. All evidence in the book of John points to the betrayal, arrest, trial and death of Christ before the feasts. Only John's account gives the evidence that that is true. John's account of the last days of our Lord and Master on this earth prior to His death begins in John 12:1;

> "Jesus, therefore, six days before the Passover, came to Bethany where Lazarus was, whom Jesus had raised from the dead. So they made Him a supper there, and Martha was serving; but Lazarus was one of those reclining at the table with Him. Mary then took a pound of very costly perfume of pure nard, and anointed the feet of Jesus and wiped His feet with her hair; and the house was filled with the fragrance of the perfume. But Judas Iscariot, one of His disciples, who was intending to betray Him, said, 'Why was this perfume not sold for three hundred dinerii and given to poor *people*?' vs9, The large crowd of the Jews then learned that He was there; and they came, vs12. On the next day the large crowd who had come to the feast, when they heard that Jesus was coming to Jerusalem, took the branches of the palm trees and went out to meet Him, and began to shout, 'Hosanna! Blessed Is HE WHO COMES IN THE NAME OF THE Lord, even the King of Israel.'"

It is very important to note that great multitudes were gathering in Jerusalem for the Passover celebration which gave Jesus opportunity to bring large numbers of the Jews unto Himself. Also it is important to note that this entry into Jerusalem gave the Jews knowledge that this was the Son of God. This account of the gathering of the multitudes to Jerusalem for the Passover celebration also places emphasis on what is about to happen to Jesus Christ.

John continues his account at John 13:1;

> "Now before the Feast of the Passover, Jesus knowing that His hour had come that He would depart out of this world to the Father, . . . vs2, During supper, the devil having already put into the heart of Judas Iscariot, the son of Simon, to betray Him, Jesus, knowing that the Father had given all things into His hands, and that He had come forth from God and was going back to God, got up from supper, and laid aside His garments; and taking a towel, He girded Himself. vs21b, 'Truly, truly, I say to you, that one of you will betray Me.' The disciples began looking at one another, at a loss to know of which one He was speaking. vs26, Jesus then answered, 'That is the one for whom I shall dip the morsel and give it to him.' So when He had dipped the morsel, He took and gave it to Judas, *the son* of Simon Iscariot. After the morsel, Satan then entered into him. Therefore Jesus said to him. 'What you do, do quickly.' Now no one of those reclining *at the table* knew for what purpose He had said this to him. For some were supposing, because Judas had the money box, that Jesus was saying to him, 'Buy the things we have need of for the feast;' or else, that he should give something to the poor. So after receiving the morsel he went out immediately; and it was night."

There are four very important statements in the above Scriptures. John said in verse one, "Now before the feast of

Passover," . . . in verse two, "And during supper" now go down to verse four, "rose from supper." In verse 30, "So after receiving the morsel he went out immediately; and it was dark." These are key Scriptures which help to determine when Jesus Christ was arrested, tried, humiliated and was crucified. We are told that Jesus partook of a supper before the Feast of Passover and that He rose from supper. Jesus identified who it was that would betray Him, and Judas, after receiving the morsel, went out and it was dark. He was on his way to the rulers of the Jews to point the way to the place where they could arrest Jesus by stealth. The other disciples confirm that they thought Jesus wanted Judas to go and buy things that were needed for the feast.

It is interesting to note here that the first three gospel accounts lack chronological order of the events that took place on the day our Lord and Master was betrayed, arrested and tried. However those accounts give us evidence that Christ did partake in the Passover. When Christ and His disciples partook of the Passover cannot be reconciled based on all the Scriptures we are given. But, the Jews did have leeway as to when they could partake of the Passover depending upon individual circumstances. In this particular case, Jesus was in control of the events John has documented. (See John 13:3.) God has conveyed in His Word, hidden truths, where He wants us to study His Word in a prayerful way so that He can reveal all the truths we desire for our daily life with Him.

From John 13:30 to 14:31 Jesus is giving His disciples the understanding of the events that are about to happen to Him. At the end of verse 14:31 Jesus said, "Get up, let us go from here." He and His disciples are leaving the place where they had the supper during which Judas went out to go to the Jewish rulers and leaders. On the way Jesus gave further instructions and teachings for understanding all that God had given the Son to perform. (See John 16:33-17:30.)

John continues in chapter 18 verse one;

> "When Jesus had spoken these words, He went forth with His disciples over the ravine of the Kidron, where there was a garden, in which He entered with His disciples. Now Judas also, who was betraying Him, knew the place, for Jesus had often met there with His disciples. Judas then, having received the Roman cohort and officers from the chief priest and the Pharisees, came there with lanterns and torches and weapons. So Jesus, knowing all the things that were coming upon Him, went forth and said to them, 'Whom do you seek?' They answered Him, 'Jesus the Nazarene.' He said to them, 'I am He.' And Judas also, who was betraying Him, was standing with them. So when He said to them, 'I am He,' they drew back and fell to the ground. We continue with verse 12, So the Roman cohort and the commander and the officers of the Jews, arrested Jesus and bound Him, and led Him to Annas first; for He was the father-in-law of Caiaphas, who was high priest that year. Now Caiaphas was the one who had advised the Jews that it was expedient for one man to die on behalf of the people. vs24, So Annas sent Him bound to Caiaphas the high priest.

Moving down to verse 28;

> 'Then they led Jesus from Caiaphas into the Praetorium, and it was early; and they themselves did not enter into the Praetorium so that they would not be defiled, but might eat the Passover.'

Up to this point John gives us the account of the arrest of Jesus. His trial before Pilate is given in the next verses, John 18:19 through John 19:13. The next verse gives us the day Jesus Christ was crucified, verse 19:14;

> "Now it was the day of preparation for the Passover, it was about the sixth hour. [About 6 a.m. Roman time.] And he said to the Jews, 'Behold, your King!' So they cried out, 'Away with Him, away with Him, crucify Him!' Pilate said to them, 'Shall I crucify your King?' The chief priests answered, 'We have no king but Caesar.' As Jesus hung on the cross He said in verse 28, 'I am thirsty.' vs 29, A jar full of sour wine was standing there; so they put a sponge full of the sour wine upon a *branch* of hyssop and brought it up to His mouth. Therefore when Jesus had received the sour wine, He said, 'It is finished!' And He bowed His head, and gave up His spirit." [This was the cup of completion.] [Clarification added by the author.] (See Table 3 page 200.)

This account by John of the events on the day before the arrest of Christ and those events on the day of His crucifixion relate in consecutive order most accurately the most significant facts of the betrayal, arrest, trial, and crucifixion of our Lord Jesus Christ. We are told in John 13:1,2 the first fact— Jesus was at supper with His disciples before the Passover. John 13:21b, Christ pointed out that one of His disciples would betray Him. In John 13:26, Christ identifies the one that would betray Him by handing Judas a morsel. The disciples could not understand that one of them would betray Jesus and thought that Jesus was telling Judas to buy the things they needed to prepare for the feast. After Judas received the morsel he went out, 'and it was night.' These events had to take place on the day before the day of Passover. At the end of verse 31 Jesus said, 'Arise let us go from here.' Jesus and the rest of the disciples now were leaving the place where they had supper. John 18:1 gives the next fact—'they went over the ravine of Kidron leading into the garden.' Verse 12 relates the arrest of Jesus. He was bound and led to Annas. In verse 28 Jesus was led from Caiaphas, the high priest, into the Praetorium, the governor's home, early in the morning on the day the Jews were preparing for the Passover. This was the day the Passover lambs were being slain and made ready to be part of the Passover meal that same day beginning at sundown. This is the day Jesus became the "Lamb of God," literally, and He fulfilled the symbolicalness that the lambs of the Jewish Passover represented from the very first Passover, the shadow of things to come. God sent His Son to be the "Lamb of God."

The blood of the lamb of the Jewish Passover gave the Jews redemption and deliverance from their Egyptian bondage. It is the blood of the Lamb of God that is the foundation of everything. We can only have salvation in the person and work of Christ. We need to have an in-depth understanding of the great importance of the shed blood of Jesus Christ, when His blood was shed for us, how to remember His sacrificial death for us and we need to know how to bring others to Christ. John's account of the day Jesus was crucified is the only clear and comprehensive account of that very important act by God. Christ died on the cross on Thursday, the very day all the Passover lambs were slain because he was truly the Lamb of God. He could not be set forth in the Word of God by a better name. Everyone who says Christ died on "Good Friday" is either an enemy of God or is ignorant of the truth in the Holy Word of God.

Christ was crucified on Thursday, not Friday. Matthew 12:40 tells us Christ was in the heart of the earth three days and three nights. During that time in the earth He set the captives free. (See Luke 4:18,19.) Christ died on the cross on Thursday. He spent part of Thursday, all of Friday and Saturday, and part of Sunday in the tomb. He spent Thursday, Friday, and Saturday nights in the tomb. This is the only way that it can be true that He spent three days and three nights in the tomb. All other thinking that clings to, He died on "Good Friday," is a sham, a fabrication of untruthful men. The term, "Good Friday," has been around for such a long time that everyone believes it is the day Christ died for the sin of mankind. The words, "Good Friday," are not in the Bible. It is a tradition of the men and women of the church. This is another example of how dangerous it is to depend on the men and women of the cloth to tell you how to live before Almighty God. We must read and study the Word of God and allow the Holy Spirit to tell us the answers to our questions and concerns for our lives. The minister, priest, rabbi and other men and women of the cloth can be misleading guides. Only guidance from God through the Holy Spirit can be trustworthy.

> "This is the disciple who is testifying to these things, [John]; and wrote these things, and we know that his testimony is true." (John 21:24) [Clarification added by the author.]

A very troublesome question is raised concerning; what reason did God have to set aside a special "ritual" for the Gentiles only, speaking in terms of the Mass, Communion, etc? To focus only on a single cup of wine and the breaking of bread within the very important Jewish Passover and Festival of Unleavened Bread as an observance for Gentiles only is without precedence throughout all of God's Word. Certainly the Apostles never instituted the Mass, Communion, Lord's Supper, etc. They would not have been able to see those two parts of the Jewish Passover celebration separated out and made into a special celebration "for Gentiles only!" We cannot forget they were Jews—they were not Romans. Only God could do that, but He had already put in place for man all that was needed and intended. Bible scholars of today accept these errors of pseudo-Christianity made many centuries ago. The errors date back to the 4th century not the 1st century. The term "Lord's Supper" is accepted by all "Christian leaders" across all of Christendom and has been established as one of the "sacraments of the altar" by most denominations and independent bodies except the Messianic Jews. It can be said with great confidence this act as set aside for once per week, once per month, or whatever interval is a ritual not an act of remembering and honoring our Lord Jesus Christ because of the very nature of the practice.

Another point to be made concerning this subject is brought to light by Paul in 1 Corinthians 11:1-34. Paul is discussing several practices of the people of the called-out-ones at Corinth which have taken the people away from Godliness. I focus on verses 20-34 because within them can be some very important enlightenment. The author uses Stern for that enlightenment. Stern wrote, commenting on the term;

> ""a meal of the Lord," [Lord's Supper] that is, pertaining to the Lord; in context it means a meal

> eaten in a manner worthy of Yeshua [Jesus] or of God, a "lordly or godly meal."" [4] [Clarification added by the author.]

The author believes the referenced meal at 1 Corinthians 11:20 is not part of a Passover celebration but a fellowship of believers meal, any time of the year, any place people of the Lord so gather together. Some Brethren practice having a meal and foot washing at the time they remember the Savior's death on the cross. There is no announcement at these Scriptures that these Corinthians were celebrating the Passover. This was an event that came to Paul's attention and he condemned the ungodly practice of drunken gluttony. The author construes the condemnation by Paul to include the failure to give the proper blessing for breaking of bread at that meal and to give the proper blessing of the wine before drinking it at the end of the meal. This second part of the condemnation is taken from verse 25, concerning when the wine was consumed.

> "In the same way He took the cup also after supper, saying, 'This cup is the new covenant in my blood; do this, as often as you drink it, in remembrance of Me.'" (1 Corinthians 11:25)

Paul is giving the Corinthians here a memory lesson on how to give the traditional blessing of the cup of wine at the end of their meal so as to remember the Lord's death.

The question that is logically raised at this point; what constitutes a Godly meal? The answer, I believe, rests within these Scriptures. Paul has indicated how ungodly and gluttonous the Corinthians were in beginning to eat and getting drunk before all were ready to eat. The next question is: How can all people gathered together at one home begin to eat at the same time? This can only happen after the proper blessing is presented to God for providing the food and since Christ we add to that blessing the thanksgiving and remembrance of what Christ's shed blood and broken body mean to us—at each and every meal—both Jew and Gentile. We only have to dig but a short while into Jewish customs to find out that bread symbolizes life itself to the Jewish people and at the time of His crucifixion Christ told His disciples that the breaking of His body is life to them and all who trust in Him. Since blood was always used to ratify covenants of God with the Israelites, Christ's blood is shed to ratify the new covenant with His people. This blood of Christ used by God to ratify the New Covenant with His people was used in the same manner and purpose as the blood shed on the mountain (Mt. Moriah) (also the mountain that Jerusalem sets on) at the time when Abraham took his son Isaac and was willing to sacrifice him to ratify the Abrahamic Covenant, Genesis 22:7-14, but God provided the sacrifice. That was the ultimate display of trusting God for all that Abraham possessed. The Noahic and Mosaic Covenants were ratified at Genesis 8:20-9:17 and Exodus 24:3-8 respectively.

When we understand the deep meaning of the breaking of bread before the Passover meal and Christ's pointing to drinking the cup at the end of that meal with His disciples the symbolism of John 6:26-58 begins to make sense and Godly comprehension shines through concerning 1 Corinthians 11. These Scriptures, 1 Corinthians 11:23-31, have been taken out of context by the Roman Catholic church and have been accepted by Gentile theologians for many years. These Scriptures are the very ones used by pseudo-Christianity to fabricate its ungodly ritualistic practice. It is highly significant to those who truly love the Lord and are living their life for and in Him to see the utter darkness of the evil brought upon mankind through pseudo-Christianity.

Again the author quotes Stern to bring the reader into fine focus on the subject of the application of,

> "The cup after the meal, the third of the four cups (see v. 17a, N), corresponding to Exodus 6:6, "I will redeem you," Thus Yeshua used the "cup of redemption," as the third cup is called, [Author Note, See Table 3 herein] to inaugurate the new covenant, which redeems from the "Egypt" of bondage to sin all who trust in God and his Messiah. The new covenant is spoken of in the Tanakh at Jeremiah 31:30-33 (31-34), but Greek kainê diathêkê can also be rendered "renewed covenant." (Mt. 9:17N) Even though it is "not like" the Covenant through Moshe [Moses] (Jeremiah 31:31 (32)), the new covenant renews and restores what the Mosaic Covenant promised to the Jewish people."[5] [Clarification added by the author.]

The fourth cup, (Christ was given the sponge filled with sour wine at His crucifixion after which He said, "It is finished") then He died. The meaning of His words, "It is finished," was given in Part One.

Also a quote from the work of Stern brings the reader into fine focus on the subject;

> ""**Breaking Bread**." Many Christians assume that this refers to "taking communion" and have an image of the early believers meeting in homes (v.

46) to eat a tiny wafer of bread and drink a symbolic amount of wine or grape juice, just as Christians do today in their churches. However, the context is not twentieth-century Christianity but first- century Judaism; and for Jews then as now, fellowship was mediated by meals. To say that the early Messianic Jews broke bread is to say neither more nor less than that they ate together.

The meaning of eating together must be grasped. First of all, when possible, religious Jews begin a meal with bread and say over it a *b'rakhah* (cited in 14:19&N and see Mt. 9:8N). Then they break off a piece of the loaf and eat it, so that the blessing of God specifically for His provision of bread to eat will not have been said in vain.

Yeshua knew and observed this practice, but He also gave an additional meaning to the act of breaking bread when He said, as He broke the *matza*h at the Last Supper, "This is my body, which is being given for you; do this in memory of me" (Lk. 22:20; compare 1C 11:24). This practice clearly became part of the "*Torah* of the emissaries," so the early believers were to recall Yeshua's death for them as they began their meal—though some fell short of the standard (1C 11:20-34). Then, after that, the entire meal time was to be devoted to fellowship, "communion" in the ordinary sense of the word (see below on "fellowship"*), not in the technical Christian sense (wafer of bread, cup of wine).

***Fellowship** (Greek koinonia, community, commonness, communion, fellowship) includes two elements, each of which fosters the other, as explained above.) (1) deepening friendship, and (2) developing a common vision, goals, and priorities.

> Yet this fellowship was not mere worldly socializing that ignores God. Consider the Mishna: "Rabbi El'azar ben-'Azaryah [1st-2nd century C.E.] said, ' . . . If there is no meal there is no [study of] Torah, and if there is no [study of] Torah there is no meal.'" (Avot 3:17)
>
> Maimonides explains that each aids in bringing about the full expression of the other and completes it (*Commentary on Pirkey-Avot, ad loc.*). In other words, if one becomes preoccupied with religious studies and ignores normal social interaction, the individual's study does society little good. But, conversely, if at the same time of socializing, the meal, one ignores the things of God, it is a sign that religious truth has not penetrated deeply into the life of the individual. Yeshua, by His identification of Himself with the bread, focuses the meal on Himself and enables this reworking of Rabbi El'zaar's epigram: If there is no time of interacting with fellow believers, one's identification with Yeshua and study of God's *Torah* is incomplete. But if the time of interacting with fellow believers does not relate itself to Yeshua's death on our behalf and to encouraging one another in living the life God wants us to live, the time has been wasted."[6]

One last thought set out by David Stern,

> "At Passover, Jews all over the world retell the story of the plagues and the exodus thus proclaim the central fact on which their peoplehood is founded (See 1 Cor. 5:6-8 N). Likewise, members of the Messianic community are to proclaim the death of the Lord as their exodus from sin and as the

> basis for their existence. Both proclamations look not only back towards a past redemption but also forward to a future one; hence the proclamation is until he comes the second time."[7]

This has deep meaning also for Gentiles.

The discussion set out here concerning the subject sacrament of the altar (Communion/Mass vs. Passover) is quite disturbing because it infringes upon what we think of as a sacred practice that cannot be in error. Our fathers, grandfathers, and great-grandfathers participated in the Communion/Mass. No one has the right to undo and upset such an important traditional event instituted hundreds of years ago by men. The practice was endorsed by Luther, Calvin, Wesley, Billy Graham, and all the popes. How can it not be pleasing to God? Each individual will have to answer that question after a complete examination of all the facts presented here, your personal knowledge on the subject and after consultations with parents, friends and pastor. I have to ask myself, how do I qualify to be the one to bring into question such an earth-shaking discovery? Better put, is there anything wrong with the Gentile Holy Communion, Mass, Lord's Supper, etc.—in sight of God? I believe Gentiles who have Christ Jesus as Lord and Master should practice remembering their Lord and Master at each and every time they break bread (eat a meal). What a thought that is in contrast to remembering our Lord once a week or once a month! Refrain from giving equal time to Satan's Easter Bunny which is a serious offense to God. Just thinking about the worldly term Easter or participating in worldly Easter time activities is offensive to God.

Anti-Semitism in Disguise

With all eyes on the earthly church and all that man has brought it to mean, the heart and mind of man has focused attention on the church and not on our heavenly home. Along with that focus, church leaders have not brought up the subject of thankfulness to the Jews and God's strong desire to bring the attention of the Messiah to the Jewish people. Hardly an oversight, this is a deliberate act by some "church fathers" thus, part of the reason for the doctrine of the word change in the Holy Scriptures from *ekklesia*, the called-out-ones, to church, the busy ones with inward never ending activities. This mind set is as strong an anti-semitic act as one could ever devise, for it is cloaked with the light of Satan himself—who would want to fight against "the church?" This is one of the great errors of part of the "church system."

We need to understand the difference between the individual's relationship with God, Jew or Gentile, through salvation in Christ Jesus, and the nation Israel's relationship with God. There is no room for a collective body, the church institution, to also have a special relationship with God. We know the nation Israel. We need to define who are the individuals—they are those persons, chosen, saved, and called out of Israel, America and the other nations of the world—thus there is no conflict between Israel and the called-out-ones. A conflict remains when we believe God created the church in His Son and believe the theologians who set forth unbiblical doctrines that say, the church has replaced Israel, God's chosen people. God did not create the church in his Son, He created the place for those who trust in His Son (spiritual kingdom here on earth and in heaven through the shed blood of His Son).

In the author's firsthand experience with pastors of many different denominations and independent faiths on the subject of witnessing to the Jew first, the answer to the question, what causes the indifference of the church to evangelize Jewish people—you and I now have the answer—parts of the church system remain in darkness and do not have a true heart for God. The leaders in parts of that system are not in harmony with God. Whether it be by design or out of ignorance, that has to be answered by those who just follow seminary instruction. To all who await the second coming of the Lord, you can hasten His return by witnessing to the Jews, for the Jewish people have to come to repentance before the Messiah can return. John the Baptist preached repentance to the Jewish people. (See Matthew. 3:2.) He also chided the Pharisees and Sadducees because they were coming to him for baptism, but they were unworthy because of the position they had taken concerning Christ. (See Matthew. 3:7,8.)

Christ cannot return until Israel as a nation declares, "Blessed is He who comes in the name of the Lord." (Matthew 23:39) Gary Hedrick declares, "The word 'until' is the key that unlocks this passage, Christ said they would not see Him again until they confess their faith in Him. The Jewish people must come to faith in Yeshua before He returns."[8] God does not want us to wait for Him to do it for us. It is out of our love for God and our belonging to Christ that we want to witness to those who are without Christ Jesus as Lord and Savior including the Jewish people. We are responding to the Great Commission. **This is part of the responsibility of man.** Could it be said, the preachers, pastors, reverends, priests, and rabbis who take the position today that we don't need to bring the Jews to a knowledge of Christ Jesus are modern day Pharisees who Christ would condemn for their misguidance of the people. This could also be part of the reason for clergy burnout. They are not obedient to God. Now, it also becomes most clear, why a high percentage of clergy do not have discipleship as a high priority in their labor for the Lord. They are busy serving the church system.

There are two types of people involved in this so-called "church age," those who promote a highly disguised hell and damnation and those who fight the good fight but do not realize (at least they do not say) who it is they are fighting against. The Reformers meant well, but they like many generals of armies who failed to define the enemy never fully defined who was on God's side and who was on the side of Satan.

Those who brought into focus the need to bring about a drastic change in what man was doing in the area of religion (Christianity) in fact, have been included in the right term, Reformers. But mankind needs to **conform** to God's Word. That is Satan's trap that most of our mainline denominations today are caught in. It should be coming quite clear how effective and paralyzing the work of pseudo-Christianity has been over the centuries and up to the present moment. First, it's a deadly counteraction of the work of God by confusing the intelligent with Gnosticism (practicing heretical Christian mystical sect), it's spreading from the demise of the Roman Empire onward—martyrdom of many true believers, then dividing true believers since the 16th century into many denominations, independent faiths and sects.

Because the true Word from God, given man through His true followers (writers of the New Testament), was very quickly challenged and debated by Gnostics even before the death of all of those writers, pseudo-Christianity projects and actually portrays such a weak and watered-down gospel and actually no gospel at all. This ungodly stance has devastating effects upon most of the denominations today, specifically in the area of hierarchical leadership and control. Those effects are reflected in the spirituality of the majority of the church attendees to the extent that they have no defense against Satan's Mormonism, Jehovah's Witnessism and Moonieism. All are very rapidly growing by people moving out of the "mainliners." Our young people are easily attracted to many of these and other cults traveling up and down the roads and streets in most of Christendom. This truth should send cold chills up and down the spine of all who are sitting numb-brained and allowing this condition to exist in the "church system." It has been pointed out before, the church system in the United States is also guilty for allowing theUnitarian church member Madeleine Murray O'Hare to commit a treasonous act against this nation when she single-handedly pushed through the Supreme Court the removal of prayer and God from our schools. Guess who was sitting on the bench at that time—Godly or ungodly men? That act falls within the definition of treason because it impaired the well-being of this great nation, America, begun by those seeking freedom of religion only 200 plus years before. We are reaping by the hand of that treasonous act, somewhere in the United States, almost daily, pain, suffering and death in a school.

Question: What are the objectives of the pseudo-church (Christianity), the American Civil Liberties Union, the secular humanists, the ungodly judges and ungodly government leaders?

Answer: Destroy or prevent everything Godly.

1. To prevent the return of Christ.
2. To prevent the restoration of the Jews to God and Israel to the land.
3. To prevent peace on earth.
4. To rule the world.
5. To destroy all of God's people.
6. To create a world-wide ungodly religion.

15

The Lingering Mystery—
Satan's Own Men on Earth

There are many reports of sightings of objects or creatures that were said to be observed in diverse parts of the world which have become mysteries. Take for example the mysteries of the Loch Ness Monster, Sasquatch man, flying saucers, and aliens from outer space. These are all unsolved mysteries, real or imagined by man. The lingering mystery of this writing is not the mystery referred to in Scriptures concerning Jesus Christ. It is, however, a mystery established by theologians over the years by misinterpreting and wrongful translation of certain words in Matthew 16:18.

Mysteries sometimes come into being because an individual or a group of people fabricate a story so far-fetched everybody believes that everything related in the story has to be true. Evidence testified to by several persons keeps the vagueness of reality growing until many more people begin to relate the story of a mysterious event, and very soon the mystery is verified by outstanding persons and the mystery is established as a verified truth.

Theologians of today and bygone years are involved with that very same predicament over the words church and rock in Matthew 16:18. So, that which God gave us as truth in His

Word through His Son and the Apostles has been altered by ungodly men and now declared throughout Christendom as the truth.

Theologians have transformed the Godly meaning and use of the words church and rock into a nightmarish mystery for many inhabitants of the earth. They have Roman Catholic and Eastern Orthodox followers believing the Holy See and the Eastern Orthodox Leader are in direct succession to the Apostle Peter. The Orthodox church did not come into existence until the eastern half of the Roman church split away from the western half in 1054 A.D. (The Great Schism). For other peoples of Christendom, the use of the word church has made it possible for men to create numerous sects. This crippling and downright fraudulent work by men of the cloth has also made it very easy for evil men to bring into being many forms of "Christian" followings which are passed off to the unsuspecting soul as "Christian." Some of the more visible today are: Charles Taze Russell of Jehovah's Witness; Jim Jones of Jonesville; David Koresh of Waco, Texas; Joseph Smith and Brigham Young of Mormonism. The invention of the word church also brought opportunities for persons to use religion to control people by marriage of religion and government such as, King or Queen, the Czar, Dali Lama, Hitler, Bonaparte, Genghis Khan, Hirohito, Mohammed and Osama Bin Ladin, and the list goes on and on. Perhaps followers of leaders within evangelical churches consciously or subconsciously allow the "senior pastor" to play the role of a god—the pastor is taking he or she to heaven with them. "Elvis worship" is a very good example of how people can fall into ungodly worship.

Christ Our Rock

Many theologians and Bible scholars have developed, over time, an irreconcilable problem with the words church, rock, and Peter in light of the terms kingdom of heaven and kingdom of God. The word rock is one of the key words in Matthew 16:18 where man began the misinterpretation of what God created through His Son in that verse. It is this very word "rock" that indeed has caused man much pain and suffering, a "mystery" produced by the "men of the cloth," while the direct opposite was God's intention, eternal life with Him. The devilish work by those on this earth who oppose God, did indeed, establish the means for man to be tormented by uncertainty concerning where they stand before God. The works of the Roman and Eastern Orthodox churches and their leaders have been accepted and sometimes adopted by many of the protestant denominations.

The ideas concerning how these men were elevated to such religious esteem in competition with God came into being via the will of man and by the traditions of men of eastern and western Europe long after the first appearance of Christ. There are very glaring weaknesses in the argument—that is the church. The most glaring weakness is throughout the development of the church institution by man; man defined and refined God's Word to suit himself not God. Man says the church institution was established and developed through apostolic succession and that this very day God has His personal representative here on earth, but He represents only the western half of what man calls the church. So God is divided! Since when are we told that God is divided? Only Satan makes man believe that and actually does divide people. Rome has gone about patching gaping holes in its armor ever since it set up business to destroy, contaminate or dilute God's work on earth. The latest being Vatican II. Rome never did recognize God's Word. Luther's biggest battle with Rome was over the Word of God being man's guide not dictums of Rome. On that one point Rome has never changed, it is the word of the Pontiff that gives meaning on how to live before God. The eastern half of the church even testifies to that truth.

The second glaring weakness is the strong earthly organization which uses mere men to override the heavenly connection God gave to individuals through His Son's shed blood. Both the eastern half and the western half of the church are guilty of the shed blood of Jesus Christ. One has made a mere man equal to God Almighty and the other regulates what people believe concerning God by unanimous vote of the people not by the pure Word of God. Almost all of the mainstream Protestant denominations have been "taken-in" by the gospel of the divided church (in strongest language, pseudo-Christianity) and have replicated the above glaring weaknesses. The one-man ministry of those denominations and the static church service and teaching are the strongest condemnations that come to mind.

The Great Whore of Revelation

In certain chapters of the Book of Revelation God tells us about His wrath to come upon the evil people of the world who are perpetrating a falsehood so great many accept it as truth. Satan indeed is the angel of light, but nothing is farther from the truth. Revelation means unveiling.[1] The Book of Revelation unveils the truth about pseudo-Christianity—Satan's own apostles—the administrators of the pseudo-church. Chapters 17, 18, and part of 19 of the Revelation relate all that the "great-whore" did, and will do, against the saints and the guilt of their blood is placed on the "great whore." Not many theologians have the courage and daring to set out the truth concerning who it is that God is revealing in these chapters nor are they in agreement as to the place where she sits—Babylon the Great—Mother of whores and of the Earth's Obscenities—chapters 17, 18 and part of 19 also tell of all the activities of the "great whore," over the centuries, against the people of God and the plundering performed by the "great whore" of all the nations of the world.

God tells us also of how great the fall is of those responsible for all the iniquity of the "great whore." Revelation relates the wrath of God that brings judgment, condemnation and destruction upon the "great whore." The author equates the "great whore" of Revelation with the people who organized and operate the pseudo-(Church) Christianity. There is but one Scripture which points conclusively to the leaders of the pseudo-church as being the "great whore,"

> "I saw the woman drunk from the blood of God's people, that is, from the blood of the people who testify about Yeshua [Jesus Christ]. On seeing her, I was altogether astounded." (Rev. 17:6, JNT) [Clarification added by the author.]

The NAS even makes the meaning more clear—verse. 6,

> "And I saw the woman drunk with the blood of the

> saints, and with the blood of the witnesses of Jesus. When I saw her, I wondered greatly." (Rev. 17:6)

There is nothing that points more vividly to the truth than the Word of God.

Bible scholars have differing views on the term "Babylon the Great" in the book of the Revelation. One says it refers to the city of Jerusalem because the antichrist rules from there and Jerusalem will be destroyed during the last half of the tribulation. While another says it has reference to Rome. Jerusalem has not given recognition to the Son of God, their Messiah, while Rome has put on the act—the Pope is God's representative on earth. One says I am working for bringing souls to God and the other denies that Christ Jesus came to earth and shed His blood for the salvation of all mankind. However, Jerusalem is the Holy city of God. It always was and it always will be, so I have to remove its name from the list of probable cities as "Mystery Babylon."

Great Britain needs to be considered for the list of the guilty concerning "Mystery Babylon." In Revelation 17:1b it says, "I will show you the judgment of the great harlot who sits on many waters." The dictionary defines the word harlot as one who plays with the susceptible areas of a man's vulnerability. The words "many waters" are key to including London as "Babylon the Great." The small land mass of Great Britain is surrounded indeed by "many waters." England has given the world mixed signals where labor for the Lord is involved. England, as well as Rome, martyred many of the precious souls of God.[2]

On the surface, England and Rome have been quite active in bad as well as good works concerning world economic power, control of many nations, and spread of unbiblical

"Christian faith." Rome evangelized people of other countries, and the increase in wealth followed. England evangelized weak countries mainly for their wealth-producing resources. England has been behind the development of many Bible versions, especially the Geneva version. England passed up the opportunity to put forth William Tyndall's Bible, the most accurate translation of the Word of God. It was the most accurate translation, in English, because Tyndall leaned very heavily upon Martin Luther's work. It is most unfortunate for all of mankind that Martin Luther's Bible translation has not been translated into the English language and other languages. I believe that, because Martin Luther spent his early years as a monk in a monastery. He discovered the evil mind of pseudo-Christianity and he found the truth in the Word of God.

Luther came clean because he found the true meaning of what God established for mankind in the shed blood of His Son. He took on the pseudo-Christianity of Rome and exposed it to the then known world under the protection of the rulers of his country who would not turn Luther over to Rome. The truth that was suppressed by the pseudo-Christians came bubbling up everywhere, causing great alarm to those who were opposed to God. This great work of Luther became the essence of the Renaissance period of European history and the great good that could have come out of its impact on mankind was again suppressed by tagging it "the Reformation." The pendulum that had swung in favor of a strong work for the Lord was turned into a worldly institution, the church. Can we begin to see more clearly who have been the enemies of God over the many centuries since Christ's first appearance on earth?

Both Rome and London fit the term "Mystery Babylon"

or "Babylon the Great" because these terms have been a symbolic name applied to Satan's domain since the time of the building of the tower of Babel, and since there is more than one reference to Babylon in the Revelation and more than one description of what is to happen to Babylon, I say, the inference can mean two different places God's judgment is coming upon because both Rome (the leader of the church of Rome) and London have played a role in bringing great damage to that which God has willed for His people and all of mankind. London and Rome have played a leading role in all parts of the world to disrupt, destroy and dilute all of the work by true followers of God in very sly ways. Who are the most influential in providing deadly ungodliness among the peoples of the world? First, certainly Romanism, including the work of the Jesuits and before them, Knights Templar. Second, the Church of England, responsible for developing and advocating the numerous denominations, independents, and sects of the "protestant church" particularly in America. These include: Anglican, Episcopal, Methodist, Church of God, Church of Christ, Salvation Army, Baptists (Northern sects), Plymouth Brethern, Christian and Missionary Alliance, Church of the Nazarene and the Assemblies of God.

There is a third view concerning "Babylon the Great." Babylon of Assyria (Iraq) will be rebuilt and play an important role in the end times. It sets on many waters also. That Babylon I would have to rule out because the Babylonians did not play a role in suppressing the people who discipled the nations to trust in Jesus Christ such as did the people of London and Rome.

The above is the foundation for much needed enlightenment concerning Satan's activities in the world via pseudo-

Christianity. The book of Revelation has meaning for the people of God. God intended those Scriptures to be a warning to mankind concerning the wrath to come. The warning shows that He loves mankind so much that He does not want it to meet up with the wrath that is spelled out in that Book in great detail which will come upon those who do not heed the warning. The person who does not heed the warning of the Rattlesnake must suffer the consequences. Just as those consequences can mean death—so the consequences for not heeding the warning set out in the Revelation can mean, **eternal death.** Just as the words in the book of Revelation are a warning to all mankind on the face of the earth so was the great World War of 1914-1945 and of the wars since then up to the present war on Terror—a firsthand warning of God's wrath to come. Disasters and destruction are coming upon all inhabitants of the world at a rate greater than ever before witnessed by mankind.

The warning being referred to here is given in the first four chapters of Revelation. This warning as symbolized in Scriptures is to the seven churches of Asia. The people living in that area at the time the Book of Revelation was written were under heavy attack by the men of Satan (Gnosticism was running rampant), but at the same time they were some of the strongest of the people who loved the Lord. So this message has a double pronged meaning and influence. It was intended to awaken the people of the cities mentioned and cause them to return to their former state. And it is directed toward the people with like mindedness of today who need to straighten out their lives before the Lord—before the Lord removes all opportunity to do so. It is not important to know when the chance to respond to the warning is taken away, the important thing is, act immediately to be certain you will be with our heavenly Father when you die.

A Lesson to Heed

There has to be greater meaning to mankind who are involved with just following along with the "church system" thinking they are safe from the wrath of God to come. The greater meaning to man is, God is laying out before us in chapters 2 and 3 of Revelation, the very carelessness of those who have received the Word of God at one time or another and in 5 out of 7 chances failed to respond to God with a complete fullness of heart and mind to serve Him as outlined in all of the New Testament. The reference to 5 out of 7 chances is the detailed descriptions of how man has responded to the call of God. The author believes God is talking to specific types of people, then and now. He is directing this admonishment to people not an organization. It is the individual God is dealing with. There was no such thing as a church when the Book of Revelation was written. For that matter, there never was until 1560 A.D. when the Geneva version of the Bible was published using the word *church*. The reference to church had to be reference to the people of the 7 cities or the assemblies (called-out-ones) in those 7 cities. This is God's way of telling us the various ways we have grieved Him by our way of living our life before Him. He uses this description of all that man has done to displease Him. Then He goes into the detailed consequences unrepentant man has to suffer for all that he has done against God or failed to do for God. God has to be directing His displeasure toward individuals not groups of people which would be very impersonal. The Book of Revelation gives pictorial consequences that individuals will suffer for the evil and sinful acts against God. This is not directed toward the chosen people as a whole, corporate sinning of an organization, or a particular agent of a group of people. It is directed toward each and every individual living on the face of the earth. There are no exceptions, nor exemptions; all who bring evil upon mankind are being addressed directly—a most personal message to those who deliberately live in sin. No one is left out of the warning of the Word of God. Following is a summary of God's Word to the seven (God's perfect number) types of people if you will. (The paraphrased statements which follow are based on the Jewish New Testament translation.)

Ephesus	(sinned)	The first type of people— you lost the love you had at first.
Smyrna	(obeyed)	No special admonishment. Only praise for their work.
Pergamum	(sinned)	Hold to the teaching of Bilam (Balaam). Hold to the teaching of the Nicolaitians (the pseudo-churchmen).
Thyatira	(sinned)	Continue to tolerate that Izevel (Jezebel) woman. The one who claims to be a prophet, but is teaching and deceiving my servants to sin (the pseudo-churchmen).
Sardis	(sinned)	You are dead. No spiritual action.
Philadelphia	(obeyed)	You have obeyed My message and have not disowned Me. You have obeyed My message about persevering.
Laodicea	(sinned)	You are neither hot nor cold. You are lukewarm.

The Big Lie

To put to rest the claim by the Western and Eastern churches that their leaders of today as well as of the past centuries are in direct divine succession with the Apostle Peter is indeed a big lie of the highest order. This most profound truth is quickly substantiated by any historic writing covering the life and times during the period from the death, burial, resurrection and ascension of our Lord to the end of Roman world civil rule. During that time the Satan-directed Roman government did not tolerate the existence of anyone who did not show outwardly a loyal worship of the Roman-declared god(s). It was not possible for anyone who loved the Lord to survive if they practiced their true faith in the Lord Jesus Christ in the open or remained in the Roman-controlled territories. It was not possible for an apostolic succession to exist or to begin to exist until after the temporary collapse of the Roman civil government rule.

When the civil government rule ended throughout the Roman Empire, the Roman pseudo-Christianity rule began. That rule has had a positive effect on mankind ever since in the area of godlessness. That is also the moment when the pseudo-Christianity head(s) began their succession, during the 4th-5th centuries, not in the 1st century as alluded to in the claim of the pseudo-Christianity. Roman apologetics goes out of its way to dodge this bone of contention,[3] thus the reason this author can be so sure in calling this claim the big lie. That string of leaders never had and never will have any ties with the true people of God. (In this case, the definition of apologetics has to be modified to add the word pseudo ahead of the word

Christianity.) Any denomination or independent church who affiliates themselves with that pseudo-Christianity organization is taking its people very close to the bottomless pit. If anyone has to go out-of-their-way as much as the pseudo-Christianity does to tell you how good, honest, trustworthy, and righteous they are, "buyer beware," Satan is in their crown whispering these sweet nothings in their ear.

For it was the act of God in dispersing those Jews who came to trust in their Messiah that God used to spread the good news all over the then-known world. The Jews, Messianic and those who remained in their blindness, were constantly moved from earthly kingdom to earthly kingdom, carried the true message of the good news around the world for their God in the early centuries after Christ's first appearance on earth. God did not use many Gentiles to perform that work of spreading the true Gospel message of the Lord Jesus Christ to all parts of the then inhabited world. It is plainly seen in the Book of Acts and in Paul's Epistles to the Gentiles that the Gentiles had a terrible time keeping the true Gospel message straight. Whereas the Jews were better prepared for the task.

A Picture Painted by History

History can paint pictures that reveal truths that we would not be able to otherwise see. Such a revealing of truth is painted for us in the history of Rome's greatest Empire builder, Augustus, for it was under the guiding hand of Augustus that the Roman rule of that day became known as the Roman Empire, the front runner and pattern for Roman Catholicism. Augustus was the greatest until the ingenuity of secular rule by

Octavian (Augustus' given name by his stepfather Julius Caesar) was mixed with the devilish ingenuity of the pseudo-Christian rule bringing into being the Holy See of Roman religion who replaced Augustus as the greatest ever. "Augustus—a word connected with religion—("revered") and the science of augury—(soothsayer-divination)."[4] The name Augustus rightly expressed his position without giving needless offence. "He was master of the Roman rule but masqueraded as a colleague."[5]

Augustus passed through the various levels of importance and positions attaining greater and greater power that came with them. He passed through the layering of power and importance very cautiously to reach the highest level of power where he represented each and every body that made up the imperial powers within the Roman society (Republic—at the beginning of his rule—he became the first Roman Emperor). He even added new representative identities with portions of the society as they came into being. In other words, he became everything to everyone. Augustus could do no wrong. He was the ultimate power. He was looked upon as "man-god." When the people of the land and those of the governing body (governing body has to be said with tongue-in-cheek for we must remember, Augustus was literally everything) desired that Augustus be elevated to yet another level in a certain religious matter, say building and dedicating a temple or altar to him, he would take a low-key stance as if he did not want it to be so but did nothing to stop it from happening. "But the name of Rome had to be associated with his own."[6] As was stated earlier, Octavian was the step-son of Julius Caesar and the Roman Senate voted Octavian, January 13, 27 B.C., the title Augustus.

> "Augustus refused official deification, but Octavian had his stepfather deified by the Senate in 42 B.C. You see, Octavian side-stepped a political trap, for if he had accepted, it would have offended the Senate members. They too, would have had to participate in the official worship. Instead, he made himself, even for the Senate, an object of religious awe. However, Senate members had Rome as the most important object of religious awe; Augustus therefore, made himself the protector of the Roman tradition and above all religion. Roman religion had always been somewhat impersonal. A superstitious reverence for 'the proper way of doing things' was the strongest religious experience of the average Roman. Republican government had been largely a structure of rituals. As a successful revolutionary, Augustus hoped to revive respect for such rituals—in others. He saw in reverence for the established order a bulwark for his regime. He therefore made himself patron of the old Roman family life and traditional class distinctions. Augustus revived the ancient Roman religious ceremonies and he had (82 temples rebuilt, old priesthood revived, cult associations encouraged, domestic worship restored by law)."[7]

It has been throughout the history of Italy a custom to hand governing power and social position down through families, a custom still in practice until this very day. Octavian was no exception to that custom.

With these few words the verbal portrait painted of Augustus also paints the portrait of the Holy See. A verbal portrait of Hitler also would not take many words for much is known about Hitler. So is much known about the Holy See but very little really understood. The combining of the two defined powers, powers of the keys of the Bible (See discussion page 96, Part One) with slight of hand misinterpretation as to application with the powers of a Caesar which were readily understood by the average Roman citizen, it now becomes very plain to see how Roman Catholicism could be brought into being. The Romans understood very well the concept of a superman (Pontifex Maximus-Pontiff) with that much religious power. Just as Augustus could do no wrong the Holy See is infallible. Just as Augustus had a college for a special group or clique, the Holy See has his college of Cardinals. It is even called the Senate of the Roman church. Roman Senators became Roman Cardinals. Roman proconsular became the Roman Bishop. The hierarchy of the Roman church still comes into being today via the "family." There are many, many more similarities which are very easy to understand once you know how all this had its beginning. With reference to powers of the keys of the Bible; it can safely be assumed that this authority given the Apostles by Christ is the great authority base pseudo-Christianity indeed did seize the opportunity to assume and is using in an ungodly manner.

It also now becomes easy to see why the Eastern group wanted to split with the Western group—the Eastern group wanted to pattern its hierarchy after the high priest concept from the Old Testament for a pseudo-Christianity while the West wanted the ancient Roman religious conception for its pseudo-Christianity. The Holy See of Rome inherited a faithful blind worship and nothing would stop it—not until Christ's second coming. This encapsulation of one segment of the history of the Roman Empire and "history of the church," brings into fine focus how mankind has been devastated by that which is set out to be the direct opposite, the universal church.

Life in Eternity

While this writing leaves room for the guilty to escape the pronouncement set out here, those who are caught in its grasp can consider the pronouncement when evaluating their own circumstances concerning **life in eternity.** The words spoken by Rome have always been hollow and without Godly foundation, and certainly without Biblical basis. For as the development of its religion is traced over the centuries, the strongest argument that can be mustered: we have been around a long, long time.

Another thought to ponder involves passing up the opportunity for **eternal life** with the true higher being in peace and pure love. This thought can be likened unto the man who has an incurable life-ending disease and will soon die, but from a distant country comes the news that a drug has been developed that cures his disease. The drug is very expensive. The patient must go and live in the distant country to have the drug administered by very special means. The question is: Will that man sell everything he has to come up with the funds to be able to take advantage of the life-saving drug? Likewise would you do everything in your power to obtain **eternal life** if you knew that it was available as a free gift or would you allow the opportunity to pass without a second thought of what **eternal life** is like without God?!

This writing exposes pseudo-Christianity to the fullest and it gives some of the evils that have been spread by it to all Christendom and beyond. All of which is most alarming because of the danger to those embedded and held in what they have been led to believe as godly instructions and basis of faith in God. I say to you, if this writing has shaken that faith but at the same time you felt some tugging by God to check the authenticity of what is said here, I have accomplished my purpose. Break the hold Satan has on mankind where man is willing to have the men of the cloth do their thinking for them. This exposure might be too late for many to find their Redeemer among all the religious ongoings set up by man in the church system, but God does still work miracles for those who truly seek Him, find Him. (See Matthew 7:7.)

This writing is not directed toward those persons who truly love God. It is directed toward those pastors and churches wherever people are being led by weakened church doctrines. People need to demand Godly leadership.

Answers to a Staggering Nation's Questions

It is highly ironical that many church men are and have been aware of the extreme danger lurking in their midst which involves the doctrines of the pseudo-Christianity but remain silent. I believe we now have the answer to the questions:

- Where were the Christians of Christendom when God's chosen people were experiencing the Holocaust?
- Where were the Christians of America when Madeleine Murray O'Hare was removing prayer and God from our schools and America?
- Where are the Christians of America when the secular humanists ride the Satanic black horse called "freedom of choice?"

- Where are the Christians of America today as freedom of religion, freedom of the press, and our freedom in general is disappearing at an alarming rate via the court system, the ACLU, and the ungodly news and information media (newspapers, magazines, and TV)?

Now it becomes easy to see why those who support the ideals of Satan love the term "separation of church and state." That term is being used to remove all godliness from America. There cannot be any such dictum of separating Godly direction from those who administer the God-given authority over the ruled. When Satan guides the minds and actions of those who administer authority over the people, the end of that people cannot be far behind. Please check out what happened and how it happened in Europe just sixty-two short years ago. In Erwin W. Lutzer's book, *Hitler's Cross,*[8] we are told in frightening detail how Hitler and his stooges annihilated the people of Germany from God. His attack on God was made by attacking the religious leadership. When only a handful responded to his Satanized attack, soon his demonization of the people was complete and he became the god and the religion of Germany.

The attack on godliness began by people like those of our ACLU, Madeleine Murray O'Hara, Mr. Jones of Jonesville, David Koresh of Waco and yes people of their own government other than Hitler. Leaders of our national government under the Clinton administration attempted to remove religious thought from the work place and strengthened abortion practices. They expanded corrupt practices via politics as if they were established by law. They instituted another language as standard along with English and court harassment of religious freedom.

As the opportunity came into view in Rome to establish a ruling body showing traditional Romanism, the Emperor look, but also implant a facelift which gave some of the ruling body an appearance of following the newly introduced king of the Jews, success was not attained until the 4th century. In between, attempts were made by Rome to assimilate this new religious and zealous people into the Roman society by Gnosticism and then by monasticism. The most powerful persuader, however; was the "Roman rule," kill those who do not conform. Two hundred or more years passed before the new religious regime would finally succeed in becoming the strong ruling religious families in the Roman Empire. From that time on the "Holy See" concept kept gaining strength and influence in the rule of the Roman Empire. The rulers of the Roman Empire did not succumb to outside powers but to the developing pseudo-Christianity hierarchal powers from within. That power swept the entire Empire and became the ruling force up to the days of the Reformation. The Eastern half of that power developed its own religious world. Both concepts survive until this day and the western half of the pseudo-Christianity introduced itself to all the nations and peoples as the religion of the New Testament.

Presented here is an entirely new approach to what God established in His Son Christ Jesus at Matthew 16:18. By the announcement of Christ in vs. 18, "I also say to you that you are Peter, and upon this Rock I will build My church; and the gates of Hades will not overpower it," God the Father set into motion that holy sacrifice of His Son, as our redeemer and God began a renewed calling to mankind unto Himself through the Son. God also made a New Covenant with His people (Jews). Consummation of the New Covenant did not take place until that moment, on the cross, when Christ said "it is finished." David Stern in his introduction to the *Jewish New Testament*, pp. XIV, XV[9], explains the use and the meaning of the term "covenant" and how that term relates to the term "New Testament":

> "Testaments and Covenants, New and Old." The term "testament" reflects a tension between the Hebrew language of the Tanach and the Greek of the New Testament. The Hebrew word "b'rit" means "covenant, contract." The Greek word for "covenant" or "b'rit" is "diathêkê." But "diathêkê" can also mean "testament" in the sense of "will."[34] (Hebrews 9:16,17) The Hebrew words "b'rit chadashah" mean "new covenant." But the set of texts translated here, called the B'rit Chadashah in Hebrew, is known in English as the New Testament because of the influence of Greek diathêkê—even though what Jeremiah foretold was a new foundational contract between God and the Jewish people, not a will: a covenant, not a testament.
>
> Moreover, a "new" covenant implies an "old" one, in this case the Mosaic Covenant made by God with the Jewish people at Mount Sinai.[35] The New Testament makes this explicit at Messianic Jews [Hebrews 8:6-13], where, in context, "Old" does not imply "bad" but merely "earlier." Since the Tanach, in which the Mosaic Covenant is pivotal, dates from between 1500 and 300 B.C.E.,[36] ["Before the Common Era," C. E. for "Common Era," modern Jewish literature uses these abbreviations instead of "B.C." and "A.D."] it is called the Old Testament,

> distinguishing it from the first century C. E. writings which constitute the New Testament." [Stern's Note 34 refers to Hebrews 9:16-17; Note 35 refers to Exodus 19-24; and Note 36 is explained.] [Clarification added by the author.]

Just before God the Father established the New Covenant with His people, the rulers, priests, and elders rejected their Messiah, Jesus and all mankind (Jew and Greek) were included in the redemption. (See Matthew 12:14-22.) The Romans and Eastern Orthodox have built their pseudo-Christianity upon the deliberate and gross misinterpretation of Matthew 16:18. The battle that true believers face concerning a true walk with the Lord stems largely from the devilish influence of pseudo-Christianity. Leaders of the mainline denominations, editors of Christian journals and many seminary leaders embrace pseudo-Christianity. The mystery truly lingers on and on via our seminaries and the men and women who blindly accept the prideful longstanding instructions and training leading to pastoral care of the people. This can be called popular religious instruction. The editor of the periodical, *Christian History*, propounds and promotes the legacy of pseudo-Christianity. See Issue 65 (Vol. XIV, No. 1) entitled, "The Ten Most Influential Christians of the Twentieth Century."

16

Confusion in the Seminaries—All Cannot Be Right

Seminary and Bible school students depend on those who are in the responsible positions guiding and directing all of the functions of a particular seminary or Bible school to make the right selection of men and women who perform in the classrooms. However God's Word is taught in the church, how the Sunday sermon is put together, the delivery technique, every mannerism, all have their beginning in the classroom. If the seminary "prof" used the snapping of fingers to keep the student awake, the finished pastor uses the snapping of fingers to keep the congregation awake or to place emphasis on a certain part of the sermon. If the pastor places great emphasis on missions, that pastor learned it in the seminary classroom. If the pastor does not create disciples, the pastor did not receive discipleship training in the classroom. If the pastor uses Holy Communion every Sunday to keep sin from getting out of control in the congregation, the pastor or priest learned it in the seminary classroom. Presbyterian seminaries produce pastors who use traditional Presbyterian doctrine of very long standing. Lutherans, Methodists, Roman Catholics, Baptists, and the long list of other faiths use the particular doctrines developed a long time ago for each different church body. Individual family relationships have accepted the hand-me-down traditions of men without any questions asked. Similarly, people accept traditions of political and governing parties the same way. The people who follow traditions of men in the church are now paying the price.

Seminary Practices That Help to Determine—What Is the Church?

Two very important principles stand out when observing the broad spectrum of seminaries of the United States:

1. Graduate men and women for service to God with the true way of walking before their Heavenly Father.
2. Continuity of training—because they all use the same source of information, the Holy Word of God.

With these two principles in mind, the question is; how come we still produce pastors, missionaries and Christian teachers who are Lutherans, Baptists, Methodists, Assemblies of God adherents and all the way to Jehovah's Witnesses and Unitarians? From all sound reasoning one would expect to find continuity of training—all would have the true way of walking before God.

These questions raised, bring into focus a highly debatable subject when we throw in the fact that pastors are experiencing "burn-out" at a rapidly growing rate and we read of the sinfulness of clergy. This continues to happen in our society that has Bible learning capabilities at the greatest level in modern history. The one and only answer to these perplexing questions, the leaders and staff of the seminaries do not have Jesus Christ as Lord and Master of their lives.

Curriculum and End Product

Today we see more and more firefighting theology than basic Biblical theology taught in the seminaries, "to know Christ and to make Him known." The true work of those trained for the ministry is more and more "picked up" by parachurch organizations everywhere. Most people of this group were self-taught because seminary training did not, in the past, (two generations) and does not today, prepare graduates for real life "winning the lost for Jesus Christ." Because of this apathy within the system of theological preparation, training people for the battle in the trenches is nearly extinct. Seminary training can be likened unto the military producing all officers and no privates to fight the war in the trenches. In our day, more officer types are being produced in seminaries to fight the social disease oriented conflicts, i.e., pastoral counseling for substance abuse, marital difficulties, and psychological and pseudo-psychology, most of which are due to the lack of emphasis on winning those people for the Lord before they reached that state.

Few seminaries offer educational study on discipling, a training our Lord put at the top of His teaching. And none of the seminaries dare mention the term soul-winning let alone offer courses of study entitled Soul-winning I, II, and III, thus the financial supporters of the numerous seminaries are virtually financing "Ivory Towers" with no one to answer to in many instances except "the Board" who love to see the flow of great "papers." More attention is being given to the production of church entertainment, i.e., special music, joking, funny stories all of which are now followed by great applause (clapping of hands in praise of man) as if it were entertainment at the theater. Most seminaries condone this lack of basic work for God because curricula are geared to a self-indulging academic atmosphere. All of which mirrors our bureaucratic system in national, state, and local governments. Some seminaries slightly recognize this pitiful state and soften the potential with a good mixture of class study and "hands on" experience. The transition from student filled with knowledge to preach, to soul-winning practitioner, slips through the "well we produced another great preacher crack." When the graduate minister arrives at the church for an interview, the call committee wants to know, "can he/she preach?" So the clergy factory uses the same mold over and over again.

The following anecdote is a verbal picture of the disturbing direction seminary leaders and church hierarchical leadership are taking the unsuspecting people in the "church system."

It was Saturday evening and when all had another full evening of their favorite television programs, they decided it was time to pass through the shower. Now when Sunday morning came, they were all scrubbed clean and each one adorned themselves with their Sunday best. Then they all arrived at the church happy and anxious to enter in through the door with great smiles and greeting one another with a friendly "Hello" and "How are you?" Then each one takes their very own seat and waits with great anticipation for the show to begin. Worship of God they call it, but the pastor tickles their ears with interrupting funny puns that bring forth spontaneous childish laughter carrying even the most reverent thoughts momentarily, to the great charisma of the "senior pastor." Then the worship turns to loud applause resounding from the four corners of the interior of the church. Visitors check the program, who is this great artist?! It is but the special music from one who dearly loves to proclaim praise and adoration to the Lord.

We could call this modern heresy and we could say apostasy has taken over the people of God. No, it is worse than either one of those blasphemous acts. This ritualistic activity by those who say they love God is now practiced by most denominations across America "From Sea to Shining Sea." This form of worship is becoming the common denominator which is playing a big part of ushering into existence the one world worship system. Just think, the very ones who say, "We are born again," are the very ones succumbing to this worldly form of worship. Participants accept this practice with great enthusiasm. I call it evangelicalism because it is sweeping evangelicals.

Results of an analysis of 42 seminaries shows only a small percentage met the one and only Biblical standard (Matthew 22:37). Statements within their published catalogs of who they are, their purpose for being, what they believe and teach, statement of faith, priorities and many other terms which give the prospective student a look at who, what and why were used to make the judgment concerning that standard (Matthew 22:37), And He said to him, "You shall love the Lord Your God with all your heart, and with all your soul, and with all your mind." The author looked for very specific convictions concerning Godliness in the 42 seminary catalogs, foremost of which:

> "Soul winning—making disciples for Christ." *This is the only business of those who say,* "I love you Lord"!

If a sign of this work did not show up in the catalog, the author assumed the seminary did not have a desire to be sure the prospective student would be so inspired and educated.

We expect that a prospective purchaser of a $30,000.00 automobile will check all the details in the brochure, the sales pitch and the vehicle itself to be very certain of the authenticity of the manufacturer's claims. A prospective seminary student makes the same analysis of the seminary to which he will pay the $60,000.00 or more for the training and preparation for serving the one true God. The catalog is one of the sources for that analysis; in fact, a university catalog is the most authentic source for information as to all legal aspects of the college or university concerning the student's expectations and what he or she will pay for the education.

The 42 seminaries were studied to determine the effectiveness of the institution's purpose and desire to graduate men and women ready to produce reproducers—soul-winning servants of the Lord. The following definitions were used to make the determination for each of the seminaries.

1. Those who show positive signs of existence to inspire, educate and disciple its students to become reproducers for the Lord. A very small number, about 5% of the 42 seminaries.
2. Those who show positive signs of existence to inspire, educate and lead its students to good works.

3. Those who show positive signs of existence to inspire, educate and lead its students to secular humanism.
4. Others who did not give sufficient evidence to place them in any one of the above groupings. A very small number, about 9% of the 42 seminaries.

The remaining 86% fall within definitions 2 and 3 above. I felt that it did not make any difference whether most of the seminaries studied fell in items 2 or 3, the outcome concerning indifference to godliness is the same for the people coming under their leadership. We are reaping that ungodliness all over America.

Table 4 reveals what the people of God are facing in the world today. Two points are made to emphasize the content of the table: one, by contrasting the data presented in the table under the column entitled Christian Theism to the woeful condition of the "Christian church" we can begin to see how easy it has been for Satan to bring in alongside our mainstream denominations that ultra-deceit represented in the other four columns in Table 4. Second, the table shows how broad the deceit is and how it matches the susceptible areas of mankind, those who are without Godly knowledge and without the Lord Jesus Christ. This all goes back to the fact mankind has decided he is as wise as God and has set out to prove it by continually creating for himself ways and means to outdo God in the area of **eternal life**. And Satan is a master at helping man achieve his goal—eternal hell instead of the eternal bliss as promised by the serpent. The data comparison also shows the enormity of the work that has to be accomplished by those who truly love God.

The only way people of God can bring about a noticeable

change in the actions, convictions, morality and spirituality in Americans is: Stop serving the church and begin to serve God. All of the differences of the faiths and beliefs displayed in Table 4 are the product of those who teach in the seminaries. While these beliefs are of non-Christian origin it shows how easy it is to twist and corrupt the Word of God by those who say "We love the Lord." You, who are instructors in the seminaries, have been given a very scathing rebuke because you are not providing the training the Lord so desires. I admonish you to take these words and turn the world upside down.

Table 4 FIVE VIEWPOINTS OF LIFE AND ULTIMATE REALITY*

Knowledge of the beliefs of prevalent worldviews is helpful in evangelism. This table compares four non-Christian belief systems with the Christian worldview.

TOPIC	CHRISTIAN THEISM	NEW AGE PANTHEISM	HUMANISTIC ATHEISM	MORMON POLYTHEISM	WATCHTOWER FINITE GODISM (Jehovah's Witnesses)
The Bible:					
Origin:	"God-breathed"	By "spiritual" humans.	Purely human product.	Inspired by the Heavenly Father.	Inspired by Jehovah.
Nature:	Inerrant (without error).	Has many errors.	Has many errors.	Many transcription/translation errors.	Texts reliable but needed own translation.
Authority:	God's final word.	One of many inspired books.	No authority whatsoever.	Below 3 other books and words of prophets.	As interpreted by the WT's governing body.
Knowledge:					
Source:	Revelation from God.	Intuition.	Observation/Reason.	Revelation, esp. words of prophets.	Bible and "theocratic direction" of WT.
Right & wrong:	Based on God's words.	Ultimately no distinction.	Determined by society.	Based on revelation to prophets.	Bible & directives of governing body.
Truth:	Determined by God.	Relative.	Pragmatism (whatever works).	Determined by prophets (presidents).	Bible as interpreted by governing body.
God:					
Nature:	Personal and infinite.	Impersonal force.	"Meaningless concept"	Many finite gods with physical bodies.	Finite Jehovah with spiritual body.
The Trinity:	3 Persons in one essence.	Denied or spiritualized.	Considered nonsense.	Father, Son and Spirit are 3 distinct gods.	Considered to be of pagan origin.
The Universe:					
Origin:	Created by God.	Emanation from god-force.	The "Big Bang"	Gods have been creating worlds eternally.	Created by Jehovah.
Relationship/God:	Distinct from God.	Contained within god-force.	Not applicable.	Each god has own world to rule.	Jehovah lives in certain place in universe.
Existence:	Dependent on God.	Illusion.	Self-existent.	Self-existent matter used to make worlds.	This universe will exist eternally.
Origin of life:	Created by God.	Emanation from god-force.	"Primordial soup"	Infinite regress of gods creating worlds.	Created by Jehovah.
Spiritual world:	Distinct from physical.	True reality.	Non-existent.	We lived as pre-existent spirits here.	Invisible parts of creation.
Jesus Christ:					
Person:	Full God and full man.	Reincarnated human being.	Just a human being.	First son of Father/brother of Lucifer.	Michael the archangel.
Conception/birth:	"Born of the virgin Mary"	Normal reincarnation.	Normal conception.	Sexual intercourse of Father with Mary.	By a virgin.
Unique?	Only begotten Son of God.	One of many avatars.	Normal human being.	Eldest brother/physical body via Father.	First creation of Jehovah.
Purpose:	Die for our sins.	"Way-shower"	Good teacher.	Make it possible to return to the Father.	Pay for the sin of Adam.
Resurrection:	Vindication of Messiahship.	Showed power any can have.	Denied.	Pattern for resurrection of all persons.	Spiritual, not bodily.
Intercession:	Only Mediator.	One of many mediators.	Not needed.	Shared with Joseph Smith.	Mediated by "God's organization" (the WT)
Second Coming:	Personal and bodily.	Spiritual/ "Age of Aquarius"	Denied.	Expected soon, to set up earthly kingdom.	Already occurred invisibly in 1914.
The Holy Spirit:					
Nature of:	Full Deity and personality.	Power source.	Existence denied.	A finite god without a physical body.	Jehovah's invisible, active force.
Regeneration:	Via the Holy Spirit.	Through own power.	Through own determination.	Via baptism by a Mormon elder.	Only needed for the 144,000.
Human Nature:	Image of God but fallen.	Inwardly divine.	Same as all animals.	Same as our Heavenly Father and Mother.	Not inherently sinful.
Salvation:					
What is it?	Sins atoned for and forgiven.	No more reincarnations.	Improvement in life.	Exaltation to godhood.	Live forever in paradise on earth.
Why needed?	The Fall/personal sins.	Don't know we are god.	Problems in life and society.	We wanted to be like the Father.	Sin of Adam.
How attained?	Faith in Christ.	Realization of own divinity.	Faith in own abilities.	Keeping ordinances and commandments.	Join WT, perseverance in good works.
Purpose:	To glorify God.	Loss of personality.	Self-gratification.	Attain physical bodies like our Father.	Vindication of Jehovah's right to rule.
Result:	Relationship with God.	Reunion with the One.	Improved society.	Continued cycle of gods fathering gods.	End of suffering.
Satan/Demons:	Personal, evil beings.	Bad thoughts.	Non-existent.	Condemned to never have physical bodies.	Soon will be annihilated by Jehovah.
The Afterlife:					
After death:	Judgement/Resurrection.	Repeated reincarnations.	Non-existence.	Second chance to receive Mormonism.	Unconscious until resurrection.
Heaven:	Place of joy with the Lord.	Union with the One.	In this life only.	3 degrees; highest--exaltation to a god.	Only for 144,000, rest on paradise earth.
Hell:	Eternal, conscious torment.	Bad thoughts.	Denied.	Punishment, but not necessarily eternal.	Annihilation into non-existence.
Human Suffering:					
Origin:	The Fall.	Law of karma.	Time + Chance.	Our desire to be like the Father.	Sin of Adam.
Final defeat by:	The Second Coming.	Human spiritual awareness.	Human efforts, if ever.	New cycle started on each new world.	Battle of Armageddon.

* *Darkness to Light,* Gary F. Zeolla, Vol. III, No. 4, 1993. *Note:* The number of sources consulted to compile the above table was too numerous to list here. But documentation for any specific point is available upon request.

Notable Objectives Most Frequently Observed in the Seminary Catalogues

- Emphasis on disciple-making non-existent for a high percentage of the seminaries studied—95%—or a very low priority?
- Careless concern for a true witness to the lost soul which should be the first order of business instead of academia first then our attention on the problem at hand.
- Very strong emphasis is placed on educational thrusts which prepares for the rigors of the ministerial office so that graduates may guide people of all ages in the rewarding and demanding ways of the Christian life, presenting the whole Gospel to the whole person, ministering to people in the home, the hospital, the community, and the world; fitting them to contribute effectively to the furtherance of the Gospel and the kingdom of God in fellowship with other Christian bodies of our time.
- Personal spiritual growth and formation of a deep walk with the Lord are attained by a passive development of campus atmosphere, fellowship, devotional life, and support-system. This learning is completely unrelated and disconnected from class work which prepares the student for a lifetime of teaching others how to achieve that very essential element of following the Lord with a true witness to the lost soul.
- Strong emphasis on seminary as a resource center for critical thought and research to maintain and nurture the historical, doctrinal character of the church.

- Narrow-mindedness is projected through clinging to confessions of faith and other longstanding (since the time of Constantine and of the Reformation) man contrived documents separated from Scriptures making it sound to the uninformed soul as true and pure Gospel which it is not! This is not deliberate, but it is time to review what we stand on, traditions of men or the pure Gospel of the shed blood of Jesus Christ.
- There is a definite overkill of Biblical scholarship which demonstrates a propensity to put great emphasis on producing great Sunday service messages (sermons) that elevate the deliverer to near sainthood.

17

Liberation of Pastors, Priests and Rabbis

Pastors, priests, and rabbis, along with the church, my burden has been very great for you. You spend a lifetime in the Word of God, pastoring the flock, counseling many parishioners on a daily basis, praying for the many needs within your flock, struggling with shortage of funds, battling abortion, anti-Semitism, drug abuse, street people, teen pregnancy and teen crime. At times it seems you should have been a policeman. The burden is overwhelming and society surrounding you adds to the list daily. It is my sincere hope and prayer for you, that you, in particular, will find some sense of direction for personal relief from the torment and struggles of mind and body within these pages.

This study is a direct result of a longtime observation of many pastors in many denominations. Some observations and experiences were very personal by actual membership in several denominations and in several parts of the United States. This experience began in the three main Lutheran church bodies beginning in 1950 and extending through 1977, the Evangelical Free Church and the Fundamental Baptist Church from 1977 to 1988. Since that time to the present I have worshiped with several different independent denominations.

All of this church experience occurred from Pennsylvania to Texas, from Washington to Nebraska, from Ohio to Kentucky, from Washington, D.C., to Maryland, and then Pennsylvania. I have sat under the ministry of many wonderful ministers during this time and my desire to find the truth and expose that which was hindering all of mankind from becoming true servants of God these many, many years kept growing. The first part of the truth I was seeking all of my life I found while attending special Bible study sessions held in the headquarters of the Office, Chief of Engineers, Washington, D.C.

The first part of the truth I found during the course of that study was: I needed to confess to God that I was a sinner, repent, thank God for sending His Son to die and shed His blood on the cross for my sins and ask Christ Jesus to come into my life and guide my life. I did not learn at that time that I had to allow Jesus Christ to be Lord and Master of my life. That was the second part of the truth I was seeking all my life. That happened probably two years later. Since that time, about 1979, I have asked God to show me any and all areas of my life He wanted to change. Until we become an obedient and humble being, we cannot please God. We might never arrive completely because we still do battle with the evil one, but God knows the motives of our heart. If we do not please God by working on agreeing with Him that we have areas of our life to be changed and become more like Jesus He cannot work in our life.

Why all this personal testimony?—only until I had Christ Jesus as Lord and Master of my life could God begin to work in my life, because until you have that personal relationship you can never be led by the Holy Spirit. (See John 3:3-8.) You see, I never found these truths sitting under all of those ministers and I do not mean to say that derogatorily. I was not guided by the church system to the truth I had sought all my life. I can only say the likelihood just was not there.

To bring into focus this point I will relate to you a conversation I had with a parachurch servant of God in Cedar Rapids, Iowa, several years ago. He told me that a pastor can only take the people of his charge as close to God as that pastor's personal walk, knowledge and conviction permit. In simple words, if the pastor does not have Jesus Christ as personal Lord and Master, he can only take his people through the motions of that experience not to the actual experience. This holds true for the membership at large of any church. If each individual is not saved they do not have the wherewithal to guide a fellow human being to the Lordship of the Lord Jesus Christ and if the pastor, priest or rabbi does not have Christ Jesus as Lord and Master of their life, they cannot be a producer of disciples for the Lord Jesus Christ.

In the beginning of his book, *A Handbook of Concepts for Living,*[1] Bill Bright makes the point that many pastors and leaders in the "Christian movement" do not know for certain that they will go to heaven when they die. The author agrees that pastors and church leaders in high places need to be discipled to focus on producing people for the kingdom of heaven instead of creating a larger church attendance with larger budgets. A few evangelists of our day recognize this problem, but because so few professional people in the Christian movement have never been prepared for the job of witnessing and discipling, this work is left undone a high percentage of the time and our church system shows it. All of this is negative rhetoric to you who have been there. One might say once more, it is easy to condemn, but to put your shoulder to the wheel is another story. It is also easy for the other side to say thou shall not judge. If in fact you are very pleased and happy where you are and what you see as a great accomplishment forget immediately what you read here and go on with the great sermon syndrome, but if you feel only a little tingle of irritation and a whole lot of burden for those people out there who need you and who need to know the complete truth in God's Word—then you need to take the bull by the horns and turn the world upside down for the Lord.

Pastor C. Marlin Hardman[2] set out ten effects on our Christian life and behavior caused by our failure to follow the Biblical principles for the true following of God:

> "1. It will cause us to get involved in non-priority issues. [Matt. 15:1,2]
> 2. It will cause us to break the commandments of God. [Matt. 15:3; Mark 7:9]
> 3. It will cause us to invalidate (or weaken) the Word of God. [Matt. 15:4-6]
> 4. It will make hypocrites out of us. [Matt. 15:7-9]
> 5. It will take us captive and cause the Holy Spirit to cease to be the controlling emphasis in our lives. [Col. 2:8]
> 6. It will make us zealous for the wrong things. [Gal. 1:13,14]
> 7. It will make us say no to God. [Luke 6:46; Acts 10:14; Acts Chap. 10 in its entirety]
> 8. It will cause us to develop unbiblical attitudes towards others. [Acts 10:28]
> 9. It will make us dull in our witness. [Acts 10:22,29–Peter was told why previously]
> 10. It will cause us to argue when we should be rejoicing. [Acts 11:1,2]"

The most important work which is receiving nearly zero attention in our churches is discipling. Our Lord gave us the complete instructions as to why we need to produce disciples and He also gave us all we need to know about how to go about producing disciples.

Facing the most popular subject of our Lord—discipling—you might raise some very important questions concerning: *Why do we need to disciple members (those who attend) of this congregation?* The reason why . . . To develop all people for the personal discovery of Biblical meaning and Biblical living in all areas of life and ministry for effective soul-winning. We also have a desire to be used of God to change Biblical living from a spectator to a participant activity thereby preparing the saints for ministry.

Before you make your decision on whether or not to form discipling classes in lieu of Sunday school classes on a regular basis, I suggest you read the following five books:

1. *Unleashing the Church,* F.R. Tillapaugh, 1982.
2. *When All Else Fails . . . Read the Directions,* Bob Smith, 1974.
3. *Rut, Rot, or Revival,* A.W. Tozer, 1992.
4. *Out of the Fury,* Eliezer Urbach, 1987.
5. *Hitler's Cross,* Erwin W. Lutzer, 1995.

Next, I list some of the very best discipling tools available anywhere:

1. *Weaving the Word into our Walk,* Reuben L. Ewert, Living the Truth Ministries, South Bend, IN.
2. *One-to-One Discipling,* Al and Lorraine Broom, Multiplication Ministries, Vista, CA.

3. *The Shepherd's Guidebook,* Ralph W. Neighbour, Jr., Touch Publications, Inc., Houston, TX.
4. *Growing Strong in God's Family,* The Navigators, Colorado Springs, CO.
5. *Advenures in Soul-Winning,* a four part video series, Ken Anderson Films, Winona Lake, IN.

If you feel comfortable that all people who attend your services on a regular basis are truly saved—you should not develop a discipling class.

One of the greatest joys of following Jesus Christ is hearing or reading the good news about someone having found the truth of the mercies of God and the work of the Holy Spirit in the life of one seeking God. Such joy is in the story of a Roman Catholic Priest, Rev. Juan Baptista Treccani-Montini finding . . .

Peace[3]

> "I was born in a simple peasant home in a small town of the valleys of Brescia, Italy, on December 8, 1933. My father, by tradition and belief a Roman Catholic, was of the patriarchal family of Treccani-MONTINI. (Pope Paul VI is from the Montini family.) My mother, who was of the Lampugnani-Barbierri family, with sincerity professed and observed scrupulously all the precepts and mandates of the Roman Church. From the two families, that of my father and my mother, have come great personalities in the Roman clergy.
>
> When I was just a very young boy my mother taught me the doctrine of the Roman Catholic church. As a little child, I went to the church to learn the rites and ceremony of the Church. There

was something in my heart which I could not explain to the people I knew. The Roman Catholic church taught about God, but I could not fully understand. My heart was hungry for something more—something better.

When I was ten years old I visited a Roman Catholic seminary. I did lots of penance and mortification in my body. I was serving the church as an altar boy; but nothing I did brought me peace. I wanted to be a priest that I might give my life to serve God. I went to my father and expressed my desire to be a priest. He said, 'Now it is wartime and you are the youngest son. Stay home!' But my heart was consumed with the desire to know God, and to serve Him. I went to a farmer and asked for work so I could earn some money to pay my way to go to the seminary and study for the priesthood. My mother prepared everything in secret for me to go. On September 8, 1943, while the airplanes were bombing the cities I left my home to go to the seminary, in the city of Alba, Cuneo, in the north of Italy. I entered the seminary because I wanted to do everything possible to please God. Here I spent five years of secondary study.

But where was God? I did not find Him at the altars of the church, or in the ceremonies. I could not find Him either in the rituals of the church, in penance, or in obeying my superiors.

When I was fifteen, I received my robes. When I came to the beautiful city of Rome, and went into the great basilica of St. Peter, my heart was moved at the great beauty I saw there. I saw treasures of silver and gold, and much beauty, but where was God?

Within a few days, I would get to see the Pope. As the golden trumpet sounded, the priests raised the Pope up to their shoulders to present him to the people; but as the Pope entered, though my heart longed to feel the presence of God, I did not.

When I looked at the Pope I could not find any kind of humility. Jesus went to Calvary with a crown of thorns, but the Pope stood before us with a crown of gold, made from forty pounds of pure gold. Even the kings of this world have one crown, but the Pope has three. I knew he was not the vicar of Christ, he couldn't be!

My heart was hungry to know God. I did penance and hurt my own body in an attempt to find God. I used chains of iron to hit myself in my search for God. They used a belt with hundreds and hundreds of nails in it, which they put around my body, as a means to find peace.

To get this peace which I could not find, I went to another seminary where they had more doctrine and more penance. But peace never came to me.

Later I went to a different sanctuary in Europe, trying to get to the feet of the Virgin Mary to find peace for my soul. My heart was moved, and I cried and wept before the statues, but when I left the church what was my position with God? The same? Or worse? I could *not* find peace at the feet of those statues.

During the month of March 1956, a few months before I was to be ordained as a priest, I received word that my father was dying. I requested permission from my superiors, but the church forbade me to go to my home to see my dying father.

For as many years as I could remember, I went to the priest and made confession of my sins. I tried to confess everything in my heart, that I might obtain peace. There was one priest to whom I confessed who really knew my heart. At this particular time I asked him, 'Please can't you give me some peace?' He could not, but he recommended I read some biographies of the saints in the Roman Catholic Church.

I followed his advice and began reading some of the stories about the Roman Catholic saints who had given their lives to the church in search for peace. I discovered they did not find peace. How could they be saints, when many were afraid to meet God?

The following day, I was to go to the altar and receive my ordination as a priest. I cried, 'Please, today, before I get ordained, give me some peace!' The priest looked at me, 'I cannot give you peace, because I do not have peace myself.'

I was ordained August 15, 1956. The Roman Catholic church teaches that the Mass is the renewing of the sacrifice of Calvary. I took the sacraments in my hands, the bread and the cup, but I knew the Lord was not dwelling at the altar. I had been taught I would see God at the altar . . . it was a holy place . . . but I could not see Him. 'Where are you God?' I cried from the depths of my heart.

At this particular time of my life, Pope Paul was the archbishop of Milan. One day he came to me and said, 'We must create a missionary center in the southern part of Argentina, in Patagonia, and we are going to send you there as a missionary to assist the Bishop.'

I arrived in Argentina in the year 1958. Here I found a people who didn't know much about religion or God. I did not know one word of the Spanish language, but I went there to find something better for my soul.

I spent the next few years in Comodoro Rivadavian, serving as the assistant to the Bishop and I was also the priest for this area. None of my duties were sufficient to bring peace to my heart. Oh, the emptiness in my heart!

One day in a little town near Esquel, I was walking in the mountains, and went to the little chapel on top of the mountain to pray to the Virgin Mary to give me peace. When I returned from praying, I met an Araucon Indian. He said, 'What are you searching and looking for in that chapel?' As I was a priest, naturally, I was ashamed to tell him what I was looking for, but I saw in his face something different. I gained the courage to tell him, 'I went there to try to find peace.' He said, 'At the feet of Jesus, we find peace.'

What kind of Jesus was he talking to me about? I knew a Christ; a statue of wood, and of metal, and many other plastic materials, but what kind was he talking about that gives peace?

The good native Indian told me that if I would go to his church and just sit at the feet of Christ and listen to His Word He would give me peace. But me, a Roman Catholic priest, in my position in the city, how could I go inside a Protestant church?

I went home, and there the Lord started to deal with my heart. It was snowing very hard that day, but there was a greater storm in my heart. I started out for the Protestant church, looking everywhere to see if anybody was watching me. This was the first time I had gone inside an Evangelical church. I expected to see pictures of saints on the walls, but when I looked around there were no pictures, no statues.

On June 21, 1961, for the first time in my life, I heard the message of the Word of God, in its simplicity. I knew the Jesus they were talking about was stretching forth His hand toward me. He was not a visible Christ made of wood or metal, but a resurrected Christ who was alive.

Still my heart was full of fear. I did not want to leave the luxury and the life I was living. My relatives, my family, my friends . . . what would they say about me? If I took this step of faith, what would happen? For several months I visited the Evangelical church. My soul was thirsty for the living water.

The day finally came when I met Jesus . . . the peace giver. On October 31, 1961, I had organized a procession of people to march through the streets of the town with a statue of one of the saints. God was dealing very strongly with my heart, and I was uneasy . . . I really wanted to be at the Evangelical church and not leading these people in this procession. We began marching with the people shouting, 'Christ is King.' However, He was not King in my heart, and I knew these people needed to know the living Christ. The Bishop and many priests were present for the procession that afternoon. I asked the Bishop, 'What is the good of all these things if Jesus is not King in our hearts?' He said, 'You sound like a Protestant!'

Immediately I left the procession and went right to the Evangelical church. The priests and the bishop followed me, and tried to get me to stop and come back, but my course was set. There was no turning back now, for I knew I had to have the knowledge of a living Christ, in my own heart. This day was different from all other days. The Lord was knocking at my heart's door, and I opened it, and let Him in. He was waiting and longing to bring me His peace.

The Indian who had invited me to the church was preaching. The Spirit of God was speaking to me. I felt the drops of the precious blood of Jesus, coming in as a stream of living water to cleanse my heart from all sin. I was a Roman Catholic priest, but a sinner without salvation. Now I knew I was a sinner, saved by grace. I felt the peace, which I had been searching for all my life. The peace which I had been looking for through the churches, through penance and mortification of my body, I now found in Christ. The chains of my religion which had bound me for many years and made me a slave, were broken. The Spirit of Christ swept over my soul like a mighty river, bringing me 'Peace, sweet peace.'

Then the brethren told me, 'The Word of God says, you must be baptized in water.' My heart was full of joy and peace was reigning. Before, I had great interest in religion; now I wanted to have great zeal for the things of God. I had tried to find Him in my religion, but I never found Him; now I found Him and I wanted to serve Him.

We went to the Esquel River, near the mountain, and I was baptized in water to show the world I had found Christ. The people who were marching through the town with the statue of the saint, left the procession and came to the river to see me being baptized. The radios and newspapers started to tell about what had taken place in my life, and I praised God in my heart.

I returned to my home in Argentina. I had a car and the necessary things to make life comfortable. While I was gone, they went into my home and destroyed everything I had. They persecuted me, and tried to do everything possible to cause me to come back to the church. The same students I had taught tried to stone me. Even the grocers and shops refused to let me buy. However, none of these things took away the peace which I had in my heart. I counted it a joy to be able to suffer for Christ, even in a small way.

I began to serve the Lord in a little town with just a few houses, nestled in the Andes mountains. Here, working among the natives of the land, I am

> full of joy as I tell them about Jesus. The Lord spoke to my heart 'The old man should die completely.' I should forget everything in the past, even what I had learned, so God could work in my life.
>
> There in the mountains, among the Indians, I started to work for the Lord. My first roof was a tree. The first seat in my church was a stone; but I knew in this church people would come to know Christ.
>
> I wanted to contact my mother in Italy and tell her what Jesus did for me. How could I do it? When a Roman Catholic priest is converted they even take their names from their family. Could my mother now understand the change that had taken place in my life? I prayed and fasted for several days and I said, 'Lord this same power that changed my life, can change my mother far away.' There is no distance with God. I wrote my mother a letter and told her what Jesus had done in my life. The Spirit of God went with that letter and worked in her heart as she read it. She wrote me that the same Holy Spirit which filled my heart with peace now also filled her heart with peace.
>
> Yes, I have found real peace at the feet of the living Christ. I cannot be silent, for there are those who need to know this peace which Jesus gives. 'Peace I leave with you, My peace I give unto you . . .' (John 14:27)"

There are millions of people all around us who are hurting spiritually as well as physically. For many this goes on for years. Those who are hurting physically you can recognize very easily, but those who hurt spiritually usually agonize through their hurt all alone. The person in the following story relates the mental agony he experienced over a very long period of time.

How A Rabbi Found Peace—A Personal Testimony,[4] Rabbi Max Wertheimer (1863-1941)

"Born in Germany of devout Orthodox Jewish parents, my first fifteen years were saturated with training in Orthodox Judaism. Then I began my studies toward a career and was apprenticed to a manufacturer doing office work. Although I continued to read the prayers and attend synagogue, my worldly associates led me into sinful pleasures, and I drifted from the faith of my fathers.

My parents sent me to America to pursue a classical education at the Hebrew Union College in Ohio. There were major adjustments to be made, but I finished my training in all phases of Hebrew learning. Four years after completing my undergraduate work I received my master's degree.

Having become proficient in the translation of Hebrew into the vernacular and with a broad knowledge of Jewish history, I was ordained and inducted into rabbinical office. I served ten years in my first charge, receiving many tokens of affection from my flock. I contributed much to their knowledge of the social, industrial, and economic problems of the day.

I spoke on monotheism, ethical culture, and the moral systems of the Jews. On Sabbath mornings, I gave addresses on the Pentateuch, and on Sundays I taught from eight in the morning to five in the evening with only an hour's break for dinner.

I became popular as a public speaker and was often asked to speak in Christian churches. Well do I recall the day when I proudly stood before an audience of professing Christians and told them why I was a Jew and would not believe in their Christ as my Messiah and Savior. I gloried in the

Reform Judaism that acknowledged no need of atoning sacrifice for sin—a religion of ethics which quieted qualms of conscience through a smug self-righteousness.

In that audience sat a humble, elderly woman who prayed, 'O God, bring Dr. Wertheimer to realize his utter need of that Savior he so boastingly rejects! Bring him, if necessary, to the very depths in order that he may know his need of my Lord Jesus Christ.'

What did I need of Jesus? I was perfectly satisfied with life. My wife was young, attractive, and accomplished. I was rabbi of the B'nai Yeshorum Synagogue, lived in a beautiful home, enjoyed a place of prominence in the community where I spoke in every denominational church, was honorary member of the Ministerial Association, served as chaplain in the Masonic Lodge, and fared sumptuously every day.

Suddenly, there came a change. My wife became seriously ill and soon died, leaving me a distraught widower with two small children. I could not sleep. I walked the streets striving to find something that would make me forget the void in my life. My dreams were shattered. Where was comfort to be found? I called on the God of my fathers, but the heavens seemed as brass. How could I speak words of comfort to others when my own sorrow had brought me to despair? I delved into Spiritism, Theosophy and Christian Science, only to find them futile and hopeless.

I decided that I must resign and take time to think things through. I was perplexed about one thing in particular: Where was the spirit and soul of my loved one who had made my existence so sweet? What had become of all her faculties, the intents and purposes of that active, keen mind? I turned to the Bible for an answer.

Again I studied Judaism, but it answered no questions; it satisfied no craving in my heart. Then I began to read the New Testament, comparing it with the Old. As I pondered over and meditated on many passages, one in particular made a definite impression. In the fifty-third chapter of Isaiah, I was perplexed by the expression, '. . . My righteous servant,' found in the eleventh verse. This was the only mention of that phrase I could find in either Testament. We have, 'David, my servant,' 'Isaiah, my servant,' 'Daniel, my servant,' but here it is, 'My righteous servant.'

I said to myself, *Who is that righteous servant? To whom does the prophet refer?* I argued, *Whoever that 'righteous servant' of Jehovah is, of one thing I am sure: He is not Israel, because the prophet declares Israel to be a sinful nation, a people laden with iniquity, a leprous nation. The righteous servant of Jehovah must be one who is holy. If it isn't Israel, who could it be?* I decided it must be Isaiah. But in Isaiah chapter 6 I found it could never be the prophet, for he confesses himself to be a guilty sinner and a man of unclean lips in God's sight. 'My righteous servant.' Who could it be?

I began to study the context and in Isaiah 50:6 I found, 'I offered my back to those who beat me.' Then I read how the chapter began: 'This is what the Lord says.' I asked, *Does God have a back? Did he give it to those who beat him?* Then I read, 'My cheeks to those who pulled out my beard,' and how he did not hide his face 'from mocking and spitting.' I asked myself, *When did Jehovah have these human characteristics? When and why did he suffer these indignities?*

In my confusion, I began to read Isaiah from the beginning. I was stopped at the sixth verse of chapter nine: 'For to us a child is born, to us a son is given, and the government will be upon his shoulders. And he will be called Wonderful Counselor, Mighty God, Everlasting Father, Prince of Peace.' Here was a most incomprehensible thing!

I was suddenly faced with the doctrine of the Trinity. What now about our familiar monotheistic slogan, *Shema Israel, Adonai Eloheynu, Adonai ehad* ('Hear O Israel, the Lord our God is one Lord')? Upon that word *ehad* ('one'), the entire philosophy of Judaism is based. I had been taught by the rabbis that *ehad* means 'absolute unity.' I began to study that word, and found to my amazement it was used of Adam and Eve who became 'one.' It was used again when the spies returned from Canaan with a cluster of grapes (*eshkol ehad*). Again it is found when the 'men of Judah' stood up as 'one man' (*eesh ehad*). Suddenly, I was struck with the error I had believed and proclaimed all through my ministry. *Ehad* cannot mean 'absolute unity,' but must refer to composite unity.

Next I began to search for the name of Jesus in the Old Testament. In my study, I found that 275 years before Christ, King Ptolemy Philadelphus summoned men from Palestine and commanded them to translate the Hebrew Scriptures into the Greek vernacular. They took the Pentateuch first, and when they came to 'Joshua' they translated it *Yesous,* written with a circumflex over it to show that there had been a suppression of the Hebrew that could not be expressed in Greek. When Joshua went into Canaan with the other eleven spies, he was called *Yehoshua* ('Jehovah is Savior'). That is exactly what the word 'Jesus' means.

I could hold out in unbelief no longer. I was convinced of the truth of God as it is in Christ Jesus. I cried, 'Lord, I believe that as Jehovah Yesous you made the atonement for me. I believe you made provision for me! From henceforth I will publicly confess Yeshua as my Savior and Lord!' Thus, after months of searching, I was convinced that Jesus was the righteous servant of Jehovah, *Jehovah-tsidkenu,* 'The Lord our righteousness.'

While I served as a rabbi, I had yearned to give the bereaved some hope and comfort, but I could not give what I did not possess. Now I could approach those in heart-breaking grief and tragedy and give them the satisfying words of the Lord Jesus, 'I am the resurrection and the life. He who believes in me will live, even though he dies; and whoever lives and believes in me will never die.' And again, 'I tell you the truth; whoever hears my word and believes him who sent me has eternal life and will not be condemned; he has crossed over from death to life.' There is but one eternal life, and one source of eternal life; that is God's Son. What a great and glorious message we, his redeemed ones, are commissioned to deliver today."

> Missing here is the testimony by a protestant pastor who found the truth concerning his salvation in the Lord Jesus Christ. I am certain there are pastors who have a similar testimony as the Priest and the Rabbi, but I have failed to find it in print. Just to mention this very important thought might be sufficient cause to arouse the conscience of some minister who can relate to this heart wrenching thought.

18

Did God Really Want Man to Create the Church and Christianity?

Historical Background Surrounding the Word Church

Up until the time of the invention of the printing press, Satan did not have any problem suppressing the expansion of true followers of the Lord or those who attempted to expand the true kingdom of God. History tells us that ungodly people, i.e. the pseudo-Christianity leaders, had them killed by burning, hanging, cutting off their head, drowning, and other means in the northern, western, and southern countries of Europe.[1,2] When the printing press came into being, about 1450, Satan's people could no longer keep up with the suppression of the spread of the truth in God's Word by barbarism (eight million books were printed and sold during the years 1450-1500).[3] At this same time the Reformation was in full swing and more and more people were now finding the truths of the Word of God. This caused Satan's people to do "something" to counteract this explosion of the truth in God's Word to all the people of the world, so the Geneva Bible was published with the introduction of the word church in the New Testament at Matthew 16:18. "I also say to you that you are Peter, and upon this rock I will build my church; and the gates of Hades shall not prevail against it." This strengthened the powerful "religious institution" already in place. The proof that a very powerful religious organization existed at that time rests in the facts and testimonies presented by Martin Luther and others who exposed the enemy of God.[4]

At about the same time (invention and early application of the printing press to publishing the constant flow of new Bible versions for a period of a little over 100 years, the furor of which is just now being equaled by the fast moving information of our "high-tech" of today) several men came to the front. God once again raised up men for Himself that Satan's people could not kill—Menno Simons, Martin Luther, John Knox, John Calvin, Ulrich Zwingli—and some, Satan's people did kill—William Tyndale, John Huss and many others during the time the true men of God fought the forces of Satan's pseudo-Christianity (the period 1400-1600s) to replace that darkness with the light of Jesus Christ. That period of time in the history of the world since the birth, death and resurrection of our Lord and Savior Jesus Christ for the Gentiles and the Messiah for the Jews shows us very clearly that a spiritual battle raged between pseudo-Christianity and the true followers of God's Word. That battle continues to rage today because pseudo-Christianity permeated the very fabric of the Gospel of Jesus Christ with traditions of men and the development of many interpretations of the Word of God thus producing the multitudes of denominations and varying belief systems. Our world remains Satan's domain for those who are without Christ Jesus.

Those true men of God, mentioned above, working in the almighty power of God brought into play a great movement among the God-fearing people of Western Europe. That movement, the front runner of and the full power of the Reformation caused the true believers to flee the suppression of their faith led by the pseudo-Christianity leaders who also held control of civil power of government, thus the great nation of America, with freedom of worship of God was born. This great land of America was being put in place by God at one and the same time all of the above events and happenings were going on in Western Europe. Christopher Columbus did not discover America by chance and by the power of men. Christian Eilers[5] points out how the Almighty power of God was behind the exposition that landed on October 12, 1492, near the shores of that land that came to be called America.

America is the only nation with so much God-given freedom to worship God in the history of the world except Israel. Many people say America is the greatest nation in the world today, but Israel is the greatest nation before God in the world; America is the second greatest. Don't ever forget who it is that gives power to nations and who it is that takes away power. America's greatness is not because of all the technology we possess, it is because of the freedom God gave each and every soul in America who claims the Lord Jesus Christ as personal Lord and Master. We do not want to overlook the fact that there is an evil force at work in this nation today which is working over time to destroy our freedom to give glory, honor and praise to God. That force, secular humanism combined with pseudo-Christianity is at work today in and through our educational and courts-of-law systems. It is at work in the church system, example: building unity of all beliefs into one ungodly world religion; the education system, example: sex education and distribution of condoms, making evolutionism a truth; prohibiting Bible study gatherings, prohibiting prayer at community events; the civil and criminal law system, example: removing prayer and God from our school system, seat belt law, nonsmoking areas, Roe vs. Wade, plea bargains, criminal investigations of private individuals without incriminating evidence (guilty before proven innocent), removing reminders from public buildings that God is our guidance in America and same-sex marriage; our social system, example: street people's condition completely accepted, drug trafficking accepted and managed by those in political power, politics accepted as if it was established by law; forms of gambling used to raise public funds behind the smoke screen, we are helping senior citizens; and the very heart of our government system, example: professed homosexuals and lesbians in high office, squandering and blatant misuse of tax monies, attempt to remove Godly thought from the work place, foreign interests more important than welfare of U.S. citizens, big business interest and dollar protection for them more important than the people.

Church attendees depend to a great extent not only on the wisdom and knowledge of those with a lifelong devotion to the search for the truth in God's Word concerning the word church, but above all else, they depend on where those individuals stood or stand with God in their personal life. This pronouncement applies even more importantly to those who performed the work of translating God's Word into the many different versions of the Bible. While God's Word was pure from the first day God gave it to the original writers to set down on parchment, all kinds of people have, in the meantime, been attempting to make the Bible more clear, put it into the modern language and many other reasons for changing and improving the original God-given meaning of the true guidance for our life with Him and through His Son. We need to be certain that the teaching we are sitting under is truth.

God did not direct man through His Word, to develop the church system. God did direct man, Moses to be exact, to construct one and only one Tabernacle. The temporary Tabernacle was just that, so as His people wandered in the wilderness for forty years the Tabernacle was set up and taken down whenever and wherever God so directed. That original Tabernacle was used over a very long period of time, until the stationary Temple was completed by Solomon in 1005 B.C. That Temple was permanent until God allowed it to be destroyed by the Babylonians in 586 B.C. The Temple was rebuilt by Zerubbabel in 516 B.C. Herod removed the second Temple and rebuilt it in 16 B.C. That Temple that Jesus taught in was destroyed in 70 A.D. by the Romans. The author supposes that God gave His people 40 years to make the transition from animal sacrifices and offerings to true worship as a son of God in spirit and truth. God used those 40 years to demonstrate the worship by those persons who accepted their Messiah as Lord and Master and who no longer had to sacrifice animals for their sins because the Messiah did this once and for all time and eternity, for both Jews and Gentiles alike. The transition of the Law of Moses to the grace of God was too much for the leadership of the Jews to understand and accept. (Discussion is given on pages 24-33.)

The synagogue concept came into use while the Judeans were in exile in Babylonia and was used for the purpose of teaching and reading the Torah. Christ used the synagogue often for that purpose. Only males were allowed to enter the synagogue for study purposes. The Jews devised this method for keeping only a small portion of the Mosaic Covenant with God since they did not have access to the Temple for sacrificing. No other Temple, house of worship, nor any other building was directed by God for man to construct for Him or for man to worship God. All that we know today as a cathedral, synagogue, temple, chapel, church, mission and the like are traditions of men. We will not find in God's Word any direction from God to build a building of any kind to worship Him in for we are the temple of the living God, those who have Christ Jesus as personal Lord and Master. (See 2 Corinthians 6:16.)

Just to say we are saved by the simple altar call, by baptism, by frequent participation in the Mass, and the like which fall short of accepting Christ as our personal savior, always remains just that—an event in our life. Those who establish themselves as a "member" of a particular church, has no meaning to God. That step in faith in accepting Christ as our Savior has to be immediately followed by making Him Lord and Master of our life. This is called discipling. We enjoy constant worship of the Lord as we go about living our life for Him.

Before Christ, man, specifically the Hebrews/Israelites, had to follow the Mosaic Law, and sacrifices and offerings at the Tabernacle/Temple were made as prescribed by God for sin. One of the differences between then, before Christ, and now with Christ, is, God forgives our sins because Christ became sin in our place (propitiation). Those who have Christ as personal savior have life. (See 1 John 5:12.) So our worship of God needs to be on a continuing basis. We should not go to a centrally located structure with the idea that is the place and the only place where the man in charge will cause us to confess our sins, once each week, and receive forgiveness.

The Birth of the Word Church

No one will find in the Word of God conclusive evidence that the word church could be derived from the Greek word *ekklesia*. *Ekklesia* was the Greek word used in the original MSS (manuscripts) at Matthew 16:18 after the death of Christ. It is the word *ekklesia* (*ek* = out of, *kaleo* = to call) that is being looked at in depth at this time. The scholars of the Bible from about the fourth century A.D. to the sixteenth century A.D worked diligently on the Greek word, *ekklesia*, trying to solve its meaning and theologians since about the last half of the sixteenth century have accepted the long-standing theologically determined meaning of this very precious word of God to mean "church." Theologians and Bible scholars of today agree that the work of translators of bygone years, did in fact find a way to come up with a different meaning of the word *ekklesia* based on elapsed time, updated and common usage, changing spirituality and modernization, to mean the word church. The words *edhah* and *kahal* (congregation or assembly) convey the most accurate understanding of how the people gathered together to worship the Lord.

We have to go back and find out what our Lord and God really provided for mankind when He sent His only begotten Son to die on the cross. Was it so that mankind could be the prime mover of the people through a worldly organized system to take the people to God through a worldly appointed guru, or was this the last call by God to all humankind through complete divine intervention which was designed to restore mankind unto God? I am only presenting the facts of current and ancient history as appears in many papers and documents for you to make judgments as to the accuracy and helpfulness in arriving at the truth of the word church.

Table 5 shows that Luther and Tyndale translated the Greek word *ekklesia*, *gemeine* (community, congregation) and congregation respectively in the early sixteen hundred's. Stern translated *ekklesia* (community, congregation, Messianic Community) in 1989 in his *Jewish New Testament* version. The Latin and Greek New Testaments use the correct words *Ecclesia* and *Ekklesia*. The New English version vacillates back and forth from church to congregation, never reaching unanimity. Tyndale and Luther did not use the word church nor the German word *kirche*. Tyndale's Bible (New Testament) was published in 1525 and Luther's New Testament Bible was published in 1532. The earliest time when the word "church" first appeared in a Bible translation was the Geneva Bible in 1560.

In the book, *The Making of the English Bible,*[6] Samuel McComb relates the names of the men who produced the Geneva version of the Bible; William Whittingham, Anthony Gilby, and Thomas Sampson. All three followed and were adherents of the Calvinistic Reformers. They were all in Geneva because the views of the Reformers were not permitted in England under the rule of Bloody Mary, Queen of Scotts, so they all went into exile in Switzerland during her reign. No original translation was performed by these men.

> "The basis of the Genevan version of the Old Testament was Coverdale's Great Bible, which was carefully compared to the Hebrew, and in the New

Testament, Wittingham's version (which was itself a revision of Tyndale's last revision), revised by the help of Beza's Latin version and of the Huguenot version of the Bible edited by Calvin." . . . "The main weakness of the Geneva Bible version was its too great reliance on Beza's text and the dogmatic colouring of its notes."[7]

TABLE 5
BIBLE VERSIONS

Bible Reference	King James Version[2]	New English[2]	Luther[1]	Jewish New Testament[2]	Latin[1]	NIV[2]	Tyndale[1]	Greek New Testament[1]	New American Standard[2]	Geneva[2]
Matt. 16:18	Church	Church	Gemeine	Community	Ecclesiam	Church	Congregation	Ekklesian	Church	Church
Matt. 18:17	Church	Congregation	Gemeine	Congregation	Ecclesiae	Church	Congregation	Ekklesia	Church	Church
Acts 2:47	Church	Added to their no.	Gemeine	Adding to them	-------	Added to their no.	Congregation	Ekklesia	Adding to their no.	Church
Acts 8:1	Church	Church	Gemeine	Community	Ecclesia	Church	Congregation	Ekklesian	Church	Church
Acts 8:3	Church	Church	Gemeine	Community	Ecclesiam	Church	Congregation	Ekklesian	Church	Church
Acts 11:26	Church	Congregation	Gemeine	Congregation	Ecclesia	Church	Congregation	Ekklesia	Church	Church
Acts 14:23	Church	Congregation	Gemeinen	Congregation	Ecclesias	Church	Congregation	Ekklesian	Church	Church
Acts 15:3	Church	Congregation	Gemeine	Congregation	Ecclesia	Church	Congregation	Ekklesias	Church	Church
Acts 15:4	Church	Church	Gemeine	Community	Ecclesia	Church	Congregation	Ekklesias	Church	Church
Acts 15:22	Church	Church	Gemeine	Community	Ecclesia	Church	Congregation	Ekklesia	Church	Church
Acts 18:22	Church	Church	Gemeine	Community	Ecclesiam	Church	Congregation	Ekklesian	Church	Church
Acts 20:28	Church	Church	Gemeine	Community	Ecclesiam	Church	Congregation	Ekklesian	Church	Church
Rom. 16:1	Church	Congregation	Gemeine	Congregation	Ecclesiae	Church	Congregation	Ekklesias	Church	Church
Rom. 16:4	Churches	Congregations	Gemeinen	Communities	Ecclesiae	Churches	Congregation	Ekklesiai	Churches	Churches
Rom 16:5	Church	Congregation	Gemeine	Congregation	Ecclesiam	Church	Congregation	Ekklesian	Church	Church
Rom. 16:16	Churches	Congregations	Gemeinen	Congregations	Ecclesiae	Churches	Congregations	Ekklesiai	Churches	Churches
1 Cor. 1:2	Church	Congregation	Gemeine	Community	Ecclesiae	Church	Congregation	Ekklesia	Church	Church
1 Cor. 4:17	Church	Congregations	Gemeinen	Congregation	Ecclesia	Church	Congregations	Ekklesia	Church	Church
1 Cor. 10:32	Church	Church	Gemeine	Community	Ecclesiae	Church	Congregation	Ekklesia	Church	Church
1 Cor. 11:18	Church	Congregation	Gemeine	Congregation	Ecclesiam	Church	Congregation	Ekklesia	Church	Church
1 Cor. 11:22	Church	Church	Gemeine	Community	Ecclesiam	Church	Congregation	Ekklesias	Church	Church
1 Cor. 12:28	Church	Community	Gemeine	Community	Ecclesia	Church	Congregation	Ekklesia	Church	Church

[1] Based on translations – existing manuscripts used [2] Based on interpretations of previous versions

TABLE 5
BIBLE VERSIONS—CONTINUED

Bible Reference	King James Version[2]	New English[2]	Luther[1]	Jewish New Testament[2]	Latin[1]	NIV[2]	Tyndale[1]	Greek New Testament[1]	New American Standard[2]	Geneva[2]
1 Cor. 14:4	Church	Community	Gemeine	Congregation	Ecclesiam	Church	Congregation	Ekklesian	Church	Church
1 Cor. 14:5	Church	Community	Gemeine	Congregation	Ecclesia	Church	Congregation	Ekklesia	Church	Church
1 Cor. 14:35	Church	Congregation	Gemeine	Congregational	Ecclesia	Church	Congregation	Ekklesia	Church	Church
1 Cor. 15:9	Church	Church	Gemeine	Community	Ecclesiam	Church	Congregation	Ekklesian	Church	Church
1 Cor. 16:19	Church	Congregations	Gemeine	Congregation	Ecclesia	Churches	Congregation	Ekklesiai	Church	Churches
2 Cor. 8:1	Churches	Congregations	Gemeinen	Congregations	Eccelesiis	Churches	Congregations	Ekklesiais	Churches	Churches
2 Cor. 11:8	Churches	Congregations	Gemeinen	Congregations	Ecclesias	Churches	Congregations	Ekklesiais	Churches	Churches
Gal. 1:2	Churches	Congregations	Gemeinen	Communities	Ecclesiis	Churches	Congregations	Ekklesiais	Churches	Churches
Gal. 1:13	Church	Church	Gemeine	Community	Ecclesiam	Church	Congregation	Ekklesian	Church	Church
Gal. 1:22	Churches	Congregations	Gemeinen	Congregations	Ecclesiis	Churches	Congregations	Ekklesiais	Churches	Churches
Eph. 1:22	Church	Church	Gemeine	Community	Ecclesiam	Church	Congregation	Ekklesia	Church	Church
Eph. 3:21	Church	Church	Gemeine	Community	Ecclesia	Church	Congregation	Ekklesia	Church	Church
Eph. 5:23	Church	Church	Gemeine	Community	Ecclesiae	Church	Congregation	Ekklesias	Church	Church
Eph. 5:24	Church	Church	Gemeine	Community	Ecclesia	Church	Congregation	Ekklesia	Church	Church
Eph. 5:25	Church	Church	Gemeine	Community	Ecclesiam	Church	Congregation	Ekklesian	Church	Church
Eph. 5:27	Church	Church	Gemeine	Community	Ecclesiam	Church	Congregation	Ekklesian	Church	Church
Eph. 5:29	Church	Church	Gemeine	Community	Ecclesiam	Church	Congregation	Ekklesian	Church	Church
Eph. 5:32	Church	Church	Gemeine	Community	Ecclesia	Church	Congregation	Ekklesian	Church	Church
Phil. 3:6	Church	Church	Gemeine	Community	Ecclesiam	Church	Congregation	Ekklesian	Church	Church
Col. 1:18	Church	Church	Gemeine	Community	Ecclesiae	Church	Congregation	Ekklesias	Church	Church
Col. 4:15	Church	Congregation	Gemeine	Congregation	Ecclesiam	Church	Congregation	Ekklesian	Church	Church
Col. 4:16	Church	Congregation	Gemeine	Congregation	Ecclesia	Church	Congregation	Ekklesia	Church	Church

[1] Based on translations – existing manuscripts used [2] Based on interpretations of previous versions

TABLE 5
BIBLE VERSIONS—CONTINUED

Bible Reference	King James Version [2]	New English [2]	Luther [1]	Jewish New Testament [2]	Latin [1]	NIV [2]	Tyndale [1]	Greek New Testament [1]	New American Standard [2]	Geneva [2]
1 Thes. 1:1	Church	Congregation	Gemeine	Community	Ecclesiae	Church	Congregation	Ekklesia	Church	Church
1 Thes. 2:14	Churches	Congregations	Gemeinen	Congregations	Ecclesiarum	Churches	Congregations	Ekklesian	Churches	Churches
1 Tim. 3:5	Church	Congregation	Gemeine	Community	Ecclesiae	Church	Congregation	Ekklesias	Church	Church
1 Tim. 3:15	Church	Church	Gemeine	Community	Ecclesia	Church	Congregation	Ekklesia	Church	Church
Heb. 12:23	Church	Assembly	Gemeine	Community	Ecclesiam	Church	Congregation	Ekklesia	Church	Congregation
1 Pet. 5:13	Church	Who dwells in Babylon	------	Congregation	Ecclesia	She in Babylonia	Those at Babylon	-----------	She who is in Babylonia	Church
Rev. 1:11	Churches	Churches	Gemeinen	Communities	Ecclesiis	Churches	Congregations	Ekklesiais	Churches	Churches
Rev. 1:20	Churches	Churches	Gemeinen	Communities	Ecclesiae	Churches	Congregations	Ekklesion	Churches	Churches
Rev. 2:1	Church	Church	Gemeine	Community	Ecclesiae	Church	Congregation	Ekklesias	Church	Church
Rev. 2:7	Churches	Churches	Gemeinen	Communities	Ecclesiis	Churches	Congregations	Ekklesiais	Churches	Churches
Rev. 2:8	Church	Church	Gemeine	Community	Ecclesiae	Church	Congregation	Ekklesias	Church	Church
Rev. 2:11	Churches	Churches	Gemeinen	Communities	Ecclesiis	Churches	Congregations	Ekklesiais	Churches	Churches
Rev. 2:12	Church	Church	Gemeine	Community	Ecclesiae	Church	Congregation	Ekklesias	Church	Church
Rev. 2:18	Church	Church	Gemeine	Community	Ecclesiae	Church	Congregation	Ekklesias	Church	Church
Rev. 2:23	Churches	Churches	Gemeinen	Communities	Ecclesiae	Churches	Congregations	Ekklesiai	Churches	Churches
Rev. 2:29	Churches	Churches	Gemeinen	Communities	Ecclesiis	Churches	Congregations	Ekklesiais	Churches	Churches
Rev. 3:1	Church	Church	Gemeine	Community	Ecclesiae	Church	Congregation	Ekklesias	Church	Church
Rev. 3:6	Churches	Churches	Gemeinen	Communities	Ecclesiis	Churches	Congregations	Ekklesiais	Churches	Churches
Rev. 3:7	Church	Church	Gemeine	Community	Ecclesiae	Church	Congregation	Ekklesias	Church	Church
Rev. 3:13	Churches	Churches	Gemeinen	Communities	Ecclesiis	Churches	Congregations	Ekklesiais	Churches	Churches
Rev. 3:14	Church	Church	Gemeine	Community	Ecclesiae	Church	Congregation	Ekklesias	Church	Church
Rev. 3:22	Churches	Churches	Gemeinen	Communities	Ecclesiis	Churches	Congregations	Ekklesiais	Churches	Churches
Rev. 22:16	Churches	Churches	Gemeinen	Communities	Ecclesiis	Churches	Congregations	Ekklesiai	Churches	Churches

[1] Based on translations – existing manuscripts used [2] Based on interpretations of previous versions

TABLE *6* Comparison of Traditional and Biblical Models of A Local Assembly of Believers*

The cure for any of these or their prevention is a return to or focus on the Biblical principles for the church. Scriptural principles for the church and each member of the body are:

CATEGORY or ISSUE	TRADITIONAL MODEL	BIBLICAL MODEL
Concept of Church	Organization (much like a "club" or a "lodge")	Organism (not without *some* organization; but seen as the People of *God;* Fellowship of the *Spirit*)
Head	The People	Jesus Christ [Mt. 16:18; Eph. 1:22,23; Col. 1:18]
Authority	Constitution plus "proof-texts" from Bible	The WHOLE Word of God [Mt. 4:4; Acts 20:27; 2 Tim. 3:16, 17]
Believers	"Members" (as in a club)	Disciples; brethren; Christians; saints (parts of the Body)
Involvement	Spectators	Participants
Government	Democracy (*of* the people, *by* the people, etc)	Theocracy (*of* God through Word and Holy Spirit)
Selection of Leadership	Election	Appointment (depending on God to raise up gifted men and cause us to recognize them as leaders)
Basic Ministry	Conducting Services	Glorifying God and meeting needs
Place of Ministry	Church Building (at *stated* times)	Anywhere (ALL the time)
Primary Concerns	Programs/Things, Buildings, etc.	God; His People; reaching others with the Good News [1 Pet. 2:4-9]
Objective	Build up "our church"	Build up the Body [Eph. 4:11-16]
Determining Factor	What the PEOPLE *want* (peace at any price)	What the people *need* (according to the Word)
Great Commission	Get converts--ADDITION	Make disciples [Mt. 28:19]--MULTIPLICATION
Field	Our Own Area	the WORLD
Purpose of Assembling	Evangelism in the Service (if *that*)	Worship God [Heb. 12:18-24; 13:15,16]; stimulate one another to love and good deeds [Heb. 10:24,25]; encourage and EQUIP the saints [Eph. 4:11-16]; administer sacraments/ordinances [1 Cor. 11:18-34]
Attitude while Assembled	"Will I get out 'on time'?"	"God, I've gathered with You and Your people, Speak to my heart; equip me; use me."
Material Presented	Cover as much ground as quickly as possible	Move on to new lesson ONLY when previous one is practiced [Jn. 13:17; Jam. 1:22].

Emphasis	Meetings/Setting and Breaking Records	God/Individuals/Families; God's QUALITY will produce QUANTITY
Pastor/Teacher	Administrator/Speaker Visitor (belongs *exclusively* to *this* Church)	Teacher/Counselor/Shepherd/Equipper (belongs to the *Body;* works *primarily* with this Assembly [Eph. 4:11]
Attitude toward Pastor/Teacher	"The" Minister (Professional) ("Bionic Pastor"; Spiritual Superman; self-sufficient due to "formal education")	One of "many" ministers/elders/pastors [Acts 20:28] (He *needs* the ministry of fellow believers)
Discipline	"I don't want to 'interfere' or be misunderstood"	Part of *shepherding* God's flock. Shepherds don't "interfere"; they "guard, watch over" the flock [Mt. 18:15-20; Acts 20:28; 1 Pet. 5:2]
Board (or Governing Body)	Keeps LEADER(S) in line; decides by majority vote if he (they) can carry out what God has shown him (them) in the Word	MULTIPLICITY of leadership; *unified;* working together with the leader(s) *as* leaders to carry out *biblical* principles of operation
Resources	Human ingenuity, "business techniques", available funds, etc.	Word, Prayer, Holy Spirit, spiritual gifts; input from other saints
Methodology	What we're USED to, feel comfortable with, etc. Ritualistic/liturgicalistic	What the *Bible* regulates. *Flexible* with methods; *true* to God's principles
Procedures	Beg, plead, cajole, twist arms, etc. for workers	Trust God to raise up gifted individuals (if HE isn't interested, WE won't be)
Leadership given to	Anyone willing	F-A-T people: Faithful, Available, Teachable [2 Tim. 2:2]
Finances	Needs dealt with only with available funds	Determine needs; then TRUST GOD to work through His people [Phil. 4:19]
Staff	"Hired employees" who carry out the policies set by the PEOPLE through the Board	Associates for full-time involvement; a TEAM to assist in functioning of the Body
Salaries	Determined by "What *I* make" or "What *I* think" Staff viewed as employees *hired* by men	Determined by *biblical* principles (e.g. [1 Tim. 5:17,18]) and actual needs. Staff viewed as those *sent* by God to whom Assembly bears a responsibility [Gal. 6:6]
Attitudes	Conditional acceptance [Jam. 2:1-4]	Unconditional acceptance [Rom. 14:1; 15:7]
Ultimate Concern	"Our Church" and "What others *think*"	Exalting CHRIST and what God says!
Attitude toward Prayer	Canned prayers prepared by hierarchy	Holy Spirit led and controlled
RESULT	Rev. 31b--Like Church at Sardis: "a name that you are ALIVE, but you are DEAD."	God glorified [Rom. 15:5,6; 1 Cor. 10:31]; Body of Christ built up to maturity, functioning as *He* intends [Eph. 4:11-16]

* Excerpts from notes and sermons by C. Marlin Hardman, Barcroft Bible Church, Arlington, VA, 197*

All of this detail on the Geneva version development provides insight as to the handling by men of the Word of God. This, by no means, is to say all Bible versions were developed in the exact same way. But there has been some carelessness handed down through the years by those persons who perform Bible translation. Any version of the Bible after the Genevan translation could apply the word "church," and did. In no way did this "modernization" of the word *ekklesia* help mankind come closer to the truth in God's Word, instead, this error, in fact, has driven mankind closer to dependence on a man—pastor, preacher, priest, reverend, and the pope instead of the shed blood of God's only begotten Son solely and completely. English kings and queens during the time William Tyndale produced and introduced his Bible version worked diligently to make sure none of Tyndale's version of the Bible was distributed to the English people. Those government leaders collected all of Tyndale's Bibles and burned them. They also captured William Tyndale and martyred him to make sure that version was eliminated. But, those very same leaders heralded the Geneva version. The men who worked on and participated in producing the "Authorized Version" in fact, used much of Tyndale's work seventy some years later.

While five out of the ten versions of the Bible studied concerning the word *ekklesia*, do in fact give the proper translation of the word *ekklesia,* the other five introduce a transliteration (to change [letters, words, etc.] into corresponding characters of another alphabet or language) of the word. One would, from all sound reasoning, expect to find a unanimous rendering of a word with such importance and with such strong bearing on the outcome of each and every soul of the human race.

For if man comes under the influence of other men carrying about with them erroneous information and teachings which is subversive to the point that the human race has greater than 50-50 chance of ending up in hell instead of heaven, mankind needs to be warned. This warning includes ministers, pastors, preachers, the clergy in general. The warning could not be more urgently needed.

Table 6 by C. Marlin Hardman[8] brings to light many of the pitfalls churches can find themselves involved in. A summarization of the contents of the table shows churches are inclined to be lead into worldly organization instead of following the guidance of the Holy Spirit.

Explanations by Bible Scholars

Kuen in his book, *I Will Build My Church,*[9] provides overwhelming evidence as to the true meaning of the word *ekklesia* and how the word "church" came into existence. Kuen wrote:

> "For decades and even centuries they have openly called church something which is not the church, and it has been so for the sole reason that they were not clear as to the meaning of the word and as to its content."[10]

Kuen further states,

> "The French word *église* (church) is the result of a double transliteration of the Greek word *ekklesia* first in Latin: *ecclesia,* then into French: *ecclésiastique* and *église.* Thus there has not been any translation

> from the Greek word, but Latinization and then Frenchifying of the original word.[11] The Romans could have expressed the Greek word by *contio* or *comitia* or literally by *convocation;* the French, by the word *assemblée* (assembly), as the Darby Version puts it. But they preferred to keep the original word, doubtlessly considering that it alone was capable of expressing the particular idea to which it was linked.[12] The Italians and Spaniards followed the same practice (*chiesa, iglesia*) while the Germans, the English, and the Flemish abandoned at one and the same time the transliteration [to change words, letters, etc. into corresponding characters of another alphabet or language] and the translation [the rendering—an instance interpretation—of something into another language] in order to link the name of the Christian community with that of the Lord to whom it belongs (*kirche, church, kerk* are derived from the Greek word, *kurios,* the Lord)."[13]

But wait a minute, we did not, I mean the translators did not, begin with *kurios,* the translators, I believe, were working with the word *ekklesia.* How can anyone begin with *ekklesia* and say they were working with *kurios?* We can now see the error most clearly that *ekklesia* cannot and was never intended by our Lord to mean church—an institution created by man.

As Kuen gives his summary of how man arrived at the word "church," he does not give an explanation of how man can accept such treachery and downright fraudulent scholarship. So here lies the answer to how and by whom we now have, since the Geneva Bible revisers, the means to develop an earthly institution by the enemies of God. Who were those enemies with the power at the time this act was committed, nobody but those who were always opposed to God to build His kingdom of saved souls, the pseudo-Christianity fathers and their successors over the last 15-16 centuries.

Kuen goes into the etymological meaning of the word *ekklesia.* Please note there is a change here in the word Kuen is now directing our attention to. At this point he has switched from the word *Church* to the word *Ekklesia* because he wants us to see the true meaning of the word God placed in Scripture at Matthew 16:18 instead of the word man placed there in later translations. Kuen wrote,

> "The word [*ekklesia*] is composed of the prefix *ek,* signifying 'out of' (found in words derived from the Greek, such as *eclectic* and *ecchymosis,* and corresponding to the Latin prefix *ex,* found in extract, exclude, etc.), and the radical *klesia,* which is the passive form of the verb *kaleē,* 'I call.' [In the New Testament *kaleē* is used in the sense of 'to call' or 'to invite' in Mt. 2:7, 20:8, 22:3; to bid or invite the guests to the wedding, Mt. 22:8-9, 25:14; Mk. 3:31; Lk. 7:36, 14:7-10.] This verb itself is derived from the old Indo-European root *kel* which contains the idea of "to cry out," or "to call out" (in Sanskrit *usakalah,* it is the rooster, the one who calls out the dawn. This root has given in the Latin the verb *calare,* to call, and the noun *concilium*; in German the words *hallen, schallen*; to ring or resound; in French, *clamer, proclamer*; to cry out). Therefore, etymologically speaking, the word *ekklesia* signifies 'one who has' been called out of."[14]

A brief summary of Kuen's discussion entitled, *Christian Meaning,* can be most worthwhile,

> "Out of 114 uses of the word *ekklesia* in the New Testament, only six have any bearing on the Greek meaning (Acts 19:39) or the Jewish meaning (Acts 7:38; Heb. 2:12). In all other cases it has a specific meaning which is peculiar to the authors of the New Testament. This meaning embodies and is more inclusive than all previous meanings, as Emil Brunner says: "The New Testament . . . has filled both the Old Testament concept and the secular Greek concept of *Ekklesia* with entirely new Christological content." So there is found in the Christian sense: "The etymological meaning." This means "called out of."[15]

God is calling. He is calling us out of darkness to light. He is assembling us unto Himself in the spiritual kingdom in heaven. Kuen has made it very clear that a sobering error has been brought upon mankind concerning the substitution of the word "church" for the word meaning "called out ones."

Van Gilder points out in his monogram, *The Church Which Is His Body,*[16] a most important revelation concerning the true meaning of the word church. Van Gilder's discussion of the terms "local church" and the "Body of Christ" brings into focus the problem of falling into literalizing symbolic words. On the surface man will struggle with symbolism in God's Word. The book of Revelation is the best example of longtime struggle with symbolical meaning.

Van Gilder gives strong argument against localists who take the position that the local church fulfills the meaning of the term Body of Christ. The arguments by Van Gilder have given part of the answer to the question, "Why the Church?" The localists and the Body of Christ theologies have been exposed by those arguments and also makes room for another look at the root word *ekklesia* which Van Gilder does.

Van Gilder wrote:

> "The localist insists that the word *ekklesia* always means assembly, but Trench insists that this is the least significant element in the meaning of the word, and the 'localist' is in no position to argue the case since he himself calls his congregation a 'church' seven days a week, most of which time it is both unassembled and invisible!"

Van Gilder continues,

> "Consider the appropriateness of this word to just that use which is set forth in this paper. . . . the word is compounded of the preposition *ek,* 'out' and *kaleo,* 'to call.' Now *kaleo* is used of believers no less than thirty times with reference to their salvation experience as resulting from the call of God, (e.g., Rom. 8:30, 9:24; 1 Cor. 1:9; Gal. 1:6; Eph. 4:1,4; Col. 3:15; 1 Thess. 2:12; 4:7). From *kaleo,* is derived a noun, *klesis,* which is translated 'calling' ten times and 'vocation' once. It is used always of the divine calling to salvation, as in 2 Tim. 1:9. From the same verb, is also derived an adjective, *kletos,* which is used no less than seven times to describe believers as 'the called' (Rom. 1:6,7; 8:28; 1 Cor. 1:2,24; Jude 1; Rev. 17:14)."
>
> "And the believer is called out. This is emphasized in every reference which stresses the fact that the believer is to be separated, and that the Christian society is not conterminous [having a common boundary] with the world. Believers have

> been chosen out of the world (John 15:19); God has visited the Gentiles to take out of them a people for His name (Acts 15:14); we have been delivered out of the authority of darkness (*ek tes exousias tou skotus,* Col. 1:13)." [Clarification added by the author.]

Van Gilder finishes his point under the heading, "*Ekklesia,* And The Usus Loquendi" with,

> "In the vocabulary of New Testament writers, in the language of our Lord's time, no better term could have been found to identify those who are thus described. 'Both the calling . . . and the called out . . .' are moments to be remembered when the word is assumed into a higher Christian sense, for in them the chief part of its peculiar adaptation to its auguster [inspiring reverence or admiration] uses lies."[17] [Clarification added by the author.]

Van Gilder agrees with Kuen's findings, but does not arouse nor does he make waves among theologians.

In his book, *The Christian Ecclesia,*[18] Fenton John Anthony Hort, University of Cambridge, England, 1897, set out a series of lectures on the word church. Hort says the reason he used the word ecclesia was:

> ". . . simply to avoid ambiguity. The English term *church,* now the most familiar representative of *ecclesia* to most of us, carries with it associations derived from the institutions and doctorine of later times, and thus can not at present without a constant mental effort be made to convey the full and exact force which originally belonged to *ecclesia.* There would moreover be a second ambiguity in the

> phrase *the early history of the Christian church* arising out of the vague comprehensiveness with which the phrase 'History of the Church' is conventionally employed."

We need to stop here and analyze what Hort is saying. To the author he is saying, man at some point in time has deliberately set aside all Biblical scholarship and decided by committee that the word *ecclesia* will henceforth mean church. This was an error of great proportions for the simple reason the change opened up the way for the error to be compounded by the whims of man over a period of time . . . 444 years. And that is exactly what happened.

Hort goes on to say:

> "It would of course have been possible to have recourse to a second English rendering 'congregation,' which has the advantage of suggesting some of those elements of meaning which are least forcibly suggested by the word 'church' according to our present use. 'Congregation' was the only rendering of *ekklesia* in the English New Testament as it stood throughout Henry VIII's reign, the substitution of the word 'church' being due to the Genevan revisers; and it held its ground in the Bishop's Bible [the next English Bible produced after the Geneva Bible] in no less primary a passage than Matt. xvi. 18 till the Jacobean revision of 1611, which we call the Authorized Version. But 'congregation' has disturbing associations of its own which render it unsuitable for our special purpose; and moreover its use in what might seem a rivalry to so venerable, and rightly venerable [commanding respect or interest because of great age] a word as 'church' would be only a hindrance in the way of recovering for

> 'church' the full breadth of its meaning. *'Ecclesia'* is the only perfectly colourless [word that conveys the original meaning] word within our reach, carrying us back to the beginning of Christian history, and enabling us to some degree to get behind words and names to the simple facts they originally denoted." [Clarification added by the author.]

This extended quotation from Hort is presented to solidify the contention that believers today need to be awakened to what "church fathers" have followed and are now following and taking all of us along with them down a path of self-serving faith.

Hort then goes on to show the meaning of the word *ecclesia* in the Old Testament and the "interplay of *ecclesia* with *qahal* [assembly] and *edhah* [congregation] and other Israelitic usages, application, and interactions over its great history of the Old Testament." As Hort proceeds with giving the sense of the use of the word in the New Testament, he gives "caution that the word already had a long history of its own, and which was associated with the whole history of Israel." It is also well to remember that its antecedents, as it was used by our Lord and His Apostles, "are of two kinds, derived from the past and the present respectively." "These words denoting 'congregation' or 'assembly' had belonged to the children of Israel through their whole history from the days they became a people." Hort ends up with just a good story. In fact, he ends up right back where he started. He did not influence nor did he change the thinking of his day on the use of the word church.

The three explanations provide very strong evidence that all three scholars agree that the use of the word church in the Holy Word of God came into usage and acceptance by deception and not by established guidelines and practices of true translators. The only answer to the question, What harm has come to mankind by the insertion of the word church in place of the term, called-out-ones?—rests in the fruit of the church system that we see in the world today. Some of the most obvious fruits are:

- Existence of great differences in the interpretation of the Word of God.
- Existence of many denominations.
- Existence of an Holy See.
- Many denominations claim to be the true church.
- Existence of anti-Semitism among the denominations.
- Existence of pseudo-Christianity.
- Existence of ungodly seminaries

Explanations From Encyclopedias

There are many sources for information concerning the origin and use of the word church. The explanations from the selected encyclopedias were chosen because nowhere else can one find a more concise meaning of the word. While the meanings provide very little help to arrive at a unanimous decision concerning its true meaning, they do help to solidify the author's position—mankind cannot put its trust in what man has created with the word church.

The 1981 Edition of the Encyclopedia Britannica:[19]

> "**church,** the Christian religious community and the building used for Christian worship

services. The Greek word *ekklēsia,* which came to mean church, was originally applied in the Classical period to an official assembly of citizens. In the Septuagint (Greek) translation of the Old Testament (3rd-2nd century BC), the term *ekklēsia* is used for the general assembly of the Jewish people, especially when gathered for a religious purpose such as hearing the Law (*e.g.,* Deut. 9:10, 18:16). In the New Testament it is used of the entire body of believing Christians throughout the world (*e.g.,* Matt. 16:18), of the believers in a particular area (*e.g.,* Acts 5:11), and also of the congregation meeting in a particular house—the 'house-church' (*e.g.,* Rom. 16:5).

After the Crucifixion and Resurrection of Jesus Christ, his followers felt compelled to preach the Gospel. They then had to provide a community for those who were converted. Rebuffed by the Jewish authorities, the Christians established their own communities, modeled on the Jewish synagogue. Gradually, the church worked out its governmental system, which was based on the office of the bishop (episcopacy).

Since the separation of the Eastern and Western churches in 1054 and the disruption of the Western Church during the 16th-century Protestant Reformation, however, the church has been split into various bodies, most of which consider themselves either the one true church or at least a part of the true church. Thus, the nature of the church has been a matter of controversy.

The fact that many Christians hold nominal beliefs and do not act like followers of Christ has been noted since the 4th century, when the church ceased to be persecuted. To account for this, St. Augustine proposed that the real church is an invisible entity known only to God. Martin

Luther used this theory to excuse the divisions of the church at the Reformation, holding that the true church has its members scattered among the various Christian bodies but that it is independent of any organization known upon earth. The majority of Christians, however, have believed that Jesus intended to found one visible church here upon earth. In the 20th century, the ecumenical movement has worked to restore the unity of the church."

The New Schaff-Herzog Encyclopedia of Religious Knowledge[20]

"**I. Meaning and Use of the Word:** The word 'church' (from Greek *kyriakon,* 'the Lord's,' i.e., 'house' or 'body') meant in original Christian usage either the universal body of Christian believers or a local congregation of believers. In the Romance languages the idea is expressed by a word from another root (Fr. *église,* Ital. *chiesa,* from Greek *ekklesia* 'the [body] called together' or 'called out'). The Old Testament had two words to express the idea, *edhah* and *kahal* (Lev. iv. 13, 14), both meaning 'assembly,' the latter implying a distinctly religious object. In modern usage the term is employed to denote also the building in which a body of Christians meets for worship. An extension has taken place in recognized usage in accordance with which men speak of the Buddhist or the Jewish Church, meaning the whole body of believers in Buddhist or Jewish teaching.

II. The Church in the New Testament: It has been disputed whether Jesus intended to found a church, i.e., a particular, organized association of his disciples, differing specifically

1. The Intentions of Jesus.

from the existing national unity of Israel. He proclaimed the nearness of the kingdom of God, and then announced that it was already present. His discourses dealt with this kingdom, with the conditions for membership in it, and with the blessings to be enjoyed within it. The question is whether there is a connection between the foundation of such an organized body of believers as has been mentioned and the heavenly kingdom which is to be set up in the world by divine power.

4. The Kingdom and the Church.

The existence and development of the church is inextricably interwoven with the realization of the kingdom of God in the world. It would be wrong to press such differences as appear between the two conceptions as though the kingdom were the inner or ideal, and the church the external or real. The kingdom has a real existence in its subjects and their actual relations; it accomplishes its destiny by means of the external preaching of the word, and announces itself by external fruits. The church, on the other hand, although like other associations of men it is an external union, is what it is only by virtue of its inner connection with Christ, who remains in the midst of it. There is nothing of an external nature which (if the words of Jesus are the only criterion) is necessary to the existence of the church which does not also belong to the realization of the kingdom. It is commonly said that the church was definitely founded with the descent of the Holy Ghost on the day of Pentecost, and in fact it did on that day enter upon its career with full powers. But it must not be forgotten that the gathering was composed of the disciples who had already formed a coherent body in the name of Christ; to whom he had already said *'Receive ye the*

> *Holy Ghost'* (John xx. 22); and from whose number, by a corporate act, the number of the apostles had been filled out after the fall of Judas. It had thus already been living and working, at first as an association within the larger one of Israel, though with its own meetings for worship and its own officers. The name *ekklēsia* was undoubtedly applied to it very early, before the beginning of Paul's ministry, since he uses it as the universally current title for both Jewish and Gentile associations. It is commonly applied to the separate local bodies of which he spoke, but he used it in the same way for the whole body of Christians whenever he had occasion to mention it, in the older epistles (Gal. i. 13; I Cor. x. 32, xii. 28, xv. 9) as well as in that to the Ephesians, which some have tried to separate in this particular from the others; and it is so used in Acts ix. 31.
>
> Whether general or local, the church consisted of those who were 'sanctified in Christ Jesus' (I Cor. i. 2) or 'called to be saints' (Rom. i. 7), with a possible allusion to the etymological connection between *klētoi,* 'called,' and *ekklēsia.*"

The encyclopedias represented here give differing opinions concerning the understanding, origin and application of the word church. It can be readily seen that these diverse opinions and understanding could make it possible for theologians and Bible scholars, over a long period of time, to influence the development of many ways to worship and serve the one true God. If the theologians and Bible scholars cannot arrive at the same truth by using the same Holy Word of God, then something has to be radically wrong with those persons making interpretations of the Scriptures. Corruptions of the Holy Word of God in fact have produced easy to detect, even by the untrained person, ungodly sects. We have many examples around us today. Our forefathers have had spiritual battles with ungodly men in ages past. Millions follow blindly the pseudo-Christianity and millions more follow Mormonism, Jehovah's Witnessism, Moonieism and we are seeing deterioration of Godliness progressing in the United States at a very rapid rate every year.

All of us who say, I love you Lord, need to examine ourselves to determine what it is we stand upon concerning our individual beliefs and who it is that has influenced those beliefs. Test those beliefs with the Word of God personally, do not allow other people to make the determination for you. Find out if they are actually taught in the Word of God—does the Bible actually say it? Above all else, come to Christ Jesus with a repentful heart and mind.

What we see today in the church system scene is a mixture of true God-fearing people and those people who continue to contend for domination of all peoples of the earth. It is most difficult to point out with all certainty, who truly belong to the one true God and who it is that is working against God. There is but one Scripture that can be relied upon to make that determination, Matthew 7:13-23. I choose to place great emphasis on verse 20, "So then you will know them by their fruits." Well, we might say, what else is new, don't hundreds of thousands and millions go to and occupy the thousands upon thousands of churches every Sunday, Saturday or Saturday night? Why should we be alarmed?

The importance of discipleship training was raised many times in this writing and discipleship training needs to be the issue. Is each and every one of those persons attending the "church service" discipled to be a soul winner? Here is where I rest my case for the Lord, "So then you will know them by their fruits." It is indeed most rare to see a high percentage of those persons attending thousands of churches truly on fire with soul-winning attitudes, abilities, and action. The bottom line question is, can we have a true salvation if we do not display the fruits that are pleasing to God? Pastors, preachers, ministers, and reverends can preach until they turn blue in the face, but they can never produce a true disciple for the Lord Jesus Christ from the pulpit.

All of the above can be used as evidence to condemn much of the church system and in particular those men and women who are actively engaged in promoting their own agenda when it comes to teaching in the churches. All of the ungodliness in existence in this country and in other nations that call themselves "Christianized" can be traced to secularization of the Word of God by evil men and women who operate within the church system.

So what was and is the agenda of those men who are responsible for fostering and spreading the church system wherever it was and is spread? What does history show and prove what it was that motivated the men who spread pseudo-christianity? We can read all about their works, but what about the legacy of those who lead in the denominations and sects—whose works will stand? (See 1 Corinthians 3:12-15.)

We read and hear that God is working in and through His true disciples in many places throughout the world. Many who truly belong to the Lord are becoming soul winners—the many who were trapped in pagan beliefs and pseudo-christianity. My heart goes out to those trapped in denominationalism, because those who are trapped do not have any way of knowing they are afflicted with the disease, "churchitis."

Epilogue

From the beginning of that which God established in His Son, the reestablishment of the spiritual kingdom in heaven and on earth, the leaders of the Jews and the Roman governors began to persecute the true followers of Jesus. They were first forced out of Jerusalem. This compelled the Apostles to form groups of disciples, with Apostles as leaders, to begin to spread the Gospel of Jesus Christ to the peoples in the neighboring countries. At this same time God sent Paul with his companion to the Gentiles of the countries on the other side of the Mediterranean Sea.

Everywhere Paul went he was opposed by unbelieving Jews, but his work in the power of the Lord, grew stronger and stronger. The Bible shows that he was very persistent and that his labors brought thousands of true followers to the Lord. God's Word tells us that these early followers were harassed at almost every turn, but severe persecution did not arise until the development of pseudo-Christianity when it raised its ugly head in the second and third centuries. At that point in history the true followers of Jesus Christ were forced to worship the Roman gods or be killed. Satan established his enemies of God to counter the works of the true followers of God everywhere they went.

This dilution of the work of the true followers of God was continued throughout all of the Roman Empire and throughout all of the nations that came into being when the civil Roman government collapsed. The pseudo-followers of

Christ established control of the people and ruled as a double-headed leader (religion and civil government vested in one person)—the pontiff or the ruling Crown. The Holy See's power prevailed until the so-called Reformation temporarily slowed down the work of pseudo-Christianity. This rule by the pseudo-Christian leaders in combination with the Crown, prevailed through the dark ages (476 A.D. to about 1000 A.D.) up through the Medieval period (anytime beginning with ca700 to 1500) to the Renaissance (1400-1700). The majority of the destruction of the true believers was done in England, France, Spain, and Italy throughout the above time periods.

It is throughout those time periods, we are lead to believe, that Roman Catholicism and Eastern Orthodoxism are and were the true godly religions. We need to be reminded that the Italians did not have a civil government monarch over the entire country as did all of the other nations throughout the above referenced time periods in that part of the world. The Italians had a "Holy See" as its head. It was, we can say, a "nationality." Italy has always been made up of satellite provinces. Because the powers that be in the provinces were constantly changing hands, the Pontiff was the only stabilizing influence in Italy. This added great power to that office and it was the controlling power, not only in Italy, but all over the world for whatever country where the Roman Catholic religion is the main religion.

At the same time, late 14th to early 16th centuries, God gave men the ability to roam, by sea, all over the undiscovered world. However, those "undiscovered" parts of the world had inhabitants when they were discovered anew and recorded in history. These newly-discovered lands provided the true followers of Christ (God's remnant of true followers) a land to escape to from the continuous suppression and persecution by the pseudo-Christian establishment in almost every country of Western Europe. The enemies of God, we are told in historic documents, continued their persecution of true followers up until the time they were able to escape to the new land that became America.

From those days until now, Americans have lived under the blessings of God Almighty. But we are seeing great inroads by the very same types of enemies of God that persecuted the true believers in Europe. The enemies of God in the United States are now destroying all godliness in America, a new form of persecution. Those evil persons are not killing the true followers of Jesus Christ; they are putting them into extreme jeopardy of losing their freedom to follow Jesus Christ as a God-given right. The rights and privileges given each and every citizen of the United States under our laws that were developed out of our constitution are being eroded away by evil persons working seemingly in a very lawful manner. Because of the very weak moral condition of America (loss of the power of God within a great number of people), evil persons are belittling our government to such an extent that evil people will be able to take away our freedom and turn it into a despotic form of government. The evil people working their works in America are bringing godlessness upon us and many Americans cannot fathom what is happening. We can lay most of the blame at the feet of those persons that operate in the church system.

To come up with answers for the reason this can be and is happening in America we have to take a hard look at the very nature of the words "freedom of religion." The people of America and all peoples all over the world who love the Lord have come to a crossroad; Do I continue on the pathway where men have made it a popular pastime to follow Christ as a religion, "the Christian religion" or do I turn to the Word of God and find the true way to walk with God—God, me and the Word of God?

Over time, from the 2nd and 3rd centuries to the 17th and 18th centuries, men have found ways to divide "the Christian religion" into two separate religions, the Catholic religion and the Protestant religion. Remember, this is not the works of Godly people, these works are by the enemies of God. It was not like that during the first century when the disciples of Jesus took the Gospel of Jesus Christ to the Gentile areas of the Roman Empire and other parts of the known world. We have very meager records of what happened to all of the early disciples. We are told, most of them were killed, but that true work of God was carried on through letters carried by the early Apostles of Christ throughout much of the Roman Empire and by word of mouth, house to house, town to town, and country to country.

After the Catholic religion (pseudo-Christianity) was formed, it was divided into two separate religions, the Roman Catholic religion and the Eastern Orthodox religion. Each of those two has been divided into several sects within those two basic beliefs mainly to accommodate the peoples of the several countries that accepted those beliefs. The Protestant religion, now, that is a long story, simply said, it is a real ball of snakes. Literally hundreds of men and women have wrongly divided the Word of God to suit themselves and each one created their own little kingdom on earth. The word protestant means to protest. Who was it that protested and what did the person protest? The dictionary says "any of the German princes who protested against the decision of the Diet of Speyer (Roman Catholic) in 1529, who had denounced the Reformation."

Most of the many beliefs that came forth from the Reformation cannot prove they have been blessed by God because few of them have produced a great work for the Lord which can be readily identified today. The greater majority are still searching for the real thing and where the gathering is being directed by a "senior pastor," the search is directed by the one person, not by the Holy Spirit working within each and every person of the gathering.

Statistics show that Christianity has some very large numbers of people following the various beliefs and faiths that embrace the "Christian religion." The Roman Catholic branch has a great numerical following and they claim they are Christians, even during the early days when they had many of the true believers killed because they did not become Roman Catholics! Do any of that denomination know what the word of God says about true salvation? We know great numbers of people in many parts of the world follow the Eastern Orthodox branch, but can any one of them tell you the answer from the Word of God what true salvation in Jesus Christ means? The Methodist branch, including many different sects, has a great numerical following, but do all of them have true salvation? Likewise the many among the different Baptists who say they are Christians, have they been trained to be a disciple of Jesus Christ or are they just a good Baptist? There are millions who say they are Lutherans, are they being trained to be a soul-winning disciple of Jesus Christ or are they just a good Lutheran? There are millions of Assemblies of God, Presbyterian, Anglican, and down through the many diverse denominations with lesser numerical numbers of followers, can any of them say we have many of us who are soul-winning disciples, workers bringing many persons to the Lord so He can bring them into His house? All of the above can say, but we support thousands of missionaries from among us that are dispersed all over the world declaring the gospel of Jesus Christ!

When we stop to consider the word "religion," we need to grasp the deeper sense and truths of how God works within the inner man. We need to be able to understand why God allows us to experience certain calamities in our life. Having a particular religion, form of worshipfulness whether Islam, Roman Catholic, or Protestant, and following those teachings blindly, can be useless repetition of traditions of men. Mankind could do just as well worshipping Elvis Presley (some do), or a sports figure (some do). Being religious as a daily occupation of the mind and following a static, man-developed ritual, "Sunday service," is only an exercise of the mind.

Following the true God is more than being part of religious ceremonies once per week at a fixed time and fixed location by a fixed leader, the one-man minister. The man-declared ceremonies usually glorify man in several ways, the minister does all of the praying, he does all of the studying of the Holy Word of God, and he does all of the caring of all of the people. He does all of the interpretation and application of the Scriptures during the preaching portion of the "service." So all of the participants go home with the attitude—our mind and thoughts have been rejuvenated again and turned toward God for an hour until the next "service!"

Being led by the Holy Spirit and turning your life completely over to Christ Jesus is the only condition of your mind and being that the true God can work his wondrous works in and through. It is the only condition of your mind where you will find peace and happiness. It is the only condition of your being where you can tolerate and go through adversities and come out the other side in a closer relationship with your heavenly Father. Our heavenly Father is the only God who sees our every need and the only God who can answer our prayers. No other god has ever functioned in that way. Answers to prayers through the man-made gods are only imagined answers. Those answers from the man-made gods usually come through a mediator (spiritualist) or a male or female seer. Never can the answer come directly to the follower of the man-made god! These are some of the very basic differences between having a religion and having a true relationship with the Lord Jesus Christ. The one is an imagination within the mind while the other is a true heart-felt way of life.

Because of all the errors evil men have introduced to mankind through the man-developed "church system," we can say, Satan has made his second strike! He did strike Adam and Eve in the Garden of Eden, and he has brought death to many who follow religious teachings, blindly, whatever the variety might be. Our guidance for our lives has to come from seeking the truth in the Holy Word of God on a daily basis and a daily time of prayer with God. This is the first step in becoming a soul-winning disciple for our heavenly Father who is calling us unto Himself. There is no other way to complete peace and happiness in this life. You can try drugs, alcohol, sex, spiritualists, Mormonism, Jehovah Witnesses, Unitarianism, even some of the many denominations we find in great buildings. But until you have the Lord Jesus Christ in your heart and mind and Him Lord and Master of your life, you just keep searching for answers forever. If the faith we follow is induced by a man; the priest, reverend, minister, senior pastor, or the like, and not by God through the power of the Holy Spirit, that faith and worship is a religion. The dictionary defines the word religion—"a specific and institutionalized set of beliefs and practices generally agreed upon by a number of persons or sects"—the Christian religion—"the body of persons or institutions adhering to a set of religious beliefs and practices."

It now becomes clear to see that just because a denomination or a group of people wrote their statement of faith and doctrines of belief and they believe that is biblical, the fact is, that puts limits on the power and love of God. Secular clubs also set down on paper rules and regulations that guide their activities. God wants us to live by His Almighty power. We need to live by His entire Word not just small bits and pieces set out as a doctrine and also given by the "Sunday sermon" and the teaching in the Sunday school class. The power of God comes to us, moment by moment, by listening to His guidance for our life each day He gives each and every soul on the face of this earth.

The world is overflowing with religious activity from the primitive voodoo form to nature worship to worship in the great cathedrals, but the true God desires our worship to be in spirit and truth. (See John 4:23.) The true worshipers are those who are the called-out-ones by God and are all truly one in Christ. They truly have a single-mindedness in Christ Jesus. They all use the same Word of God and all learn the same wisdom and knowledge of who the true God is. They all have the same objectives pertaining to following the Lord Jesus Christ. They are all knit together with the same spiritual guidance. They cannot say: "I am of Luther," "I am of Calvin," "I am of John Knox," "I am of Pope Pius XII," "I am of John Wesley," "I am of Menno Simons," and "I am of pastor John Doe."

They should all say: "I am in Jesus Christ and I stand on every word of God's Holy Word." They do not need a pastor, priest, rabbi, or reverend to explain to them what they should think concerning the Word of God. They have the guidance of the Holy Spirit. God and God's Word is their guide, not the distortion of the man or woman of the cloth telling them what they think the Word of God says. That is adulteration of the Holy Word of God—preaching for the sake of preaching. Everyone who is seeking for the truth in the Word of God should be discipled from the moment they join a group of persons who have been discipled before them.

Those persons who are seeking better direction for their lives cannot be discipled from the church pulpit or by the radio or TV preacher. Discipling is the business of everyone who has been taken through discipleship training. If your pastor is only a preacher and is not producing disciples for the biblical work of the Lord, then move on to the group of worshippers who are obedient to the Word of God and become a true disciple and then help to produce disciples. The leadership you sit under should understand that he has the God-given responsibility of using and practicing all of the truths in the Holy Word of God. The person you sit under for Godly instruction has to be held responsible to God for giving every man, woman and child complete biblical training to become a reproducer for the Lord. The woeful weakness of a great number of the churches in America today is the stagnation of their members sitting under the preacher's self-indulging ego trip Sunday after Sunday. Satan sits back and applauds the preacher's charisma.

Endnotes

Part One

Chapter 5

1. From correspondence with Glenn M. Wenger, September 16, 2005.
2. Charles Halff, *The Law of Moses and the Grace of God* (The Christian Jew Foundation, Undated), pp. 4-12.
3. *The Holy Bible* (Philadelphia: The National Bible Press, 1943), p. 233.

Chapter 6

1. David H. Stern, *Jewish New Testament Commentary* (Clarksville, MD: Jewish New Testament Publications, 1992), pp. 219-223.
2. From Message by John Royer, Mennonite Church, Kralltown, Pennsylvania, 1991.

Chapter 8

1. Stern, ob. cit., p. 231.
2. Robert Brow, *The Church* (Grand Rapids: William B. Eerdmans Publishing Company, 1968), p. 17.
3. Leopold Cohen, *Do Christians Worship Three Gods?* (God is My Help Messianic Ministries, Undated), pp. 7-9.
4. Ibid., p. 9.

Chapter 9

1. Arnold G. Fruchtenbaum, *Israelology–The Missing Link in Systematic Theology* (Tustin, CA: Ariel Ministries Press, 1989), pp. 649-651.
2. Charles Halff, *God's Predestination* (The Christian Jew Foundation, 1969).
3. Ibid., p. 35.

Chapter 10

1. David H. Stern, *Jewish New Testament* (Clarksville, MD: Jewish New Testament Publications,1989), p. xxiii.
2. Al and Lorraine Broom, *One-to-One Discipling* (Multiplication Ministries, 1983).
3. Bill Bright, *A Handbook of Concepts For Living* (San Bernnardino, CA: Here's Life Publishers, 1981).
4. Arnold G. Fruchtenbaum, Manuscript No. 106, *The Local Church*, (Tustin, CA: Ariel Ministries, 1985).
5. Glenn M. Wenger, *The Way of Truth*, Vol. 1 No. 3, Published irregularly at Richfield, PA, June 2006, p. 4.

Part Two

Chapter 11

1. Robert Brow, *The Church, An Organic Picture of Its Life and Mission* (Grand Rapids: William B. Eerdmans Publishing Co., 1968).
2. Ibid.
3. Max I. Dimont, *Jews, God, and History* (New York: Simon and Schuster, Inc., 1962).
4. E. S. Shuckburg, *Augustus* (London: T. Fisher Unwin, 1905).
5. John A. Garraty and Peter Gay, *The Columbia History of the World* (New York: Harper and Row Publishers, 1972).

Chapter 12

1. Frank S. Mead, *Handbook of Denominations in the United States*, rev. by Samuel S. Hill (Nashville: Abington Press, 1995), pp. 304, 305.

Chapter 13

1. T. S. Goslin, *The Church Without Walls* (Pasadena: Hope Publishing House, 1984).
2. Ibid., From the Foreword.
3. Ibid., (see ref. 1, section 2).
4. Ibid., (see ref. 4, section 9).

5. A. W. Tozer, *Rut, Rot or Revival–The Condition of the Church*, compiled by James L. Snyder (Camp Hill, PA: Christian Publications, 1992).

Chapter 14

1. *The Lutheran Book of Worship*, First Printing (Minneapolis: Augsburg Publishing House, September, 1973), p. 77.
2. *Passover Haggadah*, ed. Harold A. Sevener, published by Beth Sar Shalom (Orangeburg, NY: "The House of the Prince of Peace" International Headquarters, Undated).
3. Ibid., p. 1.
4. David H. Stern, *Jewish New Testament Commentary* (Clarksville, MD: Jewish New Testament Publications, 1992), p. 791.
5. Ibid., p. 144.
6. Ibid., pp. 227, 228.
7. Ibid., pp. 475, 476.
8. Gary Hedrick, "Speeding Up the Coming of the Lord," *Messianic Perspectives* (San Antonio: The Christian Jew Foundation, January–February, 2002).

Chapter 15

1. Stern, ob. cit., p. 785.
2. John Foxe, *The Acts and Monuments of the Church: The Martyrs* (New York: Worthing Company, 1850).
3. John L. McKenzie, *The Roman Catholic Church* (New York: Holt, Rinehart and Winston, 1969).
4. E.S. Shuckburg, *Augustus* (London: T. Fisher Unwin, 1905), p. 149
5. Ibid., p. 149.
6. Ibid., p. 198.
7. Garraty and Gay, ob. cit., p. 208.
8. Erwin W. Lutzer, *Hitler's Cross* (Chicago: Moody Press, 1995).
9. David H. Stern, *Jewish New Testament* (Clarksville, MD: Jewish New Testament Publishers, 1989), pp. XIV, XV.

Chapter 17

1. Bright, ob. cit., p. 13.

2. Excerpts from notes and sermon by C. Marlin Hardman, Barcroft Bible Church, Arlington, VA, 1975.
3. *The Gospel Catholic*, Vol. 3, No. 5, Conversion Center, Haverton, PA, 1967.
4. *How a Rabbi Found Peace–A Personal Testimony*, A Tract by the American Messianic Fellowship, Lansing, IL.

Chapter 18

1. Foxe, ob. cit.
2. Max I. Dimont, *Jews, God, and History* (New York: Simon and Schuster, Inc., 1962).
3. S. J. Roth, and William A. Kramer, *The Church Through the Ages* (Saint Louis: Concordia Publishing House, 1949), p. 340.
4. Garraty and Gay, ob. cit.
5. Christian Eilers, *The Interpreter,* Vol. 35, No. 3, Lutherville, MD, Fall 1993.
6. Samuel McComb, *The Making of the English Bible* (New York: Moffat, Yard and Company, 1909).
7. Ibid., p. 47.
8. C. Marlin Hardman, *Comparison of Traditional and Biblical Models of a Local Assembly of Believers*, Barcroft Bible Church, Arlington, VA, 1975.
9. Alfred Kuen, *I Will Build My Church*, translated by Ruby Lindblad (Chicago: Moody Press, 1971).
10. Ibid., (see ref. 1).
11. Ibid., (see ref. 2).
12. Ibid., (see ref. 3).
13. Ibid., p. 45.
14. Ibid., (see ref. 5).
15. Ibid., (see ref. 10).
16. H. O. Van Gilder, *The Church Which Is His Body* (Elcerrito, CA: The College Press, undated).
17. Ibid., p. 26.
18. Fenton John Anthony Hort, *The Christian Ecclesia* (London: Macmillan and Co., 1897), p. 2.
19. Robert McHenry (ed.), *Encyclopedia Britannica*, Vol. 3, 1981, p. 921.

20. Samuel Macauly Jackson (ed.), *The New Schaff-Herzog Encyclopedia of Religious Knowledge,* Vol. 3, London: Funk & Wagnalls Co., 1909, pp. 77-78.

Addendum

Personal Testimony

I sought guidance for my life during my growing-up years and I believe God sought and guided me, even at times when I was doing things my own way. I know God had his hand over me in my teens and early adult life (that time interval prior to the time when I learned the truths that I sought all my life concerning God). This testimony is about how I searched for those truths, and how God was faithful in guiding me to them.

I know God was guiding and watching over me in my young life because certain miracles occurred, and certain sinful events nearly occurred that I know now definitely had to be the work of an all-powerful God. I will not give the details of the miracles performed and the events that did not happen. These are mentioned here as background information only.

My mother and father rarely attended church together, yet both had fair background knowledge of God but did not instruct me with their knowledge. My father left the Brethren Church at an early age (maybe at the age of 18 or 19) and never returned. I always assumed it was because of his disillusionment with the church. My mother was raised in the Lutheran Church but left at an early age. I do not know the reason. My mother came to know the Lord in a very devout way in her older age (maybe in her 50's). My parents sent my sisters and myself to Sunday School at the nearest church to our home. But because we moved several times during the years I lived at home, I did not become established in a denomination. I attended high school and entered military service before finishing my junior year. During this time I attended church services with my mother at a pentacostal denomination and then at services in the military. I started to read the Bible regularly in the service, but my thirst for the truth concerning God became greater, but I was not getting any answers.

After the war (World War II) I took the necessary tests to receive a high school diploma. Shortly after that I left my home state of Pennsylvania and took up residency in the state of Texas. I was accepted for class attendance at the University of Houston, but I wanted to become a landscape architect and the University of Houston did not have a curriculum for that course of study. I transferred to Texas A&M a year later where I could pursue an Arts and Science degree in Landscape Architecture. During this time 1948-1949, God came to me in a very strong way urging me to seek His truths. I visited many denominations with friends, and none of the denominations turned me on until I visited the American Lutheran Church mission church near the campus. I was taught the standard Lutheran catechetical lessons and when finished with that I was able to become a member of the church. That satisfied me somewhat, and the urge to look deeper into God's truth went away temporarily. I attended church very regularly and all of the social activities offered to the students from the University. Then we had a change in ministers, and the urge returned to know more about God. So I asked the new, young minister, "Tell me more about God." Well, I had a few more sessions on what Lutherans believe, but I went away saying to myself this young minister cannot help me any more than the elderly minister that he replaced, so there isn't anything more to know about God. I graduated from Texas A&M University well prepared to be a Landscape Architect, but I still had the feeling that I needed to know the truth about God. I returned to my home state seeking employment, and was accepted by the State of Pennsylvania in the Department of Forests and Waters, Bureau of State Parks. After becoming established there, and moving around the state helping park managers solve some of their problems of meeting the need for additional facilities or updating old facilities, I came across some literature telling about the coming publication of the Interpreter's Bible. I said to myself, "This should give me the answers concerning the truths about God." I purchased the first volume and had to wait a month to purchase the next volume and so on, until I had the entire set of twelve volumes over a period of ten or more months. I began to read these volumes seeking the truth about God. After searching through the twelve volumes with explanations of God's Word by some of the world's greatest Biblical scholars of the 1940's and 1950's, I still did not find the truths I sought.

At about this time I was engaged in courtship with the girl that I married in 1954. We were married in the Lutheran church and became very active in Sunday School teaching, church council, church activities of a very broad spectrum, men's and women's meetings, home Bible studies with groups of couples of varying ages, church Bible Camp director, Sunday School Superintendent, and church Boy Scout committee chairman and activities. All the time I sensed God's prodding to do someing real—something more meaningful for God. Seeking the truth concerning God was still with me. At one point, about 1960, I asked one of the directors of the Lutheran Church from the headquarters of the American Lutheran Church how to apply for missionary service, and his answer was, "You can do more good here."

In the meantime, my wife and I were raising four children, and I began a private business life on top of my career with the Federal Government. Up to this point, 1966, since we had been married, we had lived in Pennsylvania; Columbus, Ohio; Omaha, Nebraska; Walla Walla, Washington; and Louisville, Kentucky. We had been a member in the Lutheran Church in America in Pennsylvania, American Lutheran Church in Omaha and Walla Walla, Washington, and the Missouri Lutheran Church in Louisville, Kentucky. We learned more and more about God, but I had not satisfied my thirst for knowing God. I have come to know that there is as much difference between knowing about God and truly knowing God as day and night. All during this time as I now look back, I became more interested in becoming successful in the Federal Government and the business world than being successful in the Lutheran Church. In 1967 we purchased a fruit orchard in Piqua, Ohio, and left the Federal Government career—I thought. That lasted eighteen months because we had two near crop failures in a row, and at the end of 1967 Pat gave birth to our third son. Because of the crop failures, we thought at that time, we were forced to sell the business. Also Bill, the new baby, was born with what we found at the end of almost one year, congenital glaucoma. At this time, God sent us to Washington, D.C. Bill's vision was damaged to the point where he was left with legal blindness. Washington, D.C., was the last place I ever wanted to go as a Federal Government employee, but God sent us there. This was His plan for saving Bills' eyesight, my life, and each family member's life. Bill had a goniotomy operation on both eyes. The pressure was arrested and his vision was saved. God and the doctor truly were great.

We were now living in the metro area of Washington, D.C., but wanted a permanent residence. We purchased a house in Frederick, Maryland. We lived there six years. Our oldest son graduated from one of the two high schools in Frederick, and I commuted to D.C. to the Office, Chief of Engineers, that is the Headquarter's office of the U.S. Army Corps of Engineers. Our family regularly attended one of the largest, most prestigious Lutheran Churches in America. In 1970, God began to prod me once more by bringing back the strong desire to know the truth about Him. This particular church also began to show us the truth concerning the where, what and why about the present day Lutheran church, particularly the LCA churches. We said to ourselves, "We must get out to more Godly surroundings." It was not the people. Many of the fellow worshipers in that congregation are still dear friends today. It was mainly the local leadership and the hierarchy of the church.

Upon the discovery that the established church is an inward directed, nearly social club in organization, and lack the effectiveness in winning the lost for Christ, guided us to joining up with a group of Lutherans in the Frederick area who wanted to see Christ raised up to the lost. This small group began to meet together in rented space and formed a Missouri Lutheran mission congregation. At this time (1972) I was accepted at Penn State University under a Secretary of the Army Research and Study Fellowship, to engage in studies in Environmental Pollution Control. The urge to know the truth about God's great love to man went away for the time being. We worshipped with a small group of very warm, God-fearing Lutherans in the State College, Pennsylvania, area, and my need for the truth about God was set aside for two years. I busied myself for those two years on a study of land treatment of waste water, and published the results of the study. After returning to Washington, D.C., and beginning the writings on the design of recreation facilities, we moved another hour's driving time north of Frederick, Maryland, to New Oxford, Pennsylvania.

I did not want this at all, but my wife insisted that we attend the auction of a small farm that was advertised in the Frederick paper . . . probably the only listing of its kind from Pennsylvania in the Frederick paper. I made one bid, and we were on our way to New Oxford, Pennsylvania . . . a two-hour commute to Washington, D.C. Immediately God gave me a commuting partner, David Alexander, who lived on a small farm forty-five minutes farther north in Pennsylvania. At this time, there were two crazy people spending four hours each day on the highways and streets, helping our fellow Americans through the Federal Government in D.C. Soon afterward we added another and then another. Now my turn to drive was coming up every fourth day . . . very comfortable.

Now we are entering 1977 and I have been a member of a Bible study group at noontime in our office in Washington about two years. Someone in the group learned that the Campus Crusade for Christ had a singing group working in the D.C. area called *The Great Commission.* We made arrangements to have them come to the auditorium in our office building for an evangelistic outreach. (Can you imagine that happening in a Federal office building?! Only God's great power and love can overcome all earthly power.) We had very good attendance and through the leader of this group we were introduced to staff members of the Campus Crusade for Christ Christian Embassy in Washington, D.C. Through this early contact and the desire of attendees of the Bible study, Jerry Regier, a full time member of the Campus Crusade for Christ offered to establish a regular meeting time at noon to study what Bill Bright, the founder of Campus Crusade for Christ, entitled "the transferrable concepts." I joined five other people to meet with Mr. Regier instead of our regular Bible study every week for fifteen or more weeks. I looked over the first of nine concepts, How To Be Sure You Are a Christian, and I thought to myself, "Well, this looks like the same old 'Sunday School Stuff.'" There was one slight difference—the first concept brought in the fact that God's Word says that we can be sure that we are a Christian when we have a personal relationship with God. This begins with asking Christ to come into our life and joining with Him to do for us what we cannot do ourselves . . . be good enought to merit God's forgiveness of our sin, only Christ can do that. When I saw this simple truth, I said to myself, "That is what I sought all these years, a personal relationship with God."

In the transferrable concepts (God's Word set out and explained in a way that I could understand what God is all about, and what God expects of me), I found the answer to the truths that I sought all of my life. I was on my way to spiritual enlightenment through a devoted daily Bible reading and prayer time in the power of the Holy Spirit.

Since finding the truth in God's Word and asking God to show me areas of my life that He wants to change, He used the commute to Washington, D.C., and the operation of a small greenhouse and nursery business, to show me His mighty power and to cleanse me of unrighteousness, to prepare me for His service, to raise Christ up to the lost on a daily basis, to study and feed on His Word daily, to pray about all things and to allow Him to direct me moment by moment.

From 1975 to 1980, during the time I found the truths concerning God's great love to man, we remained in the Lutheran Church, praying and gently urging our friends and fellow church goers to get closer to the Lord and not to allow the Church hierarchy to bring in ungoldy principles and teachings. We failed to make a dent as to our knowledge. Only God knows whether we had any effect upon individuals. After 1980 we made the decision that we could no longer stay with the Lutheran Church and the Satan directed theology creeping in and stealing God's people. We united with the Evangelical Free Church, after testing the theology and finding no ungoldy principles being taught locally nor in the main offices, which do not push anything on the independently operated local church. If you think I have any bitterness toward the Lutheran Church, you are wrong. For what you read here is great sadness concerning the blindness of people being led away from God, and into Satan's one world church. The Lutherans are again returning to the ungodliness that caused Martin Luther to break away from the Roman church. The Lutheran Church in America, along with many other denominations, are being carried away to ungodly doctrines.

From this time on, 1980's, my burden changed. My burden changed to pastors and the church. In the early 1980's I produced my first manuscript on the subject, "God's Great Love for Man." That writing became unsatisfactory immediatly upon its completion. God pushed my burden for pastors and the church into a deeper search of the Bible and books upon books in seminary libraries and a second manuscript emerged entitled, "The Serpent Strikes Twice." His first strike was in the Garden of Eden and Satan made his second strike in guiding the development of the church system. This writing occured during the last half of 1980 into the 1990's. The search for the truth of what man has done and is doing with the directions God has given us in His Word led me into a more comprehensive understanding of what God created for man in His Son.

In the late 1990's and into the early years of the new century, a new manuscript was drafted, entitled, "Enlightening Truths in God's Holy Word for Believers." I struggled daily with the people who prepared that manuscript into review form. In the midst of that struggle a new outline for the fourth and final manuscript came to mind. I believe all of the scriptures set out and discussed in the finished book could not have come from my own intelect. I am referring to those parts of the work that sets out truths from the Holy Word of God far beyond my previous understanding of that which God did through His Son's birth, life, suffering, death, resurrection and ascension. Some of those truths are:

1. How and when to remember the Lord Jesus Christ's suffering and death.
2. When was the Holy Spirit returned to earth and how was it made available to all mankind?
3. What was the day the Lord Jesus Christ was crucified?
4. The death of Jesus Christ and His resurrection restored the spiritual kingdom on earth and in heaven.

5. Jesus Christ's death broke down the barrier between man and God.
6. Jesus Christ's death and resurrection made all men one again.
7. The scriptural guided way to worship God.
8. The error of mankind to have many different doctrines for following the Lord Jesus Christ.

Family church attendance from the early 1980's to the present has been with a broad spectrum of faiths. Those churches were mainline denominations, but most worship was with many different independent groups which gave me and my wife deeper understanding of how the average church attendees have been caught up in the church system. I call it the church system because for the most part churches develop programs and activities that focus on individuals being happy with serving the church, instead of serving God—there is a big difference. I have come to realize how true this is—those institutions where individuals are trained to serve the people of any and all denominations are trained to be the church attendees priest (the individuals salvation fulfiller).

It is my sincere hope and prayer that my experiences over these many years of my life and those years devoted to searching for the truths in the Word of God will enlighten the reader to begin their own search for the truths you have a yearning for.

In the precious love of Jesus

____